10,000 STARTUPS

LEGAL STRATEGIES FOR STARTUP SUCCESS

ROGER ROYSE

ABOUT THE AUTHOR

Roger Royse is a partner in the Palo Alto office of Haynes and Boone, LLP and practices in the areas of corporate and securities law, domestic and international tax, mergers and acquisitions, and fund formation. He works with companies ranging from newly formed tech startups to publicly traded multinationals in a variety of industries. Roger is a nationally recognized authority on agtech – the technology of food production – and the legal considerations for companies in this industry. Roger is also the author of Dead on Arrival: How to Avoid the Legal Mistakes That Could Kill Your Startup.

Professional Highlights

- LL.M., Taxation, New York University School of Law
- J.D., University of North Dakota
- B.S., Accounting, University of North Dakota
- Recognized as a Northern California - Super Lawyer 2011-2019
- Martindale Hubbell® Law Directory with a Peer Review Rating of AV® Preeminent™
- Recognized as a "Top Attorney" with a "10.0 Superb" Avvo Rating
- Recipient of The Recorder Legal Innovator Awards 2014 and 2015
- Recognized by The Leukemia & Lymphoma Society as the "2012 San Francisco Bay Area Chapter Man of the Year"

Affiliations

- Certified Public Accountant (non-attest only)
- Fellow of the American College of Tax Counsel
- California Co-Chair of the Fellows of the American Bar Foundation

- American Bar Association ("ABA") Business Law Section Liaison to the Section of Taxation
- Member, Executive Committee, California Lawyers Association, Taxation Section
- Chair, City of Menlo Park Finance and Audit Committee (2021-2022)
- Palo Alto Area Bar Association, Past President
- State Bar of California Past Chair, Tax Policy, Practice and Legislation of the Taxation
- Member of the ABA Task Force on Tax Legislation (2018-2019)
- Past Chair of the Committees on Tax Practice Management and Tax Policy of the ABA Tax Section; Past Chair of the Taxation Committee of the Business Law Section; Past California State Delegate to the ABA House of Delegates

Contact Information Tel: +1 650.687.8820

E-Mail: Roger.Royse@haynesboone.com

Web: https://www.haynesboone.com/people/r/royse-roger

www.rogerroyse.com

CONTENTS

NOTES

Disclaimers

I am a lawyer but I am not your lawyer. This book provides legal information but not legal advice. You can learn from these chapters but cannot rely on them. If you want legal advice pertaining to you, you should consult a lawyer and not this book. I make no promises, representations or warranties about anything you are about to read. If you are OK with that, read on.

Warnings

The law is always changing and therefore this book has a shelf life. How long is anyone's guess. Parts of this book may be obsolete by the time it is published. That is all the more reason to check with a lawyer before relying on any legal information in this book.

As in my first book, the names have been changed except in publicly known cases. As a lawyer, I am bound by a strict code of confidentiality, so I cannot disclose client secrets even if they result in success stories.

The Tax Laws May Change

I am a tax lawyer and, thus, I mention the tax law often in this book. As this book goes to press at the end of 2021, Congress is considering significant changes to the law. The states may or may not conform to those federal changes. Consult a CPA or lawyer before you rely on the statements of tax law contained in this book.

Your Mileage May Vary

A lot of this book is law, more of it is opinion, and most of it is based on my experiences. Your experiences may be different. In particular, my experience is mostly with a certain set of venture capitalists (VCs) in the Silicon Valley. VCs may act differently in other markets. You may also disagree with me and I encourage you to do so. If you find a mistake, let me know and I will thank you.

What to Expect?

My first book, *Dead on Arrival: How to Avoid the Legal Mistakes That Could Kill Your Startup*, covered many of the common legal issues that startups encounter. Most of the information in that book is still relevant, although there have been a few notable changes in the law. Rather than restate *Dead on Arrival* (I will save that for a second edition), this book goes in a different direction; it is less legal and more anecdotal.

Appendices and Attachments

Some of the feedback from *Dead on Arrival* indicated that portions of the book assumed a lot of knowledge and the text was a little heavy going. I want *10,000 Startups* to be more readable, more accessible, and more user friendly. Therefore, much of the legal analysis is in the attachments instead of the main text. If you would like to learn more about a topic, you can go to the relevant attachment.

Credits and Thanks

Thanks to Soyeun D. Choi for helping edit this book. Thanks to Marvin Glazer and Gary Edwards for reviewing some passages on patent law and C. David Spence for helping with the estate planning chapter. Despite the other eyes on this manuscript, any mistakes are solely mine.

INTRODUCTION

The world loves bad news. Newspapers are filled with stories of failure, disgrace, and tragedy. The self-help section at Kepler's bookstore in Menlo Park is filled with books about all the things that can go wrong, how to fix broken people, mend failed relationships, and change bad habits. There is good reason for our tendency to focus on the negative. If our cavemen ancestors sat around in a Zen state of mind instead of constantly worrying about saber tooth tigers, we might not be here at all. Evolutionary psychologists say our negativity bias was necessary for survival. It was that fascination with failure that launched my first book, *Dead on Arrival: How to Avoid the Legal Mistakes That Could Kill Your Startup* (hereinafter *Dead on Arrival*).[1]

This book is not like that. This book is about the stories you do not hear about – the quiet successes: founders who worked well together; startups that avoided litigation; and products that complied with law and regulation. This is a book about the good legal planning that prevented problems from occurring.

In this book, we will walk through the basics of good legal hygiene and how some of my startup clients and other well-known companies have paved a trail to success, partly by getting the law right. This book focuses on the legal strategies I developed over many years that increase a company's chances for success.

Dead on Arrival first appeared in print in 2012. Since then, I have received many helpful suggestions. The book was written for layman and lawyer alike so, not surprisingly, some parts may have been a tad technical. This book gets to the point without being bogged down in legal detail. The law cognoscenti or those who want more background can consult the appendices for more detail, analysis, and authority. I also heavily end-noted the text with authorities to support some of the legal propositions. I can't help myself; I'm a lawyer.

Congratulate yourself for reading this book because one thing that will become apparent throughout is that the successful founders described in these pages, while usually heeding their lawyer's advice, did not depend on their lawyers to educate them as to all the questions they should ask. Your lawyer may answer a question or make a recommendation but he or she might not tell you which questions you should ask. The successful founders know that and educate themselves, as you are now doing, on the legal tools available.

10,000 STARTUPS

It's only 6:00 p.m. on a cool Friday evening in San Francisco but a popular South of Market ("SOMA") nightclub is already full of people. This is not the usual nightclub crowd; they won't arrive for several hours. This early crowd is here to pitch their startups to judges or listen to other companies pitch to judges. A dozen startups will take the stage tonight and try to convince a panel of angel investors that they have the next big thing. Every one of these startup founders believes that they do. In fact, maybe one in ten will raise money and one in ten of them will actually get to an exit, and I am being generous in my estimates. The startups that succeed will do so by executing perfectly. They will have put together a perfect storm of team, timing, and technology.

I judge on panels as well but, more often, I am responsible for preparing my clients for the pitch. That preparation starts with a solid legal foundation.

Malcolm Gladwell's 10,000-hour rule, roughly stated, holds that mastery of complex skills, like playing the violin, requires 10,000 hours of intensive practice.[2] I have a similar rule. I think it takes 10,000 startups to master startups.

I have been practicing law since 1984 and meet companies at events like the SOMA pitch most nights of the work week. I meet more companies in my office or remotely via Zoom every day. Most days, I talk to more than one company. With almost 40 years of practice and 365 days in each year, I have well over 10,000 days of interactions. While I have not kept track of every startup I have ever met, it's a safe bet that it is a very large number.

When I meet a company, I listen carefully and evaluate whether I want to take them on as clients. They also decide whether they want me to be their lawyer. I look for founders with a high potential for success. If we are a fit, I will do my best to give them a worry free legal structure. While the VCs help companies win based on solid team, product market fit, and other factors, I help them win by ensuring that they have as few legal impediments as possible.

Maybe tonight in SOMA I will find one of those companies or they will find me. Maybe they will follow the advice contained in this book and, the next time we are in a nightclub, it will be at the party following the successful IPO or sale of their company.

PART 1. PEOPLE: ASSEMBLING A TEAM

The first method for estimating the intelligence of a ruler
is to look at the men he has around him.
—Niccolò Machiavelli, *The Prince*

Chapter One

Choice of Entity: C corporations, S corporations and LLCs

The conventional wisdom in Silicon Valley is that every company must be a Delaware C corporation. The theory is that all the big tech companies started or ended up as Delaware C corporations and who are you to buck a trend that Google, Facebook, Uber, Airbnb, and many more have followed?[3] If you are the next big thing, incorporation as a Delaware C corporation is probably the right answer. But the smart entrepreneurs in the room know that the issue is more nuanced than that. A bad choice could mean the difference between success and failure or pocketing a lot more after-tax proceeds on a successful exit.

I will show you how this works but, first, here is a primer on the differences between the three types of entities you might choose for your company.

C Corporation. Most startups are formed as C corporations—partly due to simplicity and partly since most VCs can and will invest only in C corporations. A C corporation is a state law corporation that has not elected to be taxed under Subchapter S of the Internal Revenue Code of 1986, as amended (the "Internal Revenue Code" or "IRC").[4] As a state law matter, there is no difference between a C corporation and an S corporation.

The major benefit of a corporation is that the shareholders or owners of the corporation have limited liability. Generally, the management of the company is delegated to a board of directors, who further delegates the day-to-day business to the officers. The corporation should have (and under some state laws *must* have) at least three officers: a president or CEO, a treasurer or CFO, and a secretary. The same person can hold all three offices.

A C corporation is a separate taxable entity. It pays tax on its income and the shareholders are again taxed when the remainder of its earnings and profits[5] are distributed to the shareholders. This is what lawyers and accountants mean when they refer to the double tax on C corporations. One tax benefit of a C corporation is that gain from the sale of C corporation stock might qualify for exemption or rollover of gain if the stock is qualified small business stock ("QSBS").[6] More on this later.

S Corporation. The S corporation is a corporation under state law but is taxed as a pass-through for federal income tax purposes. So, it offers tax advantages over the C corporation. The S corporation form also allows for more traditional corporate equity compensation, such as an option plan, and it can be a party to a tax-free, stock-for-stock merger or exchange. S corporations can also minimize social security and self-employment (SSA) taxes paid on the business's earnings by the careful planning of bonuses and distributions.[7] The ability to avoid SSA taxes might be the single biggest reason for choosing this structure.

The downsides are that an S corporation cannot issue QSBS, it can have only one class of stock (i.e., no common and preferred stock structure), all its shareholders must be individuals who are US citizens or residents (for tax purposes), and the corporation must not have more than one hundred shareholders (hardly ever a real concern in the start-up company world). Thus, a VC or other institutional investment will terminate the S election but the shareholders may enjoy the benefits of pass-through treatment until then (like tax losses, subject to limitations). Unlike a distribution of property from an LLC, which is generally (but not always) non-taxable, distributing property from the corporation to its shareholders (on liquidation, for example) is a potentially taxable event.

Limited Liability Company ("LLC"). The LLC is a form of entity in which no member has personal liability for the debts and obligations of the company (other than as agreed).[8] The management of the LLC is vested in a manager, a managing member, or all the members under the terms of an operating agreement. The LLC is taxed like a partnership (unless otherwise elected), meaning that its income passes through and is picked up on the returns of its members in such proportions as are set forth in the operating agreement, subject to the limitations of the Code and regulations. Whereas the C corporation is subject to two levels of taxation, the LLC's owners pay one level of tax at individual rates on the LLC's earnings.

More and more, LLCs are electing to be taxed as S corporations to get the benefit of the ability to minimize SSA taxes. For the lifestyle business that will generate many years of steady income, this can be significant. For the go-big-or-go-home startups that I usually represent, this is mice nuts compared to losing the benefit of the QSBS exclusions.

An LLC is flexible and can accommodate almost any deal that the parties can think up. The downside is that due to its flexibility, every LLC operating agreement must address all the deal points that the parties wish to negotiate. The flip side of flexibility is complexity and, the more tailored the operating agreement is, the more complicated it can become. This is usually not a deal breaker but it is a point to know.

Attached as an Appendix A is a handy Entity Comparison Chart that compares each type of entity.

A Case Study – When the S Election Makes Sense

My client Ron, a serial entrepreneur, has bucked the C corporation trend for 20 years, maybe longer. He has formed company after company as S corporations and sold them as S corporations. Each sale is structured the same, each sale results in the maximum after tax proceeds to Ron, and each sale nets enough cash to fund the next company. Due to this strategy, Ron retired after his last sale. His S corporation strategy netted him enough lifetime earnings to transition from entrepreneur to investor, teacher, or beach bum, whichever he prefers. He did this by ignoring the Silicon Valley conventional wisdom of being a C corporation. Had he followed that advice he would not be retiring any time soon. Here is why.

Suppose that Ron has 5 exits over 20 years, each at $10 million cash. Suppose also that Ron owns 20 percent of each company at the date of sale, so he gets $2 million pre-tax from each exit. In the case of a stock sale, Ron can make what is known as a Code Section 338(h)(10) election and treat the sale of stock as a sale of assets. Buyers want to buy assets, not stock, because they can amortize or depreciate the cost of business assets over time, reducing their taxable income. They cannot do that with stock. Ron is mostly indifferent to structuring a sale as a stock or assets sale because of how S corporations are taxed.[9] S corporations are pass-throughs, meaning there will be one level of tax. Ignoring state taxes and the pesky net investment income tax ("NIIT") of 3.8 percent for this illustration and assuming the company has only capital assets (e.g., goodwill), Ron nets 80 percent, or $1.6 million, from each sale.

Had Ron used a C corporation and engaged in asset sales, there would be two levels of tax: one at the corporate level and another at the shareholder level. Thus, the company would have sold assets and paid tax at a 21 percent flat rate.[10] It then would have had $1,580,000 to distribute to Ron. That $1,580,000 would be taxed at 20 percent (ignoring SIT and NIIT), leaving Ron with $1,264,000.

You can see that the after-tax difference is significant and over time can add up (and in Ron's case did). Ron pocketed an extra $1.5 million plus interest by being smart about making

S elections.

So, you might be wondering, why doesn't everyone make an S election? It is rarely used in the startup world. This is for a couple of reasons. First, VCs cannot invest in an S corporation because S corporations can have only one class of stock (i.e., no preferred) and can only have individual owners (not venture funds). Second, only stock issued by a C corporation can be QSBS. That's a big deal since (as of this writing) the gain from the sale of QSBS held for over 5 years may escape federal income tax altogether. Investors love that and startups love investors.

NOTE: As of November 2021, Congress is considering limiting the QSBS benefit. A summary of the current QSBS requirements is attached as Appendix B QSBS.

A Rule of Thumb. By now, you might be wondering when to make an S election and when not to. Most entrepreneurs do not have a good working rule. Most lawyers will tell you to be a C corporation since its simpler (and that's what Google did). Your CPA may tell you to model it or run some what-if scenarios and see which option allows you to come out ahead. I agree with all of that but I have a good working rule of thumb you can use when you talk to your legal and tax advisors. Here it is: Ask yourself who you are. Are you a lifestyle business? Or a go-big-or-go-home business?

A lifestyle business will never be a unicorn or any other kind of mythical animal. It will generate income and possibly grow at some modest rate. At some point you might sell it but you will not take VC money because VCs want explosive growth startups, not lifestyle companies. If that is your case and especially if the company will generate $100,000 to $500,000 of annual net income per owner, then you might be better off being an S corporation to allow you to maximize after-tax income, deduct business losses, and minimize social security taxes.

If you are a go big or go home business, you will probably not have income. You will have nothing unless you can get an investor to fund you and VCs cannot hold stock in

S corporations. Your odds of failure are high and chances of success low but the payoff could be huge. If you can get institutional money, you will ramp up development and own the market. If you do not get money, there will only be a smoking crater in the ground where your startup used to be. There is no in between – you will either be a humongous success or a dismal failure. If this is you, form a C corporation.

So that's great but that is a tough decision to make. What if you could go either way? What if you could be a profitable business on your own or a high-flying Silicon Valley darling. It's just too early to tell. Is there a middle ground?

Case Study: Advantage LLC

My friend Steve was like that. He came up with a cool medical device he took to market quickly, given his contacts in the industry. The company was on its way to profitability, so he talked to investors. If he got VC investment, the business could scale nicely. If he did not get an investment, he could still make money in the limited fields of use and smaller markets he operated. It was just too early to tell how it would go. But, Steve for sure needed an entity to protect him from liability if the device injured someone or if someone claimed IP infringement or any of a million other business risks.

I counseled Steve to form an LLC. The LLC allowed Steve to claim early year losses for tax purposes and, when the business hit profitability, to take distributions with one level of tax. The LLC form was not perfect as compared to the S corporation or C corporation choice of entity. Steve had no ability to minimize social security taxes or issue QSBS to investors. It was, however, tax efficient.

I have counseled hundreds of Steves over the years and Steve's story has three alternative endings:

Ending #1: Steve attracted institutional investor interest. Upon the eve of a Series A financing, we converted the LLC to a C corporation and closed the round with standard Silicon Valley corporate venture terms. The stock issued to the investors (and to Steve) qualified as QSBS and, the last time I checked, the company had concluded some follow-on rounds and was headed toward a successful exit or IPO.

Ending #2: Steve could not attract a VC, so he grew the business organically. The business slowly but steadily grew and prospered. Steve distributed most of the LLC's earnings to himself (at one level of tax) for many years and paid self-employment taxes on the earnings. Many years later, Steve sold the business to a large company in a cash deal. The gain was taxed at one level and mostly at capital gains rates.

Ending #3: The company failed to attract investors and without capital, failed to achieve profitability. Steve closed the business and claimed tax losses for the amounts he invested.

As you can see, for the successful business that straddles the fence between lifestyle and explosive growth, the LLC structure works well. There are, of course, a couple of caveats to this strategy. First, many LLCs will finance their early year losses with debt. Incorporating an LLC with debt financed losses might trigger income to one or more members who claimed the tax deductions in earlier years.[11]

Second, while the founders can be issued QSBS in the incorporation, the gain that they can shield will be limited to the appreciation in the stock after incorporation. See Appendix B QSBS for more information on QSBS.

Finally, forming two entities (an LLC and then a corporation) is twice as costly as forming just one. For a multi-million-dollar VC backed company, this cost is not such a big deal. For a cash starved startup, it may be an issue.

Chapter Two

Choice of Law

Delaware: The King of Corporations (and LLCs too)

When speaking about choice of entity, you usually hear the word "Delaware" inserted before the words "corporation" or "C corporation". Why Delaware? You might ask. Is Delaware still the jurisdiction of choice for start-ups? What about Nevada? You may have heard that Wyoming is friendly to crypto, South Dakota has no income tax, and Arizona has a regulatory sandbox for fintech. All of that is true and is also irrelevant when it comes to choosing an entity.

Dead on Arrival regaled you with stories about what happens when a founder incorporates in an activist or poorly organized state, such as California, and the bad things that can follow from that decision. The rest of the time, well advised founders will organize in Delaware and their legal path will proceed something like this:

The founder qualifies the Delaware corporation to do business in the state in which they have business operations. They also register with the tax authorities of all the states that claim tax nexus. The VCs will only invest in a Delaware corporation but, since the entity was formed under Delaware law, that requirement does not delay closing their equity round. As part of the financing, the parties put in place a voting agreement, which describes the number of directors that each investor and founder may select.[12] Because of Delaware's well established body of law, the parties are relatively assured that their agreement will not be upset by an activist court or that a court might think up new, creative, or unexpected ways to hold directors and officers liable to creditors, shareholders, or other claimants for company activities. At some point, the company may place its stock ledger on the blockchain or at least issue uncertificated stock. When the company later receives an acquisition offer, its shareholders approve that offer by a majority of the shares, voting as a single class.[13]

The above scenario is what the typical VC hopes for, expects, and will require when they insist that the company be formed in Delaware. In the typical case, the path of a Delaware company from formation to exit is relatively frictionless.

Delaware is not perfect, however. In what looks a lot like a Nigerian letter style scam, Delaware has a counter intuitive franchise tax system that sometimes dupes unsuspecting companies into paying thousands more in franchise taxes than the nominal amounts legitimately due. See Appendix C Delaware Tax Memo for an example of how this works. If you get nothing else out of this book, I hope you will use this knowledge to avoid being tricked into overpaying Delaware taxes.

There are, theoretically at least, other states in which a company could organize. My home state of North Dakota, for example, has one of the most modern corporation codes in the country.[14] Don't ask me why. Nevada was a contender to be the new Delaware, especially for companies that valued privacy; however, its business license and presence rules have made it a relatively expensive state in which to incorporate. Wyoming has stepped in to replace Nevada as an easy state in which to incorporate, especially for crypto companies.[15] As much as I would like to see a western state dethrone Delaware as the King of Corporations, it is not likely to happen in my legal lifetime. There is just too much case law precedent and judicial experience in Delaware for anyone to consider going anywhere else *except* in the case of a corporation that will do business only in its home state, does not have investors, and is not so concerned about investor rights, the law of fiduciary duties, and modern internal governance statutes.

Foreign Corporations.

In 2016, a Russian entrepreneur named Ivan came to me with a Delaware corporation he bought from one of the do it yourself ("DIY") websites. He was very proud of himself for saving $2,000 in legal fees by forming his own corporation. He was less happy when I told him he had just inadvertently converted his non-taxable foreign intellectual property to taxable US intellectual property. Apparently, the DIY site did not have an app for that. Fortunately, this story has a happy ending as we caught the whole disaster in time to rescind and restart as a foreign corporation. Why did we do that and when is a foreign company appropriate?

A domestic institutional investor will have a strong preference for investing in a Delaware corporation over a foreign corporation for all the reasons discussed above. But a company may have the right metrics and legitimate reasons for incorporating in a foreign jurisdiction ("offshore"). If a foreign owned company's investment prospects are as likely offshore as onshore, it may be advisable to stay offshore as long as possible. I might keep a foreign owned corporation offshore until a US investor demands that the corporation migrate to Delaware. If the corporation has a US founder, there are, as usual, tax considerations.

Before 2018, using a foreign corporation could have avoided US taxation on the company's earnings until those earnings were paid or repatriated to its US owners. Thus, foreign corporations would regularly reinvest their earnings offshore on a tax-free or tax-reduced basis. The 2017 Tax Cuts and Jobs Act ("TCJA") changed that landscape dramatically. Under current law, US owners of a controlled foreign corporation[16] may be taxed on most of the foreign corporation's income, excepting only the income deemed attributable to tangible property (usually a small amount for my tech startup clients). If the shareholder is an individual, the rate of federal tax on that income could be as high as 37%.

If the foreign corporation has a US trade or business, it will be taxed in the US on its income that is effectively connected with a US trade or business ("ECI").[17] If the foreign corporation intends to conduct a US trade or business, organizing as a foreign corporation will not avoid US tax on that business's income. Corporations organized in countries with which the US has an income tax treaty enjoy the benefit of a higher standard and are not taxed on US business income unless that income is attributable to a permanent establishment. If the metrics are right, we could limit that tax by forming a US subsidiary to conduct the US trade or business.

Returning to our Russian client, Ivan, his foreign IP (now) resides safely in a foreign corporation, far from the tax tentacles of the IRS. Ivan now has an efficient strategy for rolling out his business in the Silicon Valley without upsetting the investors, breaking any laws, or evading any taxes. The plan Ivan adopted is as well scripted as a Russian novel.

Book 1: We meet the protagonist. Since Ivan is foreign and his business is worldwide, we left most of his operations in a set of foreign entities that include an intellectual property ("IP") holding company. Then, we formed a US subsidiary to conduct his US business. The IP holding company protects the IP from creditor claims if the business should not do well and, similarly, protects the operating business if the IP is infringing. The US subsidiary is what we call a blocker because it blocks Ivan's parent companies from tax or liability while operating in the US. The US respects such entities if corporate formalities are observed (which the DIY website probably did *not* accomplish) and the US subsidiary earns an arm's length amount of taxable income. We paper the deal and Ivan moves to the Silicon Valley, pitch deck in hand.

Book 2: Enter the Villain. It turns out that Ivan succeeds in attracting US investor interest, subject to a reorganization into a Delaware corporation that owns all the business, including the IP. This is a big step for Ivan because it means he must subject his foreign IP to US taxation. He takes a deep breath and decides the benefit of having VC investors is worth the US tax cost and asks us to make it happen.

Book 3: The Plot Thickens. We propose a flip transaction, in which the foreign company ("ForCo") (1) forms a new Delaware corporation ("NewCo"), (2) contributes all its assets, including the IP holding company ("IPCO"), to NewCo in exchange for stock and (3) ForCo distributes the stock of NewCo to shareholders of ForCo. There are many variations of this transaction but the general idea is that we convert the foreign company into a Delaware corporation and move everything onshore. See the Appendix D for a schematic of a Flip Transaction.

This is a simple transaction from a US standpoint. The difficulty, if any, is on the foreign side. Many countries will tax the foreign shareholders on transferring property or shares to the Delaware entity. When that happens, we have a work around. See the discussion of stapled entities below.

Book 4: They all Live Happily Ever After or Die a Horrible Death. With the company now reconstituted in Delaware and Ivan at a desk in Silicon Valley, the VCs conclude their venture round. Then, Ivan discovers how expensive a house is in Silicon Valley and wishes he had never met a VC. He moves back to Europe, the VCs replace him as CEO, and Ivan takes his vested shares and starts over, vowing to read my book first before talking to VCs again.

A Note About DIY Legal Websites

You will note in the tale above that Ivan started with a DIY website company. So far, I have assumed that you will hire a lawyer to form your corporation. There was a time when you basically had no other choice. Thanks to the Internet, we now have numerous websites that allow you to form your company online and inexpensively. The American Bar Association, forever in a dreamy, idealistic world of its own, has praised such sites as facilitating access to justice.[18] However, most lawyers view do-it-yourself law as good of an idea as do-it-yourself brain surgery and protest loudly over the whole practice. To be sure, you will make mistakes if you try this at home. But, nevertheless, I am all for DIY websites for legal assistance. They make my job much easier and here is why.

Ten years ago, the number of new incorporation clients who failed (and thus did not pay me) was probably ten times higher than it is today, maybe more. Today, the rate of failures, while high, is not nearly as high as it once was. The reason is that the online incorporation tools have weeded out the tourists and eliminated from the herd the players who are not really serious about their startups. I would guess that most DIY incorporated companies fail, do so quickly, and were never expected to succeed. If they did expect to succeed, they would cough up the $2,000 it takes to incorporate properly and hire a lawyer. That the founders are unwilling to bet even that amount on themselves tells me something (and it is not positive).

A lot of quality companies that end up on a DIY website ultimately become successful and then must seek a lawyer to clean up their documents and/or prepare them for something more sophisticated. I, or someone like me, will help with that. The DIY has filtered out the low-quality startups and has not precluded lawyers from helping the high-quality ones. So, for that, I am all for DIY legal sites.

Chapter Three

Building a Team – Co-Founders

Steve Hoffman runs Founders Space, one of the top startup accelerators in the world. The eponymous captain of Silicon Valley is nicknamed Captain Hoff. I asked Captain Hoff if a startup should hire a technical consultant or find a technical co-founder. Steve firmly believes that unless your business is selling technical expertise to other companies, a consultant just won't have enough skin in the game to give a startup the attention it needs. Steve says, to be fundable, a startup should have a technical founder or co-founder.

Another person essential to the startup team is the person with industry expertise. I regularly work with AgTech or Agri-tech companies, which develop technology for food production. Early in our program we noticed that many companies were building tech solutions for problems that did not exist, like iPad apps that told farmers what they already knew, didn't care about, or couldn't access anyway because of a lack of cellular coverage. The successful companies, however, usually had someone on board who knew the market. Sometimes that person was a farmer themselves or a person who was in an agriculture related business.

That formula is the same for any other tech company that hopes to disrupt an industry. For example, fintech companies should know financial services and healthtech companies should know health care. Like Captain Hoff says, only a founder will invest the effort needed to get the tech into an industry.

A startup is usually a team effort, meaning that a company must attract and retain several people, including a techie, an industry specialist, and a visionary. The startup must then ask those people to work long hours, usually without pay, in a highly risky venture. How do you do that? One word: Equity.

<u>"Get Equity"</u>

Los Gatos is the kind of town that screams Silicon Valley. It sits at the base of the Santa Cruz mountains, just a short drive to either the communities of the Silicon Valley or the towns on the coast. One of the few businesses not pushed out by gentrification is the Black Watch Bar, the South Bay's number one biker bar. One warm summer afternoon I was enjoying the Black Watch's signature Kamikaze drink (no more than one is recommended). A row of Harleys were parked on the street outside. Seated to my right were two tattooed, chained, rough looking bikers engaged in a lively discussion, seemingly about a job offer. "Make sure you get equity," one of them exclaimed. "Ya, equity," said the other. That is the depth of the equity culture in Silicon Valley.

What exactly does that mean?

<u>What is Equity?</u>

Silicon Valley was built on equity compensation and most of that has been in the form of a magical instrument that allows a person to participate in the upside of a company without having any downside risk. The magic is optionality and the instrument is an option. There might be no two words more powerful in Silicon Valley than "stock option."

Technically, an option is a right to buy some shares ("option shares") of stock at a certain price (the "exercise price" or "strike price"). Under current rules, the exercise price of an option must be the fair market value of the underlying option shares as of the date of grant of the option. Thus, if the value of the shares increases (as expected), the option becomes more valuable ("in the money"), allowing the optionee to wait and see before exercising and buying the option shares. If the stock value increases, the optionee will exercise the option and participate in the increase in value. If it decreases, the optionee will not exercise and not be out any money. This is optionality.

An option is a security and, thus, must be granted in compliance with federal and state securities laws, even though it provides no voting rights, imposes no fiduciary obligations, and does not participate in corporate distributions. Some states, such as California, require a securities notice to be filed with the state. No federal filings are required for private companies but there are rules on what must be in an option plan and what aggregate value of shares may be optioned.[19] Importantly, a written plan is required and, under the most common federal securities law exemption for equity plans, options may be granted only to individuals.

Current tax rules require an option to be granted at fair market value as of the date of grant (see the discussion on Internal Revenue Code section 409A below). If an option is granted to an employee at less than fair market value, the employee will be subject to taxes, penalties and interest. The company will also have withholding obligations. Because of the potentially large tax exposure, most venture-backed companies will obtain a professional valuation to support their option price, as all companies should.

The requirement of a valuation is a problem for a lot of startups since the company might not have enough metrics for a valuation professional to come up with a value. Also, valuations can be expensive and startups are cash starved. There are some ways to deal with that problem.

The startup might avoid options altogether and simply grant stock. A stock grant, unlike an option grant, is taxable to the recipient but does not require a 409A valuation. Alternatively, the startup can promise to grant an option at a future date when it does have a valuation. In that case, the option is not granted until it is *formally* granted, meaning that necessary corporate action has been taken. An offer letter promising to make a grant does not result in a completed grant that locks in the strike price. That price will be measured not at the date of the offer letter but at the date of grant and no backdating is allowed.

Options come in two flavors: Incentive Stock Options ("ISOs") and Non-statutory Options ("NSOs"). Most stock plans allow for the grant of both ISOs and NSOs. The amount by which the value of the option shares exceeds the exercise price (the "spread") on an NSO is taxable as ordinary income on exercise. The spread on an ISO, however, is not taxed until the option shares are sold, which is why ISOs are popular. However, the spread on an ISO is an adjustment to alternative minimum taxable income, which may cause alternative minimum tax so, except for relatively small grants, it is not quite accurate to view ISOs as tax free.[20] In addition, an option is only an ISO to the extent it is exercisable as to $100,000 worth of stock in any calendar year.

If the shares received on exercise of an ISO (the ISO shares) are held for at least one year from exercise and two years from grant, gain on sale of the shares will be taxed at favorable capital gains income tax rates. If the shares are disposed of before the expiration of those time periods, however, the transaction is called a disqualifying disposition and the gain is taxed at ordinary rates.

Options can and regularly do vest, just like stock or, to be more accurate, the underlying option shares can be made subject to a right of repurchase at cost that lapses over time based on continued employment. Options can be exercisable for vested shares under a vesting schedule or can be exercised for non-vested shares. An exercise for unvested shares is known as early exercise.

The TCJA gave us a new type of startup equity compensation plan. Section 83(i) allows qualified employees the option to defer the recognition of taxable income from qualified stock for up to five years past the date substantial vesting occurs. By electing to defer the income, the recipient of the stock option or restricted stock unit ("RSU") defers the date for which the income is recognized but the deferral does not affect the amount or character of the income recognized. The amount of income recognized is the difference between the fair market value of the stock and the price paid for the stock at the time it was substantially vested. Even if the stock declines in value during the deferral period, the amount of income is based on the value at the time the stock became transferable or substantially vested.[21]

A few important notes on §83(i) elections. First, these can only apply to privately held corporations whose stock is not readily tradable on established securities markets. Second, it is only available if 80 percent of the company's employees receive stock options on the same terms. As this election requires broad participation, it is specifically geared to benefit employees of private firms in the start-up arena. Third, an election to apply these rules must be made no later than 30 days after the first date that the rights in the stock are transferable or substantially vested, whichever occurs first. Lastly, employers who provide qualified stock must comply with employee notification require-ments. Failure to do so will result in significant penalties.

For more information about option plans, see Appendix E Stock Option Plans.

My rule of thumb with options is that they are for smaller stakeholders. While there are exceptions to my rule, C-level executives should hold stock instead of options. Higher-level participants should put skin in the game by buying stock. An option, in contrast, carries no risk until exercise. The more commitment we want from management, the more we want them to be stockholders.

How much Stock Should Management have?

Here is a scenario that plays out all day, every day, in Silicon Valley. StartupCo authorizes[22] 10 million shares. It issues 8 million to its founders and reserves 2 million for its stock or option plan. Thus, its fully diluted[23] cap table looks like this:

	Class	Number of shares	Percentage
Founder	Common	8,000,000	80%
Stock Plan	Common	2,000,000	20%

StartUpCo raises money by selling 4 million shares of Series A preferred stock. Now its cap table looks like this:

	Class	Number of shares	Percentage
Founder	Common	8,000,000	57%
Stock Plan	Common	2,000,000	14%
A Investor	Preferred	4,000,000	29%

StartupCo blows through its initial funding and then does a Series B round. It sells another 4 million shares. Now it looks like this:

	Class	Number of shares	Percentage
Founder	Common	8,000,000	44%
Stock Plan	Common	2,000,000	11%
A Investor	Preferred	4,000,000	22%
B Investor	Preferred	4,000,000	22%

The real world is more complicated than that. The option plan will likely increase by the time you get to Series B. The company might have convertible instruments on its cap table. The company might do down rounds. The point to make here is that the founding team will have over 50 percent after Series A but will lose control after Series B.

Many years ago, one of my mountain biking pals told me how he had financed his company by selling common stock to friends and family. He had a lot of friends and sold quite a lot of stock. He sold so much stock that, in my sample cap table above, his management team would have been squashed down to a small percentage after a Series A financing. The VCs would never go for that because they need management to have enough common stock to be incentivized to perform. If passive investors held a large amount of common stock, there would not be enough upside to keep the founders working through the many Top Ramen days and long nights ahead. We went back to his friends and convinced them to recapitalize. Instead of common stock, we gave them convertible notes which converted to preferred stock in the later rounds. The moral of the story is that management must keep enough common stock to keep the company investable.

Plan on giving 20 to 40 percent to the Series A holders and 20 percent to optionees. After that first round, plan on management having over 50 percent. Plan on selling about the same amount in Series B (although that is far more speculative) and plan on losing control in that round. I hope you will not need a C round but by that time you will likely be off the management team anyway. You can set these amounts by backing into the numbers, starting with a series B cap table, as I have done above.

How Much Stock should each Founder have?

Of those 8 million shares, how much stock should each founder have? That is the million-dollar question (or more). Here are ways that founders can split up equity:

Equal Split – are all founders created equal?

The most common way of dividing equity is by simply splitting it up equally. For example if there are three founders, each gets 1/3. On top of this split you will add vesting (see below) and an equity comp plan (see below) so adjustments can be made along the way. This method has the advantage of simplicity and avoids the uncomfortable conversation about the relative value of each founder's contribution. It is, however, inexact and may actually inhibit value creation.

Thomas Hellmann, of the Sauder School of Business at the University of British Columbia, and Noam Wasserman, of Harvard Business School, have studied the issue and have found that equal splitting is associated with lower first round valuations from investors.[24] On average, companies that split founder equity equally are valued at about 10 percent less than companies with negotiated splits. It's not clear whether the equal splitting is a cause or an effect. Parties who negotiate splits with their founders might be the kind of people that negotiate harder for valuations with their investors. Or maybe, in an equal split situation, someone will feel like someone else is getting a windfall and be less motivated to work hard. Or maybe the investor is adjusting their valuations to account for the extra shares held by the slacker founder, since more shares must come from the company to compensate someone else to do his job.

In my experience, about a third of all startups use an equal split method. There is no issue with that approach as a legal matter but, when I see an equal split, I will recommend vesting restrictions (discussed below), so we can reduce the number of shares held by non-contributors, if necessary, and an equity plan so we can increase the shares held by contributors, if necessary.

Methods for splitting equity are discussed in greater depth later in this book.

In the "doesn't matter much" category, you should keep in mind that start is usually a long way from exit in the typical startup and the company's ownership will look much different at exit than it does at start. Contributors will come and go, options will be refreshed, shares will be repurchased, and the investors may reset the cap table with every financing. Whatever method makes you feel good will probably be fine if your first investor is just going to make a pancake out of whatever you have devised, which is often the case. The VCs are notorious for re-shuffling economic decks that have already been dealt. My job as company counsel is not so much to care for the refinements of how the cards are dealt but to ensure that the structure has the flexibility to accommodate changes, if necessary.

In the 2010 motion picture *The Social Network*, one Facebook founder (Eduardo) ended up with a small amount of equity after the investors became involved. The situation came as an unfortunate surprise to Eduardo but not to any startup lawyer in the audience, since these situations play out frequently. The investors did not consult a grunt fund method or argue over what the opportunity cost of the founder's time was a year earlier. All that mattered was where they were at the time of the financing. Thus, as for the company, whatever the split, it must allow for changes.

By the way, I have no idea whether *The Social Network* is an accurate depiction or not. Your takeaways here should be that (i) founders need to split equity, (ii) the company should have the flexibility to adapt to new events (new founders, investors, etc.) usually through vesting restrictions and equity bonus pools and (iii) company counsel is looking after the interests of the company, not necessarily the interests of the founders.

Pro Tip – Outsourced Cap Table Management Tools

There was a time when cap tables were kept on excel. The lawyers had a copy, the client had a copy, and they often diverged. They were also often wrong and consumed a lot of time and expense in the updating at financing and liquidity events. These days, commercial cap table solutions are available online that keep track of cap tables in the cloud. Some good solutions include Carta, Pulley, and Captable.io (renamed LTSE Equity), among others.[25] While they are only as good as the information fed into them, they have solved the problem of multiple dueling cap tables and have taken much of the pain out of cap table maintenance. You should look into outsourcing this function.

Chapter Four

Vesting

Here's a good one. Three guys walk into a bar. They decide to form a company. They divide the equity three ways and pencil out their idea on a napkin. The next day, they visit their lawyer who recommends that the founders all vest into their shares over three years with a *one-year cliff*. Six months later one founder gets bored with the business and moves to Indonesia to live on the beach. He terminates his service with the company. The company buys his shares back at a nominal amount and sells those shares to a new person who will act as his replacement. The team comes up with a minimum viable product ("MVP") soon after, obtains some angel money, which leads to venture money, and exits a few years later at a large valuation. We all celebrate with a closing dinner in San Francisco.

There is no punch line to that joke because vesting is no joke. It is an essential part of every startup's organizational structure. Without vesting, that company may have lasted all of six months. With vesting to protect the management equity pool, it lived on.

Here is how vesting works. The founders purchase their common shares for a small amount (since the company is new, it has a low valuation). If a founder leaves before a certain period of time has expired (usually three or four years in the Silicon Valley), the company may buy back the unvested shares at cost (not value). The founder would then lose those unvested shares.

The repurchase right lapses and the shares vest over time so that after the vesting period—say, three years—all the shares are vested and are not subject to repurchase. If the founder leaves after two years, two-thirds would be vested and one-third would be unvested. You get the idea.

It is a good idea to agree to vesting restrictions right up front, even though you might get kicked out of the company and lose all your unvested shares. For starters, an investor is likely to ask for a vesting restriction from all the founders and, if one of you is difficult or unreasonable, that is just one more thing that must be negotiated. Second, any company is at risk of losing or replacing a founder in the first year. Startups are hard and not everyone has the stomach for it. When someone leaves, you will want the departing person to return his shares so the company can use that equity to replace him.

You Need to File an 83(b) Election!

The tax rules regarding unvested stock are tricky. If you are a service provider (e.g., a founder, employee, advisor, contractor, or consultant) and you don't want to get creamed on taxes, you must file an election with the IRS called an 83(b) election. Unless your mother works at the company, you cannot assume anyone will take care of it for you. The company will likely tell you that it is your problem, not theirs. Here is what all the fuss is about.

In tax language, stock that is subject to a substantial risk of forfeiture is treated as transferred to the owner when the restrictions lapse. For unvested shares, that means they are treated as transferred as and when the shares vest. In other words, the general rule is that a founder does not own stock for tax purposes unless and until it vests. If the stock appreciates between the time of grant and date of vesting, it will be treated as having been transferred at a value higher than the price paid, which is a taxable event for the founder. For example, if the founder buys unvested stock for $1 and it is worth $1.50 when it vests, the founder may have $0.50 of taxable income at the vesting date because he is not treated as owning the stock until it vests. At vesting, he is treated for tax purposes as having received $1.50 worth of stock for the $1 he paid, resulting in a $0.50 taxable gain.

Worse, because the founder will be an employee, vesting is an event that creates a withholding tax obligation for the company. The tax code allows a person to avoid this harsh result by electing to treat the issuance of non-vested shares as a transfer of the shares at the time of grant or issuance, rather than later when the shares vest. Thus, the compensation element in the transaction closes and there is no further tax event when the shares vest. This election is called a Section 83(b) election. The Section 83(b) election must be in writing, signed by the taxpayer, and filed within thirty days of issuance—if it is one day late, it is wholly ineffective. In addition, the taxpayer must prove that it has been filed (best practice is by certified mail return receipt or a file-stamped copy).

The 83(b) election is a beautiful thing. If the founder has made a valid election, when he or she sells his or her stock at exit (after a one year holding period), all the gain will be taxable at capital gains rates instead of the much higher ordinary income rates. The difference can be huge.

Taxes and the Belated Founder

The receipt of stock for services is taxable at ordinary rates. The stock in that scenario is valued at fair market value as of the time of receipt. After the stock is received, if a recipient holds it for a year (the holding period) and then sells, he or she will have capital gain or loss on the sale. As of this writing, capital gains are taxed at a lower rate than ordinary income.

One of my clients, a renewable energy company, was in the three guys walk into a bar scenario and their problem was not that they needed the departing CEO's stock back (they had it) but that they needed to issue new stock to his replacement. The tax law is not kind to the incoming shareholders in this scenario. The difference between what the service provider (the new CEO) pays and the value of the stock received is taxable income as if the company paid him for services in stock instead of cash. Never mind that the stock is illiquid and cannot be sold to generate cash to pay his taxes. The incoming shareholder either must pay fair market value for the stock in cash or be taxed on the value of the stock received.

Venture backed companies run into this problem all the time since they regularly replace management after they gain control of the board. Part of the compensation package offered to new management will usually consist of stock. So how do they deal with it?

That was the question my renewable energy company had for me. How do we get stock into the hands of the new CEO? As a lawyer, I won't tell you or them what to do but I will lay out options, explain the consequences, and help evaluate the risks.

Option 1: Stock grant. The benefit of an outright grant of stock is that the CEO is not out of pocket any exercise price but the downside is that he or she is taxable at ordinary rates on the value of the stock at the date of grant, even though the CEO is getting no cash out of the deal. The holding period starts on the date of grant.

Option 2: Stock sale. The CEO has no tax consequence because of the sale but has to pay the company fair market value for the stock. The holding period starts on the date of sale.

Option 3: Stock sale for a promissory note. This is the *Wimpy* solution. J. Wellington Wimpy, generally called Wimpy, was a character in the comic strip and television cartoon, *Popeye the Sailor*. Wimpy's regular line was, "I'll gladly pay you Tuesday for a hamburger today," and we knew he would not pay anybody on Tuesday.

Similarly, in the promissory note scenario, the CEO gets the stock on day one but need not pay for it until later. If the note is recourse, meaning that the company can seek repayment from the personal assets of the debtor, the note must be paid at some point. If the note is nonrecourse, however, the CEO may never pay for it.

The term nonrecourse means that, upon default, the company can take the shares back (subject to collection procedures imposed by law), but cannot hold the executive personally liable. As a tax matter, the IRS does not view the nonrecourse note arrangement as any different from an option and will tax the transaction as though it were an option. Thus, for tax purposes, the executive is treated as buying some stock each time he or she makes a payment on the note. This means that the executive gets no holding period credit until he or she actually pays the note. If the value of the stock has increased between the date of the note and the payment date, he or she is also treated as buying the stock for less than its value and may have gain on each payment date when he or she is deemed to own the underlying shares. Obviously, that is not a great result.

Option 4: Use a phantom plan or bonus plan. Phantom stock, as opposed to real stock, is a contractual right that mimics stock in one or more ways. Thus, if there is a sale of the company and the holders of the real stock sell their shares for cash, the holders of phantom stock would get a distribution as if they held real stock. Phantom stock works well for small stakeholders but not so well for larger ones. The payment on phantom shares is compensation, not dividend or sales gain, and is subject to tax withholding by the employer. The amounts received are taxed at ordinary income rates.

So, faced with these options, the CEO of the above renewable company had to make a choice: (i) pay cash or sign a recourse note and enjoy capital gains tax rates if the company is a success and suffer the cost of the shares if the company is a failure; or, (ii) take an option or sign a nonrecourse note, in which case he will have ordinary income if the company succeeds and no out of pocket loss if the company fails.

This story could have ended in many ways. In this case, the CEO chose the nonrecourse note. He turned out to be a wise man because soon after the transaction, an influx of cheap Chinese semiconductors decimated the US solar manufacturing industry, sending his company into bankruptcy. Under the nonrecourse note, the CEO walked away unscathed.

The compromise solution to this problem would have been to allow the CEO to purchase his shares with a promissory note that has limited recourse. By limited recourse I mean that the creditor (the company) would be limited in the amount of personal assets of the debtor it could seize to satisfy payment of the note. For example, a 50 percent recourse note would mean that the debtor is only personally liable for half the note and the creditor could sue and recover that limited amount from the debtor's personal assets. The recourse required for the IRS to respect a note as payment (and not a mere option) is not entirely clear but 51 percent is generally assumed to be safe in a start-up company environment.[26] That means that the CEO would eventually have to pay that amount regardless of what happened with the shares.

Chapter Five

Advisors, Directors, Consultants and Employees

Advisors

"It's a rare man that is smart enough to do what he is told," a wise man once told me.[27] For the founder who will take counsel, there is no shortage of people who will tell a founder what to do. Those people are advisors, consultants, and counselors.

An Advisor has a special expertise or brand that is valuable to your company and who advises you as needed on very specific issues. An Advisor typically works for equity, if they take compensation at all, and is consulted periodically. An Advisor's term is usually, but not always, relatively brief. Unlike officers and directors, advisors have no authority to bind the company or act on its behalf. An Advisor is not the same as a consultant.

An Advisor may be an industry luminary who will advise a founder on how best to approach a market. He or she may be connected to money and may help the company find investors or a certain type of investor. The Advisor may have some technical knowledge that would be useful or market connections or a big rolodex.[28] Even though we call it a board of advisors, unlike a board, the advisors may never meet each other since they are selected due to their narrow expertise on specific issues.

Advisors are most often paid in equity as stock or options. Stock or options granted to advisors are between 0.10 percent to 1 percent, with a standard of 0.25 percent and sometimes more for high value advisors. The Advisor's equity should vest monthly over 2 years. Vesting may accelerate upon sale of the company, since the buying company will not likely have any need for keeping the advisor around post close. Since the Advisor does not report to work regularly like an employee or deliver a result like a consultant, the company should establish some metrics for the advisor and should tie vesting to those metrics. For example, the metric might be a certain number of hours per month of meetings. If the Advisor's expertise is in knowing the market, the metric might be sales to a certain number of customers.

Directors

Directors are elected by the shareholders (owners) and are responsible for the management of the corporation. For LLCs, the managers usually have this role. Directors differ greatly from advisors because they have fiduciary obligations to the company (it is questionable whether advisors have such duties), have authority to act, may bind the company to its decisions, and must act as a group. Directors may be chosen due to their stake in the company. For example, the directors will usually be founders or investors as they may have the right to fill board seats. Some directors are chosen because of their expertise and some serve as tie breakers.

Here are some rules about directors that will keep your board running smoothly. First, have an odd number of directors. If you have an even number, you run the risk of deadlocks. A deadlock (e.g., 2 in favor, 2 against a proposal) means that the proposal does not pass. The worst case is that the company is so deadlocked that it cannot kick out a departed founder, sell its assets, or operate the business. There, a court may be invited to step in and solve the problem by appointing a receiver or ordering a liquidation and dissolution. An odd number of directors largely solves that problem.

Second, choose carefully. Directors have enormous power over a company, so you would want to ensure that you have responsible people at the helm.

Keep the board size small. Three is plenty for a new startup (but not two – see rule 1 above). Five is large but ok if people are not wedded to the position. Seven is pushing it. Nine is way too many. When you have large boards, you exponentially increase the effort required to reach quorum[29] and convene a meeting. Startups need to be nimbler than that.

Note that someone must come off the board eventually. When the VCs come into your company, they will want board seats and that means someone must leave, hopefully without contention.

Directors draw fees when the company can afford it and take stock or options on independently negotiated terms until then. Since directors are often stockholders, the market standards for equity ownership are not standardized. I start with the advisor guidelines and adjust from there. Vesting may apply (similar to advisors) and directors should sign NDAs and sometimes invention assignments (if the director has other roles). For both advisory or director roles, the prima donnas will push back on signing NDAs and invention assignments. This is especially true of VCs since they may have director positions in companies in similar spaces and do not want to expose themselves to potential claims. If you do forego these protections, know who you are dealing with and whether you can trust them.

Finally, directors have fiduciary duties, meaning they can be sued by unhappy shareholders, creditors, and third parties. Those duties include a duty of care and a duty of loyalty.[30] The business judgement rule[31] protects directors from most good faith business decisions but a good defense will not stop a lawsuit. Thus, directors should have indemnification agreements whereby the company agrees to indemnify the director for actions taken in good faith on behalf of the company. Importantly, every director should insist that the company procure and cover them with directors and officers liability insurance ("D&O insurance").

A case in point

One of my clients operated an online platform for trading in a certain consumer product. Not being very astute financially, the CFO had mistakenly (or not?) booked consignment receipts as revenue. The nature of consignment receipts is that they do not belong to the consignee company; rather, they belong to their consignors. That meant that revenue was overstated on the company's financials. That is bad, but it got worse. When the company hit some cash flow issues, it was unable to pay some consignors and the problem started to mushroom. The board consisted of at least three venture capitalists, none of whom thought to look into the financials. I counseled the company that a fraud claim based on these facts was imminent and would make it difficult for the board members to get D&O insurance in the future. That would make it difficult if not impossible for the directors to serve on other boards. Investor's counsel did not see the issue and thought me to be a tad bit alarmist until, at my insistence, they spoke to an insurance broker. After that conversation, the VCs settled the potential claims before they became asserted claims and they all lived to fight another day. Although the company did not survive, the VCs were so relieved to have avoided the fraud claim that they stepped up and paid my fees personally, even though they did not have to, which almost never happens.

Officers and Employees

The board of directors delegates the day-to-day business of the company to its officers. As noted above, the corporation should have at least three officers: a president or CEO, a treasurer or CFO, and a secretary.

Some companies have Co-CEOs when I cannot talk them out of it. Co-CEOs are allowed by law but they invite deadlock, confusion, and conflict. If you are ok with that, then go ahead and have Co-CEOs.

Officers are employees, not independent contractors, of the corporation. However, specific services may be provided through contractors. For example, there are temporary, outsourced, and rented CFOs that are not employees and there are outsourced management solutions that might not be employees. See below for a discussion of this issue. As employees, officers are entitled to be paid at least minimum wage, in cash, absent a narrow founder's exception.[32]

Besides cash salaries, officers should have stock in the company and that stock should be subject to a vesting restriction. Equity compensation saves precious cash for the startup and aligns the individual's interests with the company's. There are numerous calculators online that will help you determine how much stock to grant to employees and officers. The analysis is so company specific, however, that I prefer to model the grants. A typical model would predict an exit value of the company, the expected dilution to get to exit, and the present value of a grant based on exit value. Subtract the employee's base compensation and the formula should come up with a stock grant.

As a practical matter, only the most sophisticated employees will engage in that sort of analysis or even understand it. The more likely metric that employees will use is to compare their grants to what their co-workers have received. Employees will talk, so assume full transparency and keep everyone's grants within established guidelines. And if you think you can control that process through NDAs, know that California law prohibits enforcing agreements by employees not to disclose their compensation.[33]

For larger equity holders (1/2 a percent or more) I prefer that the company sell or grant stock to the service provider. For smaller stakeholders, options make more sense since they allow an employee to share in the upside of a company's appreciation without having to invest cash (unless they want to). Options may also be granted under a broad securities law exemption from registration to holders who might not otherwise be able to acquire stock under federal or state securities laws.

Consultants

The Silicon Valley hosts a contractor culture. Gig economy technologies have made it easier and easier for individuals to turn their side hustles into full time jobs and be their own bosses. The state of California, however, hates the idea of individuals taking ownership of their jobs and has mounted a heavy assault against the gig economy and the contractor culture. The California Supreme Court, in *Dynamex*,[34] dramatically altered the standard for determining worker classification in the context of California wage and hour law. In replacing the decades-old, multi-factor *Borello* test, the *Dynamex* decision implemented a simplified three-part test that effectively narrows the definition of an independent contractor. The *Dynamex* ABC test presumes that a worker is a statutory employee under California wage and hour law unless the hiring entity is able to prove and overcome all of the following factors:

the worker is free from both the control and direction of the hiring entity in connection with the performance of the work, both under the contract for the performance of the work and in fact;

the worker performs work that is outside the usual course of the hiring entity's business; and

the worker is customarily engaged in an independently established trade, occupation, or business of the same nature as the work performed.

In 2019, California law AB-5 codified the *Dynamex* case, subject to numerous exceptions contained in AB-2257. The view of California's lawmakers is that employees lose the valuable protections afforded employees (benefits, wage and hour, health care, etc.) when they are classified as contactors instead of employees. Thus, no matter how much the parties want to have a contractor relationship, state law might prohibit that conduct. California tends to lead the nation in trends, so every entrepreneur needs to be aware of the developing trend in state law to classify contractors as employees. In fact, as of this writing, there is also a proposal to make AB-5 the model for federal legislation that would apply to startups in every state in the country. This is an evolving area.[35]

Despite Sacramento's best efforts, the contractor economy is not going to go away. For now, startups should be prepared to deal with contractors and know how to pay them in equity. Unlike employees, contractors need not be paid minimum wage, need not be paid in cash, and need not be paid currently. The bad news is that typical equity plans are designed by law to be available only to employees or employee-like individuals. Thus, a startup can grant private company stock to a contractor only if they fit within federal and state securities law exemptions from registration. The most common federal exemption is Rule 701,[36] which exempts certain stock or option grants to individual service providers. The grantee will have the same tax issues as employees described above, except that a non-employee cannot receive ISOs.

With non-individual service providers, however, more creativity is required. First, the Rule 701 federal exemption will not apply, so the recipient must fit within another exemption. See below for Regulation D exemptions. Generally, the contractor in this case should be accredited. For an entity, this will generally mean that the entity is 100 percent owned by accredited investors or that it has $5 million of gross assets – a heavy burden. In addition, the transaction must meet state blue sky securities law requirements.

If the company clears the securities law requirements, the recipient still has a tax issue because the value of stock received for services will be taxable income, as discussed above. A recipient may be able to avoid this result by the use of warrants and convertibles.[37]

A Startup on a Shoestring

My client RobotCo is in the innovative field of robotics. Because it is so new, it will be a while before they ever see meaningful revenue and a lot longer to get to EBITDA.[38] RobotCo is also following the Silicon Valley model of foregoing annual operating income in favor of reinvesting and building a great product. They are early and unproven so their value is low – too low to sell a lot of stock to raise money. Even the angels willing to invest in convertibles want a guarantee that their investment will equal a certain low percentage of the company. They call that a valuation cap and there will be more about that later.

It takes a village, apparently, to build a robot and RobotCo has a village of service providers helping them. There are at least three founders who got their stock tax free in a tax-free Code Section 351 incorporation. See Appendix F 351 for the requirements of a Section 351 transaction. Some C-level people came along later and RobotCo sold them stock in exchange for partially recourse promissory notes. Some flamed out within the first year and departed, giving their unvested shares back to the company to re-issue to their replacements. The company adopted a stock option plan, under which it liberally granted options to its team to keep its cash compensation low. The company's consultants and contractors have taken large portions of their fees in stock but, to avoid a current tax on receiving non-liquid stock for fees, they were issued convertible instruments designed to defer the tax impact until they converted to stock. That won't happen until the company is more mature or its stock becomes liquid.

RobotCo won't become a unicorn without a solid business plan and perfect execution. In addition, it will take more than a plan and execution to get traction on its limited cash resources. With the careful and strategic use of equity comp, RobotCo can get to a minimum viable product on its available cash. RobotCo is talking to VCs and is well on its way to a successful financing.

Chapter Six

Putting Out Fires

Reid Hoffman's Masters of Scale podcast is required listening for every startup entrepreneur. The podcast features interviews with the founders and leaders of wildly successful tech startups and focuses on some things they have done to scale their companies. Reid is an early participant in PayPal, Facebook, LinkedIn, Airbnb, Flickr, Zynga, Convoy, Nauto, and Last.fm and knows a thing or two about scale himself.[39] In one episode, called "Let Fires Burn," Reid makes the point that startups must know which fires to put out and which to let burn.[40] PayPal is an example.

In the early days of PayPal, the product had issues. As Reid notes, it is okay be a little embarrassed by your first product. If you are not, you waited too long to release the product. In PayPal's case, the online payment solution had a few bugs. It sometimes may have over charged customers. The company was too young to have a big product support team, so dealing with customer complaints fell on the founders. Unhappy customers called the offices and no one answered. Eventually, customers got ahold of the founders' cell phone numbers, so they changed them. Customers found their office address, so they locked the doors. The way Reid tells it, had they taken the time to fix version 1 of their product, they never would have had time to release version 2. They could not put out all of the small fires. They had to let those fires burn.

Reid is quick to point out, however, that not all fires are equal and not all fires can be ignored. The entrepreneur must be able to distinguish small fires from big ones and, among the big ones, some fires are Chernobyl.

Chernobyl refers to the worst nuclear disaster in history. In 1986, near the Ukrainian town of Chernobyl, a nuclear reactor melted down. The environmental damage was disastrous and the effects of the incident are evident even today. I have visited the area and met some people who were there at the time of the incident. They know that their lives have likely been shortened by the event.

I am not crazy about the Chernobyl analogy. For starters, fire was not their biggest issue - radiation was. Secondly, unless you are from the Ukraine, you might not have been aware of Chernobyl. Finally, Chernobyl has still not recovered, but Silicon Valley is nothing if not forgiving and even failed entrepreneurs have risen again and again to start new companies from the ashes of the old. I think a much better metaphor is the *Dixie Fire*.

The Dixie Fire occurred in the summer of 2021 and was the largest non-complex wildfire in California's history, and the second-largest over-all. It burned for months and was not fully contained until the onset of the October rains.

So how does a founder know the difference between a fire you can let burn and the Dixie Fire?

How to Spot a Fire

In the Silicon Valley, a small but quickly growing professional services firm sought our advice on an employee classification issue. Like many such firms, it started by using subcontractors on an as needed basis. And in accord with industry standards, it treated those professionals as independent contractors and not employees. The result of that characterization was to allow the firm to provide a varied service offering it could not otherwise have provided. It also allowed the firm to avoid federal and state wage and hour laws, such as overtime, minimum wage, and mandated meal and rest breaks. It avoided having to pay benefits, procure workers compensation, and pay payroll taxes. Some experts estimate the cost savings of using contractors instead of employees is as much as 30% of payroll. More importantly, contractor classification allowed the firm to assemble multi-disciplinary teams quickly and effectively compete with much larger firms.

But, there was a fire burning and that fire grew larger and larger with every new hire. The early service providers easily met the somewhat arbitrary tests for independent contractor treatment by requiring professionals to provide their own facilities. The group was small and a lot of the relationships were based on trust instead of agreements. As the firm grew larger, however, it found economies of scale in centralizing facilities and asking its professionals for exclusivity – two factors that counter-indicate contractor status. The legality of the firm's treatment was becoming uncertain.

While the cost savings of classifying service professionals as contractors is substantial, the cost of getting it wrong is larger. A misclassification audit can result in back taxes, interest, and penalties. It can attract large workers compensation claims and even criminal liability for willful avoidance. It can result in large wage and hour claims. Worse, aggrieved employees may be able to sue the company in a class action[41] on behalf of all other similarly situated persons, even those that do not complain. The importance of getting this right is high. Many a company has failed due solely to this one issue.[42] This is not a small fire. This is the Dixie Fire.

The founding partner of the firm saw this issue coming and, unlike many contemporaries, proactively insisted that all professionals be reclassified as employees instead of independent contractors. The demand was met with substantial resistance. Virtually no one wanted to be an employee. Nobody wanted their wages to be subject to withholding. They did not want to be foreclosed from using their own private retirement programs as opposed to employee plans. Mostly, they did not want the designation "employee."

The process was expensive. The firm lost good people who simply refused to agree to the new terms. The cost of compliance was a drag on the firm's profitability and limited its ability to adopt new and innovative technologies. It also brought growth to a temporary halt. It was painful but necessary.

A few years later, all hell broke loose. The Federal Department of Labor made misclassification of employees a priority issue, with punitive edicts coming directly from the White House. The states also saw this area as a source of new tax revenues. Firms that were audited were often driven out of business. Whereas a tax authority acts like a collection agency, the Department of Labor acts more like an avenging angel. State agencies can be even worse. The California courts and legislature have added fuel to this fire by expanding the definition of employee beyond logic and modern commercial practice. See the discussion of *Dynamex* and AB-5 above. One court has even ruled that the new tests for employee classification can be applied retroactively, meaning that practices that were legal for many years were, with the stroke of a pen, potentially illegal.[43]

The firm in this example, however, foresaw this series of events. Long before the meltdown occurred, this firm saw the numerous warning signs and took radical action to mitigate the risk. When the taxing and labor authorities finally came knocking on its door, as they inevitably would, the firm in this example showed that it was squeaky clean. It had little liability. It prevented a Dixie Fire.

So how did the firm know that the fire of misclassification was about to burn out of control? Startups regularly violate the existing Byzantine web of wage and hour laws and get away with it. How is a company to know which issues to ignore and which to address?

Few entrepreneurs would have thought to even ask the question. Had it asked the question of its lawyers, it as likely as not would have gotten the wrong answer. Some would have advised the startup to strictly comply with all wage and hour laws such as rest and meal breaks –a heavy burden – or to take an aggressive position on classification. Neither solution would have been optimal since some of these issues are small and some are existential. If that strikes you as unfair, remember that we are governed by a rule of law, not a rule of fairness.

The moral of this story is one you have heard before – that you, the entrepreneur, must take responsibility for knowing what questions to ask and who to believe. You are doing the right thing by reading this book and the books like it. You should not rely on your lawyer to advise you on where the Dixie Fires are. For many lawyers, every problem is a Dixie Fire or a Chernobyl, and a game theory that eliminates all risk also eliminates all rewards.

In this case, classification became politicized. First, politicians have positioned this issue as a battle between big corporations and powerless employees. The crackdown was supported as protecting workers' rights and little was said about freedom of contract, the importance of gig economy jobs, or the unfairness in trying to apply a fuzzy and non-uniform standard. For a summary of factors on the employee classification issue, see Appendix G Independent Contractor Guidelines.

We have seen similar crackdowns that started as political theory and morphed into legal actions in areas such as immigration, tax planning, and intellectual property. No one today would expect that they could backdate options, employ an undocumented nanny, hold unreported foreign assets, or go dumpster diving for trade secrets, yet those practices were common 20 years ago. They could all land you in jail today. Keep your eyes open and stay informed and you may spot the next Dixie Fire in time to avoid it while letting the small fires burn. Do not assume that a lawyer will warn you of risks that you do not ask about specifically. Being informed is your responsibility.

Chapter Seven

The Smartest Lawyer in the Room

I am sitting at the head of the conference room table (the power position) with three software consulting business founders who are forming their new company. I have worked with these guys for many years and I know them well.

Rex is the business/financial guru of the three. He is a wiz with numbers but maybe not the best vision guy. I have a feeling that he may be a little too good with numbers. I get his Christmas letters (he is old school that way) and I can see he likes the high life. I know he has a new house, a boat, a fancy car, and an RV. Rex is a big guy, the physical embodiment of excess, and on his second or third wife. My gut tells me that his appetite for money is as voracious as his appetite for food and drink. He is in this for the money and a quick exit.

Dave is the visionary. He is also a pure sales guy and, not to stereotype sales guys, but I notice he spends a lot of time entertaining his customers and he seems to have more attractive young women on staff than a sales guy should need. He has a wife he never mentions whom, oddly, in all these years, I have never met. I suspect that his wife is more married than he is and I can tell that he is likely to be a target of the Me Too movement. I also note that Dave has a certain nonchalance about rules, protocols, and procedures.

Joe is the techie of the bunch. He is stereotypically focused on product. While the company could probably find another finance or sales guy, it needs Joe. Unfortunately, Joe doesn't look so good. He is pale and underweight and smells of stale tobacco smoke. He looks like he has been working too hard and he is too old to be working too hard.

These three founders did not have to come to me. They could have hired a robot or an artificial intelligence system to incorporate their company and draft their contracts. My friends in deep learning and AI assure me that an algorithm can replicate anything I can do, or soon will be able to. My friends tell me that an algorithm (let's call him Al Gorithm) is the smartest lawyer in the room. I don't know Al and I don't care if he has rhythm but I doubt he will get this right. Based on my real-world flesh and bone, protoplasmic experience, I believe that this company has a high likelihood of having to deal with death or disability, an angry spouse, or a founder who wants liquidity too soon. This company needs something that is atypical in Silicon Valley – a Buy-Sell Agreement.

A buy-sell agreement is an agreement among stockholders to sell their shares of stock to the company (and possibly the other shareholders) upon the occurrence of certain events. A vesting restriction will allow the company to buy unvested shares (at cost) but not vested shares. A buy-sell will allow the company to buy vested shares at fair market value.

The buy-sell we crafted for the Rex/Dave/Joe business had to have three things:

A right to buy a shareholder's stock upon death or disability.

I am mostly worried about Joe. If he dies or flames out, we need his shares to hire another Joe. We asked each shareholder to agree that the company can buy their shares if they cannot work due to an unfortunate event.

A spousal consent and the right to buy a shareholder's spouse's shares.

In the event that Dave's wife finally kicks him out, she could have a community property interest in his shares if they are domiciled in California or another community property state. That means she could end up as a shareholder. My Spidey senses tell me this would not be good, so we had all the shareholders' spouses agree that the company could buy the spouse's interest in the shares. We could have had the spouses agree that the shares are separate property over which they have no claim but this is tricky stuff requiring each spouse to have their own lawyer and such agreements are sometimes hard to enforce. This scenario looks likely enough that I asked each shareholder to hire lawyers to represent their spouses to advise them on their consents to the buy sell.

A limitation on a shareholder's right to sell his shares.

We don't want Rex to exit too early because we need him to have skin in the game. I also worry he might try to sell his shares to a competitor if the price were right and, since shareholders have certain information rights, that could be very detrimental to the company. We need to restrict the sale of his shares. You may be thinking we could simply have the shareholders agree that their shares are non-transferable but that is the rookie kind of mistake that Al Gorithm might make. I learned in law school that unreasonable restraints on alienation are void – or was it voidable? In either case, a court may refuse to enforce such a restriction. So, instead of trying to prohibit secondary sales of stock, we draft to make a secondary sale difficult. The usual way to do this is to impose a right of first refusal (ROFR) in favor of the company and, sometimes, also in favor of the other shareholders. The ROFR requires a shareholder to offer his or her shares to the company (and/or other shareholders) before they can sell to a third party. The ROFR chills any potential third party offers because who would want to go to the trouble of conducting due diligence and making an offer if the company will just snatch the shares away from them? We also will add a requirement that the shareholder get an opinion of counsel that the sale will not violate securities laws, which is expensive. I might also require the buyer to sign up to the same egregious terms as the shareholders. That ought to do it.

There are, of course, numerous details that must be filled in. You can see an example in the Buy Sell questionnaire attached as Appendix H. For example, how do we determine a fair price for the stock? Who decides if someone is disabled? How does the company finance a buyback of shares? Maybe Al Gorithm, the smartest lawyer in the room, can help with that language now that the executive thinking is done.

I might even go a step further and turn this into a Shareholders Agreement, which is expressly authorized by statute.[44] A Shareholders Agreement will define the rights of shareholders to manage the company, such as the required vote for certain actions, the number of shareholders that can be elected, etc. Most startups do not have Buy-Sell or Shareholder Agreements and are content to rely on the vesting provisions in their restricted stock purchase agreements. There are many reasons for this. A company's value during the vesting period is speculative, so buying a founder out at a low fair market value would deprive them of the real value of the opportunity inherent in the shares. The company also expects to experience rapid growth and exit fairly quickly, placing less risk on long term shareholder issues.

I know you are wondering how it turned out for Rex/Dave/Joe. Well, no lawyer in the world (not even a robot) can tell you what *will* happen; we can only tell you what *might* happen and my presumptions were not far off. The company did buy Rex out. Dave's wife did finally divorce him. She did not challenge being excluded from participation in the company. Joe, on the other hand, is as healthy as a bull and will probably outlive us all. Two out of three ain't bad. Twenty years later, the company is still alive and doing well as a lifestyle business. It is a happy ending.

One More Example of a Good Use of a Buy Sell in a Non-Startup Scenario.

EqualSplit was founded by two longtime friends more than 20 years ago. I cautioned against a 50/50 split. "At least make it 51/49 to resolve deadlocks," I pleaded. They did not take that advice and, for ten years, they got along fine. For ten years, I was reminded annually at the stockholder/board meetings that the risks I warned against existed only in the head of a paranoid lawyer.

The co-founders believed an equal split was the right answer because both were equally dedicated and worked equally hard at the business. However, a lot can change in ten years and the time came when they no longer shared the same vision. The company did not exit as planned and instead became a lifestyle company, albeit a very valuable lifestyle company. One founder wanted to sell; one wanted to hold. There it was: my deadlock. Worse, the parties had different views of the company's worth. Predictably, the founder who wanted to exit valued the company higher than the founder who wanted to hold.

Fortunately, although we did not get a very workable stock ownership structure ten years earlier, I did talk them into agreeing to a buy sell agreement on formation. Under the terms of that buy sell, in the case of a deadlock, the founders would agree to a third-party valuation. There are many varieties of a third-party valuations in a buy sell. In the simplest version, the parties simply agree on a valuation expert. Well drafted buy sell agreements will anticipate that, by this time, the founders cannot agree on anything. The agreements will allow that if the founders cannot agree on an appraiser, they each get to pick one and the two appraisers will come up with a valuation. Sometimes the value is the average of those two appraisals; sometimes, if the appraisals are too far apart, the two appraisers will select a third who will definitively resolve the matter. It is good practice to give the appraisers some rules, like whether or not they may apply discounts to their valuations for marketability, minority ownership or the opportunity for control (alone or acting with others).

One of the founders triggered the valuation process and, while nobody liked the numbers the valuation experts eventually came up with, we all had to agree that it was a fair process. The transaction closed and the company is still alive and well today.

PART 2. TECHNOLOGY: BUILDING VALUE THROUGH LEGAL PROTECTION

"The mystic, endowed with native talents ... and following ...
the instructions of a master, enters the
waters and finds he can swim."
—Joseph Campbell, *Myths to Live By*

Mystics, shamans, and alchemists have long been with us. In the ancient world, societies looked toward various forms of magic, mythology, or religion to transmute base metals into gold, create elixirs of immortality, and cure disease. So universal is the need to create that the great psychologist Carl Jung termed the magician a universal archetype.[45] Technology is the modern magic and tech entrepreneurs are the new magicians.

Technology is about turning lead into gold, manipulating nature, and practicing magic. We start with the laws that protect and enable the development of technology – intellectual property rights.

Chapter Eight

The Startup Executioner:
A Case Study of Ignoring Intellectual Property

Susan was only in her early 20s but had already paid her startup dues. She lived a Top Ramen life, working long hours at a local incubator writing code and pitching ideas. None of her ideas ever gained traction until one day she came up with an idea for a fitness app that would help people track fitness and diet goals.

The first thing she did when she thought of the idea was to assemble a hackathon team to develop and present the idea. A hackathon is a caffeine and sugar soaked event where software developers work to develop a software product in a short period of time, often times collaborating with other developers with complementary skills, such as design, coding, particular APIs, etc. Susan and her team stayed up all night working on the idea and finished a minimum viable app for presentation the next day. While Susan came up with the idea and contributed to the design, the heavy lifting was done by more experienced coders. One coder in particular, Evan, contributed much more than the others. Without Evan, there would have been no product but, due to his tireless efforts and competitive drive, the app was finished by morning.

Spectacularly, the product won the hackathon and everyone was happy. At least for few days. There was much celebrating that evening. The team excitedly spoke about the great concept they had created and how they would jointly improve on and commercialize it. Surely, the VCs would back them. Someone said they should get a patent and maybe trademark the cute name they came up with. Evan took it all in.

Immediately after the hackathon, Susan contacted her team members about taking the next steps to turning the product into a company. Although everyone was excited about the app at the hackathon and shared Susan's and Evan's big plans, what happened next was *nothing*. It just sat there. The other team members went off to their next big thing. Time and life intervened. They stopped returning emails and answering calls and texts. Susan and Evan, however, continued to promote the idea. Susan approached angel investors and worked on designs. Evan improved the software, raising it beyond hackathon standards. And then one day even Evan stopped communicating with Susan about the app. Soon thereafter, Susan forgot about the idea and went on to other more promising matters.

And that is where it sat until one day when Susan happened across a website featuring her app. The product was being promoted by a company Evan had formed. To be sure, the product and concept had come a long way from the simple app that Susan helped create at the hackathon. It was far more robust, with a much more appealing design. It probably was still based on some of Susan's code but it was hard to be sure.

Susan immediately contacted Evan. "What gives?" she asked. "We were supposed to do this together." Evan countered that he decided to develop the idea himself. Her role in the product was minor, he said, simply coming up with the idea and design and writing a small bit of code. In any case, he was unwilling to pay for it and certainly unwilling to grant her any equity. That's when Susan came to me.

Any lawyer will tell you that the first step in any legal analysis is to determine the rights and obligations of the parties. That is not quite correct. The first step is to understand what the client wants. Do you want cash? Do you want equity? Or do you want to kill this company? Sometimes, our view of the rights and liabilities of the parties depends heavily on what the client wants. They call that advocacy.

Fortunately for Evan, Susan did not want to kill the company. She certainly could have. It was using her intellectual property, which she had not assigned. Evan had also potentially breached his fiduciary duties to Susan by going off and building the company by himself – he had been a bad partner. If Susan owned some of the technology, the company could not claim exclusive ownership. If Evan had breached a fiduciary duty to Susan and she made a claim, Evan would be required to defend. Most importantly, if Susan threatened suit, few investors would be interested in this company. Who wants to fund a lawsuit when there are so many other good ideas around? VCs invest to make money. Every VC knows that when companies get sued, the only people who make money are the lawyers and most VCs would rather eat their Audis than give money to a lawyer.

Armed with these facts, I now stood over the company, executioner's sword held high above its exposed neck. With one demand letter, the company would be no more.

Evan was lucky. All Susan wanted was equity. Susan could have been a competitor trying to keep the product out of the market and we could have done that. She could have demanded cash and Evan would have had to pay it. Instead, she wanted something far more precious and much less valuable – equity. Now it was just a matter of how much.

Any good lawyer will tell you that there is support in the law for Susan demanding an equal share of the company. After all, they are co-venturers with no agreement. The law might imply 50/50 ownership. Any good lawyer will also tell you that there is no obligation for Susan to agree to any restrictions on her share of the business. She doesn't have to accept rights of first refusal, lock ups, vesting … none of the things that we discuss in this book. Again, they are all wrong.

Not so much wrong on the law but wrong on the approach. In fact, they are so far off they are not even wrong. The question is not "What is Susan entitled to?" It is "What is Susan's claim worth to Evan?" More to the point, what is Evan's breakeven point? What is the maximum amount he will give to Susan rather than walking away from the project and starting over? How much is it worth to keep me from killing his company? And now we have a negotiation, albeit one in which I hold a sword over the head of the company. If Evan doesn't settle, his company is dead.

There is scarcely a week that goes by that I do not counsel someone on an execution, and I don't mean execution as in implementation. Friends make handshake deals that never get documented. Companies borrow or create IP freely without assignment documents. Entrepreneurs leverage their sweat on fatally flawed endeavors without knowing it until it's too late.

Similarly, there are few weeks that I do not have to deliver the bad news to the hapless entrepreneur that his company does not own its technology, does not have a clean cap table, or carries the cancer of a legal claim waiting to metastasize and take over the company.

Almost always, the execution could have been stayed and the prisoner pardoned. Agreements could have been signed, deals could have been made, or businesses could have been changed to navigate away from problems instead of right into them.

Getting back to Susan and Evan, the parties opted to stay the execution by granting Susan an equity interest in the company. In this case, although Susan might have been legally entitled to some large percent of very little, we opted instead to take a small, vested percent of something that Evan would hopefully grow to be very large. We settled on 5%. It was fair. The executioner would rest that day.

Chapter Nine

Intellectual Property

The largest room rental company in the world (Airbnb) owns no real estate. The largest rideshare companies (Lyft and Uber) own no cars. The most popular video rental company (YouTube) has no sets or studios. So where does all that value come from?

Very few companies that walk into my office have bricks and mortar operations. In the new economy, property, plant, and equipment ("PPA") is not the biggest item on the balance sheet. In a startup, it is not likely to even be on the balance sheet at all. A typical balance sheet will, at formation, have cash and capitalized costs. Because generally accepted accounting principles ("GAAP") record items at cost, that company will similarly have little on its balance sheet when it gets to the financing stage. The investors will demand that sort of balance sheet.

Imagine that the founders capitalize their company with $1,000 and borrow $10,000. Here, is an admittedly oversimplified version of what a typical GAAP balance sheet should look like at financing stage:

Cash	$1,000
Capitalized Costs	$10,000
PPA	$0
Total Assets	$11,000
Current Liabilities	$10,000
Long Term Liabilities	$0
Shareholder Equity	$1,000

That is what the investors want – a very simple set of accounts. On a cost basis, the founders have contributed a little cash and a lot of sweat. The sweat does not show up on the financials and the company value does not reflect those efforts. If we restated this balance sheet based on fair market values, however, we would have a much different story. Imagine our company above is allowed to book up its assets to fair market value. Its accounts would look more like this:

Cash	$1,000
Capitalized Costs	$10,000
PPA	$0
Intellectual Property	$10,000,000
Goodwill	$10,000,000
Total Assets	$20,011,000
Current Liabilities	$10,000
Long Term Liabilities	$0
Shareholder Equity	$20,001,000

Every lawyer in Silicon Valley will tell you how important intellectual property ("IP") ownership is and IP is the one area where a lawyer's services actually create a valuable, alienable asset. Similarly, it is also where the founder's services create a valuable asset. This section describes what that asset is, how to create it, and how to protect it.

Chapter Ten

Types of IP [46]

Intellectual property ("IP") comes in different forms. The basic categories are patent, copyright, trade secret, and trademark. In tax law, we often refer to valuable intangible property, which includes IP but also includes value harder to fit within a legal category.

Intellectual property is legally considered a property right and can be sold and assigned like any other property right. Intellectual property is *not* the same as technology and is not the physical components in which technology is embodied. Terminology is important when enforcing rights. The following is a description of the main categories of legal rights.

Patent

A patent is a government granted right, especially the sole right to exclude others from making, using, or selling an invention for a limited amount of time.[47] For example, a patent might describe a method for building a computer chip. Its value would be in keeping another person from using the patent holders' design and know-how in building that same chip. We may view a patent as both a property right that can be assigned like any other property and a government regulation that restricts others from using an invention.

A patent is an exclusive right granted by the US Patent and Trademark Office (or a similar office in a country other than the United States) to the first inventor for a limited period of time in exchange for public disclosure of an invention. A patent does not grant a right to use the invention; rather, in the US, it is a right to exclude others from making, using, selling, offering for sale, or importing the patented invention for the term of the patent. Like anything else protected as a property right, it may be sold, licensed, mortgaged, assigned or transferred, given away, or simply abandoned.

In the US, Patents are now issued to the first inventors *to file*, not necessarily the first inventor to invent. Under the first to file system, a patent may be issued to someone who was technically not the first to invent. Consider the following hypothetical. Assume that Inventor A conceives of a new method for building a computer chip in January but does not file his patent application until June. Assume further that Inventor B conceives of the same invention in February, gets his act together and files his patent in March. Under the current law, Inventor B is the owner of the patent even though he did not invent first. Inventor A may avoid this problem by disclosing to the public before Inventor B files his patent application; however, this approach may result in the loss of the ability to obtain patent rights in countries outside of the US. The system has many critics but the reality is unavoidable; file your patent application as soon as possible.

Unlike copyright, trade secret, and trademarks discussed below, patents require registration. All patent applications require a written description of the invention sufficient to allow one of ordinary skill in the art to make and use the invention. Non-provisional applications require at least one claim that provides a legal definition of the invention. Most applications also include technical drawings that help illustrate and define the invention. Non-provisional patent applications require at least one patent claim reciting a legal definition of the invention. Most applications also require technical drawings if a drawing would assist in the understanding of an invention. The average wait time for a patent after filing can last as long as three years and the patent process can be expensive. Attorney's fees alone – not including filing fees –will almost always cost you over $15,000 depending on the complexity of your invention.

The person(s) named as the inventor(s) on the patent application have ownership in the patent for the invention until they assign those rights to another entity. Employers often require their employees to assign all rights of patents created within the scope of employment under an employment agreement. Even if the employer does not get an assignment, it may still use the patent without compensating the inventor under its shop rights when the invention was made using the employer's time, materials or labor. When the value of a company depends on the value of its intellectual property (particularly its patents), which depends on the ability to keep competitors out of the market, getting an assignment from the inventor will be important. This is particularly important for start-up companies where the inventors are one or more of the founders and securing ownership of the IP is essential to success of the company.

For the startup on a budget, there is the provisional patent application. The filing of a provisional application with the USPTO establishes an early filing date, often without incurring all of the costs of filing a non-provisional application, but does not itself result in the issuance of a patent. If the applicant files a corresponding non-provisional patent application within one year, he or she will obtain the benefit of the early filing date. A one-year deadline for filing applications outside of the US is also triggered by this filing. A provisional application includes a specification but does not require formal patent claims, inventors' oaths or declarations or any information disclosure statement. The attorney's fees and the PTO fees are much less than the fee required to file a non-provisional patent application.

Attached as Appendix I is a description of the patent process.

Patents are discussed in more detail in Chapters 13-15.

Copyright

"You should copyright that." How often have you heard someone say that? Contrary to popular belief, copyrights are granted *automatically*, i.e. without registration, when an original work is put into permanent form.[48] Original works include songs, paintings, books, photographs, motion pictures, computer programs and even source code. These works are said to be copyrightable meaning they are eligible for copyright protection. Copyright protection attaches to a work when the work is put into a permanent form. For example, a song must be recorded onto a CD, a story must be put to paper, and a movie must be filmed.

What is more important is what copyright does not protect. Copyright does not protect ideas, methods, facts, words, short phrases, or two-dimensional geometric shapes. This should illustrate the main distinction between copyright and patent. Patent protects the functionality of the idea or invention. Copyright does not protect functionality; it protects only the idea's manifestation onto whatever medium you choose. For example, while copyright does protect source code as an arrangement of letters and numbers, it does not protect how the algorithm actually operates. This means that a competitor can come along and replicate how your algorithm operates so long as the letters and numbers are not arranged so it is substantially similar to the original.

The copyright owner receives a bundle of rights: (1) the right to reproduce the work; (2) the right to adapt the work; (3) the right to distribute the work; (4) the right to perform the work; and (5) the right to display the work. Copyright owners possess these rights for the author's entire lifetime *plus 70 years*. An owner may license the copyright or sell it in whole or in part whenever he or she pleases. Thus, anyone who reproduces, adapts, distributes, performs, or displays a work without permission or license violates copyright law as a direct infringer. Also, anyone who helps another violate a copyright owner's rights is liable as a contributory infringer.

Although registration is not required, registering a copyright with the Copyright Office provides additional protection. First, registration is needed to file a civil lawsuit against a copyright infringer. Second, registration is proof in court that a copyright is valid. Third, registration is required to obtain statutory damages and attorneys' fees. Practically speaking, not every copyright need be registered. But if you believe the copyright to be valuable, it is well worth the application fee to register the copyright.

In start-ups, copyright raises some important issues. For one, if an employee creates a copyrightable work as a part of employment, who is the owner? Generally, the person who causes the work to be put in permanent form is the author and owner. In this hypothetical, the employer owns the copyright at the expense of the employee. The same rule may apply to independent contractors. Second, if you are likely to create a website for your business or if a website is your business, the intersection of copyright law and Internet law is important. Without a law saying otherwise, a website that hosts or links to infringing material may be liable as soon as the material is put online. Luckily, Congress has provided a safe harbor for Internet service providers[49] who host or link material from copyright owners so long as they comply with certain other provisions in the law. Thus, if a website will be an integral part of your business, it is imperative to develop a plan to comply with the law to get this protection.

Trade Secret

What if the technology is not patented or copyrightable? Is it worth anything? Most states provide trade secret protection for *valuable* information, including formulae, patterns, programs, devices, methods, or techniques. In addition to state law, the federal law of trade secret should be considered. The Defend Trade Secrets Act of 2016 ("DTSA") allows U.S. employers to protect against and remedy misappropriation of trade secret information in federal court. Before the enactment of the DTSA, in the absence of diversity jurisdiction, employers seeking redress were required to sue in state court. Bringing suit under the DTSA allows a party to avail itself of the federal courts, which can be advantageous since federal courts often are more adept at addressing highly complex technical issues arising in trade secret cases. While the DTSA provides trade secret owners with a new federal cause of action, it does not preempt existing state trade secret law regimes. As a practical matter, this means that a trade secret owner can bring parallel state and federal claims for trade secret misappropriation in federal court.[50]

In this context, "secret" means that the information is not readily known to others in the same industry. As with any other secret, the owner must try to preserve its confidentiality. The recipe for Coca-Cola is the oft cited example. It is said that very few people within Coca-Cola itself know the actual recipe and that the ingredients are kept under lock and key, so valuable is the actual formula. Whether that is true, the key lesson is that the owner of the trade secret must take steps to preserve the confidentiality of the secret. This prong of the definition may be the most important and most neglected requirement of the law of trade secrets.

The owner of a trade secret can prevent whomever – employees, outsiders, thieves – from acquiring, disclosing, or using the trade secret, but only when foul play is involved. Trade secret law does not protect against reverse engineering or independent creation. Employers, however, do have additional protections at their disposal to combat the dangers of employee mobility. First, employers may, and often do, create Non-Disclosure Agreements

(NDAs). NDAs may be one-way (meaning that only one party promises not to disclose) or mutual (each party agrees not to disclose the secrets of the other) and they may protect information that does not constitute a trade secret. Second, employers may require their employees to agree to non-compete clauses. These prohibit an employee from competing with his former employer for a specified period after leaving the job. However some states, including California, do not allow such provisions except in narrowly defined circumstances because they burden an employee's mobility.

An NDA protects confidential information or technology, restricts the use of the information to a limited purpose, and prohibits the disclosure of information to third parties. However, NDAs typically contain an exception for disclosing information independently developed or already in the possession of a signing party. For example, an inventor may meet with a company representative to share his ideas for development. The company representative and the inventor may sign an NDA. However, the inventor may not know that the company has been working on perfecting a very similar product. He or she may now have shared essential propriety information without realizing that the company could beat the inventor to the prototype with no legal liability. Thus, a prudent inventor (1) should not rely solely on the NDA to protect valuable material and (2) should research the party with whom he or she is entering business negotiations.

Interestingly, an invention can be legally protectable as a trade secret and, as a matter of cost, a company might rely on trade secret protection instead of patent. That might not be a great strategy, since a competitor's patent registration could appear at any time, effectively putting them out of business. Trade Secrets and patents are discussed later in this book.

Trademark

A trademark is a distinctive mark used to identify a product or service's unique source and to distinguish those products or services from those of others.[51] A trademark is a type of intellectual property and can include a name, word, phrase, logo, symbol, design, or image and in certain cases can be colors, sounds or potentially even scents.

A person acquires rights to a mark by using it, even without a federal registration. Eventually, that mark (and name) may become so associated with the company and its products as to be a large part of the company's goodwill. If that mark (name and/or logo) should be challenged or diluted, a large part of its goodwill might disappear. When a technology company is sold, it usually has little on its balance sheet in hard assets. Instead, it is selling intangibles, such as intellectual property and goodwill.

The owner of a registered trademark can sue for infringement to prevent unauthorized use of their mark. Registration is not required but an unregistered mark may be protectable only within the geographical area within which it has been used or in geographical areas into which it may be reasonably expected to expand. Thus, a competitor could exclude a company from using an unregistered mark in future markets.

To obtain federal registration on the US Federal Patent and Trademark Office (the "PTO") Principal Register, the mark must not be merely descriptive. In addition, even after a registration, under the fair use doctrine, the owner will not prevail on an infringement claim if the alleged infringer can show use of the mark to accurately describe an aspect of his or her own products or is engaged in explicitly comparative advertising. Thus, a name merely descriptive of a company's products (and its competitors' products) may not be a great choice for a mark. The issue is important to resolve early in the company's life since a large part of its future goodwill may be tied up in the mark and the company or its acquirer would not want it to be subject to challenge.

Because so much of a company's goodwill may be tied to trademark, good practice dictates that a founder search a name or mark with a search engine and then conduct a more formal trademark search (a "knockout search") with the PTO. If nothing comes up in the knockout search, the company may proceed with registration.

Unlike other forms of intellectual property (patents, copyrights, etc.), trademarks are entity-specific. Even for a registered trademark, an attempted sale or transfer of a bare trademark is legally ineffective under U.S. law. Also, trademark rights arise from use in commerce or an application to register the mark stating that the applicant is using or has the intent to use the mark in interstate commerce. This minimizes the potential for placeholder filings and developing markets for buying and selling mere trademark applications.

Open Source Software

Open source software is free for the public to access, develop, and redistribute. This peer review development model promotes an efficient and reliable evolvement of the product, encouraging the advancement of a bug-free program without the complications of intellectual property law, licensing issues, or financial motives. The information-sharing nature of the open source community may be much more efficient than highly confidential proprietary development, allowing many people to test the code and address any flaws. Open source code also has the added benefits of increased quality due to thousands of developers examining the product and getting it closer to what the users actually want. Thus, a startup might consider the implementation of open source software in its own business, which could be further customized to suit its needs without the license restrictions of a proprietarily registered product.

Other Intangibles

Accountants and economists often lump intellectual property rights in the category of general intangibles that add to a company's value. Market intangibles may include goodwill, brand recognition, and customer lists. Data is an intangible asset that might have legal protection. Workforce in place (i.e., relationships with employees and the expectation of retention) may be a valuable intangible.

Legally and strategically, a company will use traditional legal vehicles to protect its other intangibles. Workforce in place, for example, may be strengthened by employment contacts or, in some states, non-competes and non-solicits.[52] Brand and goodwill rely heavily on trademark rights. Intangibles that derive from relationships depend on strong contracts.

Data – the New Gold

One intangible deserves special attention. Data has gone from being a byproduct of a business to a business, especially actionable data and data analytics.

If a company produces or sells data, how can it protect its rights to its product? Data ownership has traditionally been determined through contractual agreements between parties. However, as technology has evolved, the traditional rights of possession, use, and ownership have evolved to include additional considerations beyond contractual rights and obligations.

Contracts discussing the use of data, either through collection or processing of such data, often define the data, detail the manner of aggregation, prohibit the use of data except to provide certain services, require obligations for maintenance and security, limit the duration of retention of the data, and set minimum requirements for the destruction of the data. These concepts are included to protect the underlying data and prevent unwanted parties from exploiting access. As data science and artificial intelligence have evolved, new complications in this paradigm have arisen. More than ever, licensors must also contemplate that third parties may use licensed data to train artificial intelligence or data analysis software. These products and other derivative products may develop to a point where the original underlying data is no longer necessary. Therefore, unless data licensing contracts contemplate the ownership of derivative works, licensors may be left in a position of unintended and self-imposed obsolescence.

Generally, privacy laws are triggered when data includes information about individuals. At the federal level, data privacy laws address particular industries or sectors. For example, federal law provides differing regulations for protecting personal information in video rental records, consumer financial transactions, credit records, law enforcement records, and medical records. Among the federal agencies that enforce these privacy laws, the Federal Trade Commission has played the most prominent role through its authority to enforce against unfair and deceptive trade practices. The FTC has used this authority to police commercial privacy policies, creating a new standard for commercial entities to consider when determining the fitness of their privacy policy. Congress has also granted authority to the FTC to enforce privacy regulations since the 1970s from the Fair Credit Reporting Act of 1970 to regulating the collection and use of information about children through the Children's Online Privacy Protection Act (COPPA) in 1998 to regulating spam marketing via the CAN-SPAM Act of 2003.

In 2003, California was the first state to pass a law requiring commercial websites to conspicuously post a privacy policy if the website collects personally identifiable information from individuals living in California. California again led the way when it passed the California Consumer Privacy Act ("CCPA") in 2018 and the California Privacy Rights Act ("CPRA") in 2020, which substantially enhanced the privacy rights and consumer protections of residents in California. Significantly, the CCPA and CPRA allow users to prohibit the sale of their personal data. The trajectory of privacy law in the United States appears to be similar to that of the European Union and the General Data Protection Regulation (GDPR), passed in 2018. The GDPR offers substantial rights to individuals that allow the individual to control the use, disclosure and destruction of personal information. These privacy regulations are increasingly challenging and limiting the traditional rights of owners of data.

When dealing with personal information, state data security laws are increasingly dictating certain minimum requirements for security of personal information. State data security laws require parties to take reasonable data security measures to protect personal information and require entities to develop, implement, and maintain specific data security programs. Closely related to these laws, states may also require entities to take certain actions when breaches lead to the unauthorized disclosure of personal information.

<u>Closely Related Rights</u>

Some common law rights are similar to IP such as unfair competition (discussed below), the torts of misappropriation of ideas, invasion of privacy, defamation and trade libel, and unauthorized use of name, voice, signature, photograph, or likeness for commercial purposes. There are also business torts such as interference with potential economic advantage, interference with contractual relations, and breach of confidence.

Chapter Eleven

An Ownership Strategy

<u>IP Holding Companies, SPVs and Bankruptcy Proofing</u>

Almost every company starts with the founders assigning their IP to their company in exchange (at least partially) for stock. Little thought and, if you use a popular online incorporation service, little explanation typically go into that decision. When my client and friend, Peter, determined to launch his medical device company based on his patented technology, he saw that the tech, a minimally invasive surgical tool, could support multiple different verticals. For example, the market for cardiovascular solutions differed greatly from the market for joints, which differed greatly from the market for ear, nose and throat ("ENT"). Instead of assigning the patent to the underlying multi-use tech, Peter licensed all substantial rights in a single field of use for the most promising application, which was cardio.

The company attracted investment. By the time of the Series B financing, Peter was no longer CEO and no longer had a controlling stake. The new CEO could not execute and it soon became apparent that the company would not get to profitability nor would there be a favorable exit. Failures are not uncommon in venture capital but what is uncommon is what happened next.

The company had the rights to use the tech in the cardio business but it turned out to be more valuable in ENT, and the company wanted part of that action. Having been counsel to Peter, and not the company, I was tasked with informing the company that it did not have rights to any other fields. Peter had licensed the IP to an entirely different company for ENT.

The cardio company failed soon after that. The VCs lost all of their investment. Peter's ENT company, however, became very successful. Peter eventually exited that company a wealthy man. The VCs lost their money and the entrepreneur got rich.

How often does that happen?

For the well-advised, quite often. For Peter, we used what I call a *Scoggins* partnership, named after the case that made them popular at one time.[53] The structure is illustrated on Appendix J Scoggins Partnership. While the tax law has since changed to eliminate much of the tax benefit of the structure, the business benefit is obvious. The IP sits in a separate special purpose vehicle ("SPV") to serve as an IP holding company so that, if one business based on the tech fails, the whole company does not fail. The founder would be free to start over with the same tech in a different business. Without this structure, the first failure would be the last, as the tech would end up in the hands of creditors or, in Peter's case, the hands of the VCs. We call it bankruptcy proofing or bankruptcy remote entity planning and, when it works, it is a thing of beauty.

The concept of SPVs and bankruptcy proofing is not new, but most VCs will insist that a company own its IP. That often means that the company must have the rights to all fields of use of a relevant patent and that it take a broad invention or trade secret assignment. One variation is to isolate the IP in an SPV but give the VC an interest in the SPV so we can at least shield the IP from the hungry creditors of a failed venture.

Securing Ownership

Before you shed tears for the VCs in the above example, note that the parties got exactly what they bargained for and the end result went exactly as planned. The IP was clearly divided up at the start of the company and there were (or should have been) no surprises. There are many famous examples to the contrary. Facebook, Snapchat, and Square are all examples of companies that had founder disputes around IP ownership (and other matters).[54] They settled their disputes and went on to be successful companies; however, the better example is the company with such clear documentation that it had no disputes.

Most trade secret theft is by employees or partners.[55] Thus, to protect against misappropriation, everyone who touches the IP should assign their rights to the company. More importantly, everyone who might later claim they have touched the IP should execute an IP assignment. For employees, the IP assignment will often be contained in a proprietary or confidential information agreement and invention assignment ("CIAIA"). Basically, the agreement will define what information belongs to the company or employer and will assign the service provider's rights to any IP to the company. For independent contractors and consultants, the operative IP ownership clauses may be contained in the independent contractor agreement. Founders will also execute an assignment of IP created in connection with their service to the company.

A well drafted agreement will define the information to be protected and will do so broadly. Confidential or proprietary information includes not only technological information, like technical data and processes, but also financial and market information. Customer specifications can be valuable trade secrets. Employee information can be valuable (identity, contact information, salaries, expertise, etc.). The agreement should include employee information in its definition of protected property and should specify that the media containing the information, such as documents, are also proprietary.

The employee or service provider should keep records of any inventions and disclose those inventions to the company and no one else. The agreement will state those inventions are the sole property of the company and are assigned to the company.

The agreement will also specify what information is *not* subject to the agreement. Generally, a fair agreement would not try to claim ownership of everything in the employee's head before and during his employment with the company. In California, the state Labor Code does not allow an employer to assign an invention that the employee develops entirely on his or her own time without using the employer's equipment, supplies, facilities, or trade secret information except for those inventions that either relate to the employer's business or research or development or result from work performed by the employee for the employer. Any contrary agreement is unenforceable.[56] The Labor Code only applies to employees so non-employees, such as contractors, should be a little more careful about how their invention assignment clauses are drafted.

Most such assignments will carve out an employee's prior inventions by requiring they be listed on a schedule. It is a good idea for both employer and employee to actually complete that schedule. For the employee, read literally, if the schedule is blank, the employee has just assigned everything he owns (subject to the statutory exceptions noted above). That is not necessarily good for the employer because, if the schedule is blank, a court might decide that the parties did not have a meeting of the minds, that the contract is ambiguous, or that the contract should be reformed and rewritten to reflect the parties' true intent, whatever that is. Careful entrepreneurs will pay attention to these provisions.

Chapter Twelve

Trade Secrets

A big part of a tech company's value will often, if not always, be tied to trade secrets. As defined by the United States Patent and Trademark Office (USPTO), trade secrets consist of information and can include a formula, pattern, compilation, program, device, method, technique, or process. To meet the most common definition of a trade secret, it must be used in business and give the owner an opportunity to obtain an economic advantage over competitors who do not know or use it.

For federal law, a trade secret includes many forms of information if the owner has taken reasonable measures to keep the information secret and the information derives value from not being generally known.[57] California similarly defines trade secret to mean information that derives independent economic value from not being generally known to the public or to other persons who can obtain economic value from its disclosure or use and is the subject of efforts reasonable under the circumstances to maintain its secrecy.[58]

Breaking this down, for information to be trade secret, it must be valuable, not generally known and the owner must take reasonable steps to keep it secret. It is that last prong, the reasonable steps, that requires the most effort. The well-advised startup will have a trade secret policy in place that documents its reasonable efforts to keep its trade secrets secret. It should go without saying that it should also follow its policy and ensure that its trade secrets are not easily accessible.

The high stakes case of *Waymo LLC v. Uber Technologies, Inc.* illustrates the value and importance of a good trade secrets program.[59] Waymo LLC is a self-driving car startup owned by Alphabet (originally known as Google's Self-Driving Car Project). Waymo sued Uber for violating the Defense of Trade Secrets Act[60] and the California Uniform Trade Secret Act[61] as well as for patent infringement. Waymo alleged that a former Google employee secretly downloaded highly confidential data from Google's hardware systems and used the information to launch a self-driving startup that Uber later acquired.

In connection with its trade secret claims, Waymo laid out steps it took to secure its information. According to its complaint, it restricted access to secret and proprietary information only to those with a need to know. Systems were encrypted and required passwords and dual authentication. The physical facilities were secured. Everyone with whom Waymo dealt signed NDAs before they received confidential information. The information was secret and not generally known and was valuable in that Waymo derived economic benefit from the information.

The case settled just four days into trial so we will not know all the facts. Clearly, Waymo had a good system. However, it would not have had this problem if it had restricted the departing employee's access to the information. A good practice that I advise is to ask the employee to attest to the prior employer that they have taken no information upon leaving that employment and, correspondingly, the hiring employer should require a similar statement that the new employee is bringing nothing with him from his former employer. It gives the hiring company a defense if they are dragged into a trade secrets theft case as a result of an employee's alleged acts, like Uber was.

We will return to the *Waymo* case later in this book. It is full of lessons.

Chapter Thirteen
A Patent Roadmap

Patents add to a company's valuation and make the company attractive to an investor. Further, they can discourage competitors from developing similar technology. However, patents are also expensive to enforce. Litigation attorneys will tell you that a patent case can cost $1 million to $10 million (that is not a typo) in legal fees to litigate and take years to settle. Few companies can afford to pursue that case and few VCs will underwrite that cost and, even if they do, over 75 percent of the time the alleged infringers prevail.[62]

Patents should cover the things that make a product successful. The patent should not only reflect the technical knowhow of the inventors but should also be informed by the marketing and sales team. A useful tool for illustrating this is a flow chart. Let's assume that the company manufactures a complex product, requiring several features, including a monitor. We talk to the sales team and they tell us that the main things the monitor must have are an attractive design, a sensitive microphone, and a big sound. A patent roadmap might chart those features and the patents would flow around the features that are important to the product. In this example, the components each have both utility and design patents associated with them. They would also all be linked by a central design patent. A component may also have IP that is protected as a trade secret. With this map, the parties can visualize where and how each part is protected and the lawyers can proceed to protect the IP that is important to the product.

Chapter Fourteen

Kinds of Patents [63]

Patents are good but not all patents are created equally. The United States Patent and Trademark Office (USPTO) recognizes utility, design, and plant patents. In each case the invention must be novel, useful, and non-obvious to qualify for grant as a patent.

Utility Patents are the most commonly filed patents and protect four types of functional inventions: processes, machines, manufactures, and compositions of matter. Utility patent protection extends beyond tangible objects, as method claims can be directed to processes of making things, processes of using things, and computer-implemented processes. Recent court opinions on computer-implemented processes have created uncertainty in what processes are patentable, which has made patents on computer-implemented processes more difficult to obtain. Business methods are an example of computer-implemented processes that have come under scrutiny for being disproportionately used for questionable litigation. For example, in the America Invents Act of 2011, Congress set forth a special proceeding within the USPTO to hear challenges to business method patents.

There are two types of utility patent applications — provisional and non-provisional applications. Provisional applications are not actually examined and do not issue as a patent; instead, they provide an informal way to claim a filing date for a later-filed non-provisional application on the subject matter disclosed in the provisional application. Provisional applications are beneficial to companies because they are less expensive to prepare and file, allow the company to assert "patent pending" status, and may protect foreign rights if there is a subsequent public use, disclosure, or sale of the invention before a foreign application has been filed. Non-provisional applications must conform to a large body of rules and are, therefore, typically prepared by a lawyer.

Provisional applications may be less formal than utility applications, but they can be a trap that results in loss of patent rights if the provisional application is not sufficiently prepared. In order for a later filed utility application to successfully claim priority to the provisional application, the provisional application must disclose the subject matter of the invention claimed in the following utility application in sufficient detail to support those claims. In other words, the provisional application must include a sufficient level of disclosure to support the later applications. Loss of the priority date, if there is intervening public disclosure of the invention, can result in loss of patent rights to that invention.

A non-provisional application that claims the benefit of an earlier provisional application must be filed within 12 months after the provisional application was filed. A non-provisional application may initially be rejected by a patent examiner but after some back and forth on the application's claims, the majority of applications issue as patents. Utility patents are enforceable from the patent's issue date to 20 years from the filing date of the earliest nonprovisional application to which the utility application claims priority, provided that the maintenance fees are timely paid over the life of the patent (e.g. at 3.5 years from issue, 7.5 years from issue, and 11.5 years from issue). In many patents, the 20 year term described above may be adjusted by the patent office to compensate for slow prosecution of the patent application by the patent office.

Unlike utility patents, design patents protect non-technical, non-functional, visually ornamental designs on articles of manufacture. Famous examples of products with design patents include Apple's iPhone, iMac and iPod; Coca-Cola's bottle shape, and the Volkswagen Beetle.

There are two types of designs for an article: those that concern the configuration or shape embodied in an article and those that concern the surface ornamentation applied to an article. Surface ornamentation designs must be inseparable from the articles to which they are applied; thus, a design patent covering an ornamental pattern on a chair does not extend to the use of the same pattern on a basket. If granted, the patent only protects the application of the surface ornamentation to the specific article indicated by the inventor. Design patent applications are examined for novelty and non-obviousness, like utility applications, but are granted more quickly and readily and are also less expensive to prepare. Items that have designs dictated exclusively by the functions they perform are typically not eligible because there must be an aesthetic element to every patentable design. Two notable categories of design patents are type fonts and icons, as applied to a computer display. Sometimes, a product can be covered by both design and utility patents. Design patents last 15 years from their date of grant if the application was filed on or after May 13, 2015; earlier-filed design applications have a 14-year term only from grant.

Plant patents protect newly invented and asexually reproducible plants that are not tuber-propagated. Although the legal language on these patents uses the term discovers, this refers to the discovery of a distinct and new plant variety because of cultivation, meaning that plants discovered are not patentable, whereas mutants and hybrids discovered in a cultivated area are. Because they are recognized as plants, algae and macro-fungi are patentable. Bacteria are not regarded and, thus, are unpatentable. Plant patents last 20 years from the filing date of the application.

Chapter Fifteen
Patent Defense

The patent law does not require a patent holder to exploit the patent. Patent holders who have no intention of developing the patent are called non-practicing entities ("NPEs") or sometimes patent trolls. Patent trolls typically acquire patents to prosecute patent infringement suits against parties they maintain have infringed the patent. The US Federal Trade Commission ("FTC") uses the term patent assertion entities ("PAEs") to distinguish patent trolls from other NPEs, such as universities and other research organizations.

For most startups, patent trolls are not their biggest problem until they establish traction and are on the radar of the patent holders. For larger companies that are potential targets, there are strategies to deal with the risk.

Some operating companies have made public pledges to use their patents purely to defend against claims. For example, in Twitter's Innovator's Patent Agreement ("IPA"), Twitter committed to its employee inventors that it will not offensively use any patent without the inventor's permission.

A company can also make a multilateral pledge by agreeing with members of a network not to offensively assert their patents against any other member of the network. One example of this multilateral pledge is the Defensive Patent License ("DPL"). There, the companies opt into a network where each promises not to sue any other company in the network for patent infringement. Another example is the License on Transfer Network ("LOT"), under which the participants agree to license their patents to any other member of the network when the patents are transferred to a non-member third party. The Open Invention Network ("OIN") has acquired patents it will license for free to any company that promises not to assert its own patents against Linux technology.

Another approach is a patent pool where members agree to cross-license to each other patents related to a particular technology. Generally, a group of patent owners will determine which patents are essential to a technology and agree on how those will be licensed. If the patent pool has most or all of the essential patents to a technology, being a part of the pool can be a huge benefit because it gives the members additional exclusivity.

Chapter Sixteen
Goodwill, Logo and Brand

My client GreatApp (not its real name) is well on its way to becoming a unicorn[64] if it is not already. It has more than a hundred million downloads and ranks high in the App Store. The idea is so simple you will wish you had thought of it yourself and the name, well, the name makes it even more attractive because of its cleverness. It seems like the kind of company that was destined to succeed from day one, but it wasn't always like that. The world will never know how this company was almost finished before it started and a billion dollars of market capital might never have existed.

What's in a name? When you google something, you are relying on Google's search engine and placing your faith in that brand. When you order a Coke, hire a professional, or buy a BMW, you are again placing your faith in the brand as a signal of a certain level of quality. If Coke or Google or BMW suddenly could not use their name, their market share would disappear, at least temporarily, until they rebuilt another brand. If a competitor could freely use their names on their products, those companies would certainly lose business. A company's major asset – goodwill – is inextricably linked to its name, brand, and sometimes logo. Trademark law protects that value by allowing the trademark owner to prevent others from using their names and marks and protecting their right to use them.

GreatApp obtained federal trademark protection early in its life. It later learned that a competitor was using a similar name for a similar product. It was obvious that whoever had the rights to the name would likely go on to be the market leader. Because GreatApp had secured its trademark rights, it was able to prevent the competitor from doing business under a similar name, which effectively ended its competition.

Chapter Seventeen
Marketing Intangibles

Marketing intangibles include brand, trade name, customer data, customer relationships, and customer lists. Accountants and economists talk about marketing intangibles more than lawyers, maybe because they are smarter but certainly because they are more focused on the numbers.

Founders will also be focused on numbers when it comes time to exit their companies. The number they are focused on is likely the deal value. That number will be directly affected by the development of intangibles many years earlier. Here are a few ways:

Customer contracts. Customers means revenue and customer contracts means that there is a binding agreement or an expectation of recurring revenue. Those contracts mean something and have value.

Workforce in place. Workforce in place is the value of having an assembled, proven, and ready to work labor pool. Without this intangible, a company would have to engage in a lengthy staffing and training process.

Employment agreements. Depending on the state, employment agreements can add a lot of value to a company. In states that allow employment related non-competes, an employment agreement effectively ties valuable people to a particular company. That can be a very valuable asset.

NDAs and invention assignments. The value of these types of agreements has been discussed above. For a tech company, ownership is key to its existence as well as to its value. Well drafted agreements shore up that value.

Licensing agreements. For companies that license their IP, a license means recurring revenue, which is a number that can be capitalized and valued. On the inbound side, a license agreement is the next best thing to IP ownership as it provides for the right to use IP and exclude others from using IP.

Joint venture agreements. Similar to license agreements, a joint venture is a revenue stream as well as route to additional markets, IP, and business units.

The one thing that all of the above intangibles have in common is the need for a contract. This is one area where a lawyer can not only protect the company's existing value but also add new value though the creation of legal rights via contract. A contract can be a good thing but, as illustrated in the next chapter, can also work against a company if not thoroughly thought through.

Chapter Eighteen

Licensing Strategy

Most of my job is protecting startups from third parties. Often, my job also includes protecting founders from themselves. A common mistake made by founders is to get so excited about their first sale, licensing deal, or other venture that they give away the secret sauce, meaning that they grant too many rights to their counter parties. Those rights may include exclusivity, either in a market, vertical, or a geography. They may refer to the term of the license. Is it limited in time or does it last forever? Is the license limited geographically or is it worldwide? Is the license revocable or irrevocable? Is there a royalty?

I work a lot with agtech companies. Agtech, the technology of food production, is an early and fiercely competitive space where the winners will be the companies that can gain early market share in a market that is extremely hard to access. Because customers – in this case, farmers – are so hard to get to, many agtech companies will give away the farm trying to get that business. More than once I have seen agtech service providers assign their IP rights to the farmer customers in their service agreement just to get the business. Since an agtech company without any tech is not a great business model, they can be said to have won the battle but lost the war. The whole experience makes me wary of any arrangement that requires IP sharing or assignment.

Thus, when my AdTech client brought me a proposed joint venture, I was similarly concerned that they were giving away too much. The deal included a royalty free, exclusive, perpetual, and irrevocable license of the startup's core technology to a large retailer. The tech was an artificial intelligence system that could target customers in a fiendishly brilliant way with ads for what they were likely to buy, when they were ready to buy, and where they would undoubtedly see them. The license was limited to a specific country and a specific application of their IP to a certain set of products. The client, however, had thought this deal through very strategically. If the retailer could prove out the tech in its one vertical, the startup would have the proof of concept it needed to finance and launch in other countries and other markets. On its face, it seemed like a give-away but, in fact, we would get far more out of the deal than we were giving up.

This example involves a fairly narrow scenario where an expansive license makes sense. The next chapter contains a different example.

Chapter Nineteen
Why LicensingCo Cannot Get Funded

Back before cleantech became a dirty word, my cleantech client had developed a low energy and environmentally friendly technology that had a large number of possible uses. Cleantech was hot at the time and I managed to get them many meetings with the Sand Hill Road crowd of Silicon Valley VCs. Their go to market strategy was to license their awesome tech to major industrials. They only needed a few million dollars to build it out and do some marketing. The upside would be lower return than what the VCs like but also lower risk. After several weeks of meetings, they ended up with zero term sheets. Nobody was interested in their company. How could that be? They were asking for a modest amount for a relatively safe deal. How could Silicon Valley VCs throw larger amounts of money at riskier deals and pass us by?

It was a mystery but did not remain so for long, as one VC took it upon himself to blog about the company. The VC wrote that a major problem was that the business model was a licensing play and VCs simply don't like licensing. For sure, the company must rely on its patents in a licensing company and that may invite lawsuits from larger companies. More importantly, however, licensing is typically a lower risk but lower return investment than a product company. In other words, a pure licensing company will have investment in R&D but not in plant and equipment. As a result of only being able to license, its revenues will never be as high as a product company.

VCs do not want safe, low return investments; they want explosive growth. They want product companies.

My cleantech client, after reading the blog post, went back to the drawing board on their basic business model. Instead of licensing, they would now increase their ask to $10 million and invest it into plant and equipment. With that new model and new projections, they received several term sheets and closed a financing with a major VC. The company is still around today and is a market leader in its space.

Chapter Twenty
Patent vs. Trade Secret

Several years ago, I represented a company that had a valuable patent but the real value was in the know how that allowed the company to exploit the patent. The know how was not patented and probably not even patentable. When they were approached by a potential buyer of the patent, we negotiated a sale of the patent rights. It did not occur to the buyer that they should also get a license to the knowhow. That is, it did not occur to them until after the patent assignment was completed and they realized that the patent could not be commercialized by itself. They then had to come back to us asking for the right to use the trade secret know-how which, of course, required another negotiation. My client did well, since at that point he had a lot of leverage. The moral of the story is that sometimes patents are not enough.

No doubt, the VCs like to see patents. They add value and are a real, lien-able asset of the company that can be sold if things don't go well. They give the company a limited monopoly on commercializing their invention and they make the company a more attractive acquisition target.

Legally, the pros and cons between patent and trade secret is pretty straightforward. A patent grants its holder the exclusive right to make, sell, or import a product or process for 20 years. The patent holder must disclose the invention publicly and incur legal fees obtaining the patent. A trade secret does not have a 20-year shelf life; it can last forever, provided that it is kept secret. A trade secret need not, indeed cannot, be disclosed publicly. If it is, the protection is lost. However, it is perfectly legal to reverse engineer a trade secret, meaning that someone could independently figure out how to make the invention. You cannot legally do that with a patent. In a nutshell, a trade secret can last longer than a patent but is more fragile since its protection can be easily lost. So what is a company to do?

Coca Cola is an example of a company that opted in favor of trade secret protection over patent protection. The Coca-Cola formula is probably the most famous trade secret in the world. No single person has the full recipe. Each supplier only knows parts of the blend. The formula is reportedly stored in a vault in Atlanta where only a few executives can access it. It is easy to see why Coca Cola did not patent its formula. Without secrecy, there would be more imitators than Coca Cola could police. And 20 years is a blink of an eye for a company like Coca Cola – the formula has been around for more than 100 years.

By the way, my friends in the industry tell me that they could easily replicate the Coca Cola taste and many companies have, to some degree. The Coca Cola formula in a vault legend is good marketing for the company but that secret formula may not be its biggest asset. Its biggest asset might be its name, logo, goodwill, and mark, as discussed above. I will let you decide.

But assuming that you are not Coca Cola and your product will not be relevant in 100 years, what should you do? Should you patent that invention?

The secret in Silicon Valley is that it is not all about the patents. In fact, most companies might have patents to get their monopoly but are really powered by their trade secret know how. The strategic company will likely utilize both patent and trade secret protection. This is especially true in software. As an example, if an invention covers a set of processes (that are susceptible to reverse engineering) and an underlying code or neural network that cannot be discovered, the inventor would patent the processes to obtain a public monopoly and rely on trade secret for what is underneath to maintain a strategic advantage.

Chapter Twenty-one

Sales

Sanjay was a sought-after speaker on the Silicon Valley circuit since he started, built, and sold a successful company before becoming a VC himself. Sanjay frequently speaks about how he obtained that initial traction.

As a product engineer at a large Silicon Valley tech company, Sanjay did not have a lot of authority but he did have the ability to procure on behalf of his employer. On his own time and with his own equipment, Sanjay developed a product that he thought his employer might like. Since he had the authority to place orders, his first instinct was to simply buy the product from his company. Sanjay thought better of it and, with the employer's conflict of interest policy in mind, fully disclosed to his manager that he co-owned the vendor company and convinced his manager to place a small order. On the strength of that order, he was able to tell investors that he had, as a customer, a large Silicon Valley company, again not withholding the fact of his relationship with the buyer. Sanjay parlayed those first few sales into a successful startup.

Had Sanjay elected to skip a few steps, it could have easily have gone bad instead of great. State laws impose obligations on businessmen that might be easily overlooked. Here are a few.

Unfair competition and unfair trade practices. An unfair or deceptive trade practice refers to a deceptive, fraudulent, or unethical method to obtain business. It usually comes up in the consumer context but the concepts have been applied more broadly in commerce. The California Unfair Practices Act, for example, prohibits unfair competition and any unlawful, unfair or fraudulent business act or practice and unfair, deceptive, untrue, or misleading advertising.[65] Consumer facing companies in particular should be aware of these types of laws.

FTC Act. Under the Federal Trade Commission Act ("FTC Act"), the FTC is empowered, among other things, to (a) prevent unfair methods of competition and unfair or deceptive acts or practices in or affecting commerce; (b) seek monetary redress and other relief for conduct injurious to consumers; (c) prescribe rules defining with specificity acts or practices that are unfair or deceptive and establishing requirements designed to prevent such acts or practices; (d) gather and compile information and conduct investigations relating to the organization, business, practices, and management of entities engaged in commerce; and (e) make reports and legislative recommendations to Congress and the public. Many statutes are enforced under the FTC Act.[66]

The FTC authority is surprisingly broad and even extends to health care data breaches. For example, the FTC filed a complaint against a medical testing laboratory that suffered a data breach alleging that the company failed to reasonably protect the security of consumers' personal data, including medical information.[67]

<u>Good faith and fair dealing</u>. Some states, such as California, impose on every agreement an implied promise of good faith and fair dealing. This means that neither party will do anything to unfairly interfere with the right of any other party to receive the benefits of the contract. Good faith means honesty of purpose without any intention to mislead or to take unfair advantage of another. Generally speaking, it means being faithful to one's duty or obligation.[68] As a practical matter, the covenant prevents a party from negotiating with no intention of concluding a contract.

The combination of these statutory tools can be very powerful in the hands of a court. For example, in one case, an Illinois company required its California employees to sign an unenforceable non-compete clause. Unlike California, non-compete provisions are enforceable in Illinois. Not only did the court rule that the covenants not to compete were unenforceable, the court also found the employer liable to the employees for an unfair business practice by simply including the non-compete provisions in the employment agreements.[69] Non-California lawyers will often include unenforceable non-competes in contracts simply for the *in terrorem* effect, and never seem to want to believe me when I tell them how much trouble they can get into that way.

Chapter Twenty-two

The Importance of Documentation

Employment lawyers have a saying: "When your employees walk out the door, your trade secrets go with them." If they don't have that saying, they should, because it is very true. Even with tight CIAIAs and NDAs, there is the evidentiary problem of proving when something was developed and by whom. That hole can be plugged with proper documentation.

The Uber-Waymo litigation described in Chapter 12 provides a very public example of how this works. In late 2016, Waymo accidentally received an email containing an attachment that looked suspiciously like Waymo's design relating to LiDAR (Light Detection and Ranging). LiDAR measures the distance between objects and is important to self-driving car development. Waymo alleged that an employee took Google trade secrets related to this technology and brought them to Uber.[70]

Trade secret theft is hard to prove in California, because there are strong protections for employees to take their skills and knowledge to different companies. A company really needs a smoking gun to win a case like that. As it turns out, the company had that smoking gun in the form of thousands of sensitive documents downloaded to a personal computer. The case was settled with Uber giving Waymo $245 million worth of Uber stock and agreeing to ensure that Uber does not infringe Waymo's intellectual property.[71]

PART 3: MONEY

Money often costs too much.
—Ralph Waldo Emerson

If a company has attracted and retained great people and secured its intellectual property, it will soon need money to scale. If the company's growth is expected to be slow and steady, with low risk, early profits, and modest returns, it might be able to fund through operations or debt. While there is no shame in that model, the VCs and high-flying startup angels will be seeking companies that promise high risk, explosive growth, and huge returns.

Ralph Waldo Emerson wasn't a startup entrepreneur but he was right on the money – it can cost a lot. While the established low risk business can borrow at low rates, the startup is generally left with financiers who demand equity returns. The focus of this Part 3 is how to attract that sort of investment.

Chapter Twenty-three

The Chicken and Egg of Traction

For every winning idea, there are many more that fail. A winning idea is not enough in a synchronistic Web 2.0 world where ideas spread and are duplicated immediately. Facebook was not the first social media platform, Google not the first search engine and Uber not the first ride share platform. Those companies succeeded through great execution as much as anything. Investors want to know you can execute and the only way to show that is by having traction.

When investors demand to see traction, they are asking for affirmation that the business can attract users. The easiest and best metric of traction is revenue. Revenue means that people will actually pay for the product or service. Attracting those first few customers can be exceedingly difficult but, until the company has revenues, it may not be able to attract the money needed to finance its sales and marketing efforts. It needs money to make money.

<u>Cold Calling</u>. By the time I first met Chromium (not its real name), it was already being acquired by Yahoo. The company had started as a one-man shop, offering its online marketing solution to small and mid-sized businesses. The company's founder had a difficult upbringing. As a child, he was bullied and had to learn martial arts to protect himself. After being turned away from a job at McDonald's, he dropped out of high school to start a business buying and reselling printers on eBay. His difficult upbringing, no doubt, gave him the resolve to make his company a success. When asked how he managed to build the company so quickly, he responded, "cold calling." Cold calling is not fun or glamorous, but the founder did what was required.

<u>Build value not revenue</u>. The first board meeting after a VC investment is always an interesting place. Expectations get set and CEOs get educated. My client had developed a winning app and attracted a top tier VC into its first financing at a $50 million valuation. He quite proudly presented the

financial forecast and explained how the company would attain profitability soon. But, to his surprise, that is not what the VC investor wanted to hear.

First, profit means income and that means taxes on income at ordinary rates (21% federal, plus state, as of 2021). VCs hate paying taxes.

Secondly, profit means that the company is attracting fewer customers at higher rates. Instead, running at a very low price could attract more customers and freeze out the competition. Giving up short term profits for long term value is a strategy as old as the monopolies of the late 1800s.

Finally, investors are not interested in the relatively measly profits that a startup might earn. They are concerned about the value of the shares in an eventual exit. For many companies, the number of users has much more to do with that metric than annual profits.

One great measure of value is the number of users, even if those users are not paying much. The freemium model exploits this idea by offering a free basic subscription with paid upgrades. Anyone who has ever downloaded a free app is familiar with the model. As a legal matter, the model seems suspect under anti-trust laws as anti-competitive but has remained unchallenged.

Another way that startups build value is through creating legally protected assets. The most obvious is patent, as discussed above. The most common is trade secret, again, as discussed above. Contracts add value, as well as agreements that secure the workforce in place. Combined with a solid brand, the company can prove its value to an investor. The next chapter drills down a little further on how that can be quantified.

Customers. This is a book on good legal practices, not marketing, but it is worth mentioning that the law restricts marketing practices in a few ways. The law requires claims in advertisements to be truthful. They cannot be deceptive or unfair and must be evidence-based. Companies that advertise directly to children or market child-related products to their parents should not only consult truth-in-advertising standards but also the Children's Online Privacy Protection Act.

Endorsements and testimonials, including those by social media influencers must meet certain FTC requirements.[72] The FTC's Telemarketing Sales Rule gives consumers certain protections under the National Do Not Call

Registry. Companies also should be familiar with rules banning most forms of robocalling.

Chapter Twenty-four

Getting the Cap Table Right – Founders Stock

Zipcar – a company that did everything wrong but still managed to succeed.

Imagine that you are living in a sprawling metro area where the costs of owning and keeping a car are very high. You do not need a car often but, when you do, you do not want to deal with the high costs and hassle of a rental car. Enter Zipcar, a slick alternative to the rental car market in which members can use their app to reserve a car on an hourly, daily, or some other timeframe. It's one of those ideas that I wished I had thought of.

Zipcar was founded in 2000 and, by 2016, had one million members across 500 cities in nine countries offering nearly 10,000 vehicles. It went public in 2011 and was acquired by Avis Budget Group in 2013.[73] By any measure Zipcar was a big success.

Or was it?

The company was founded by Antje Danielson and Robin Chase. Danielson kept her day job while Chase worked full time for the company, but they split the equity ownership 50/50. By the end of 2000, it had occurred to Chase that she should have had more shares than Danielson since she was working much harder. Danielson was fired in 2001. Chase lasted another two years before the board replaced her. At the time of Zipcar's exit in 2013, Danielson ended up with 1.3 percent and Chase had less than 3 percent.[74] In a deal worth $500 million, the founders made millions, but not the kind of money they might have expected. But, like my uncle used to tell me—"if you can't be a good example, at least be a horrible warning." Zipcar is a warning. The case of Zipcar is a gift to founders everywhere for the lessons it has given us.

Let's start with that 50/50 split.

Splitting the Pie

> "A quick, even split suggests that the founders don't have
> the business maturity to have a tough dialogue."
> — Noah Wasserman, Harvard Business Professor

Most startup companies have co-founders. Look at Apple, Microsoft, Facebook, Google, and many others. For a tech company, one of those co-founders should be technical. A quick Google search will disclose opposing opinions on this issue but, in my experience, it is difficult to hire what you need. You will need someone with the dedication that only founders have. Similarly, this goes for design skills, business acumen, and domain expertise. But mostly for technical people.

There are always exceptions to the rule so, if you are the rare founder that can do it all – technical, domain, design, and business – then, congratulations. You can skip this chapter. But the rest of us will have to make the difficult decision about how to divide equity among the co-founders.

Equal Split. The simplest, most commonly used way founders divide equity is an equal split. For example, two founders each would receive fifty percent; three founders would receive a third each, etc. It is simplest because we can avoid the uncomfortable discussion about the founder's value relative to each other. But according to some experts, an equal split may be the worst method.

Harvard Business School Professor Noam Wasserman has argued that the founders who keep the most control over their company make the least amount of money because they split equity based on short term rather than long term contributions.[75] Based on data gathered from thousands of startups, Professor Wasserman asserts that non-negotiated splits result in lower valuations at the first round of financing. He argues that a negotiation over equity is a trial by fire and surviving that discussion proves that the team can work together for the long term. While that is certainly important, I have found that founders will resent the fact that they are carrying a disproportionate share of the load. More importantly, investors will punish a company that gets its equity split wrong through lower valuations. Whatever the reason, the data backs me up.

Sometimes a non-negotiated equity split is the right answer. Sometimes it is not the right answer but is the only answer that will allow the founders to move on. In those cases, the founders should definitely be subject to vesting so that the split can be easily corrected down the road. If you do have the luxury of being able to negotiate a split, there are many ways to go about it.

Non-Formula Negotiated Split. The negotiated split is exactly as it sounds. The person who can pound their shoe on the table the loudest (or has attended one of my talks on negotiation skills) will end up with the most equity. As noted above, some very smart people believe that negotiated splits demonstrate the founders ability to work together. Larry David, from *Curb Your Enthusiasm*, expresses another view that "a good compromise is when both parties are dissatisfied."[76] If both parties are getting exactly what they expected coming into the relationship, the negotiated split works great, but then it is hardly negotiated. If, however, the split is unfair, even if negotiated, the company will have the same problems associated with an equal split.

Subjective Formula Equity Split. One step up from the shoe pounding split is a split based upon an agreed upon subjective formula. The use of a formula has much to recommend itself from law and negotiation. If the founders will agree on a fair formula, well then, the rest is just math. That is how it works in theory, anyway. The formula need not be complicated. A common one goes something like this: founder A works full time; founder B works half time; therefore, the split is 2 to 1 or 2/3 for A and 1/3 for B. I like to believe that if Zipcar had followed this formula, they would have avoided being mentioned in this book and the founders would be that much richer.

Here is another example. Founders Jack and Jill might agree that the full-time founder gets 20 points and the part-time founder gets 10 points. The founder with the idea and patent application gets another 10 points. The one with the extra garage gets 10, the one with the beta customer gets 10 and the one with the money gets 20. We then add up the points:

	Jack	Jill
Time Commit	20	10
Patents	0	10
Space	10	0
Customer	0	10
Initial funds	0	20
Total	30	50

This method ostensibly has objectivity and simplicity going for it and is a way to move past a negotiation impasse if the parties can agree on the formula criteria. Agreeing on the criteria might be as arduous as agreeing on the split itself. This method also begs the question of what happens if the inputs change. That brings us to the dynamic or changeable split.

Dynamic Split – the Holy Grail. All the previously mentioned valuation methods share the problem of myopically focusing on the short term. Professor Wasserman argues that the remedy for this shortcoming is to use a formula that adjusts as the facts change. You learned in earlier chapters how vesting can allow for this but vesting is a blunt tool. It adjusts harshly by requiring a termination of service to correct share ownership to match performance. In such a case, vesting acts as a hammer when sometimes a scalpel will do. The dynamic split models take a more precise approach.

Dynamic split means that the relative percentage ownership of a group of founders will change based on their relative contributions at any given time. It is measured by valuing each contributor's inputs, usually on a weighted average, pre-assigned value basis and comparing them periodically to each other person's contribution. See Appendix K for a summary of some models used in a dynamic split.

You can find numerous dynamic split models online. Here are few of them:

The Founders' Pie Calculator was created by Frank Demmler, Professor, Tepper School of Business at Carnegie Mellon University. Under this system, a founder's value add is divided into 5 categories:

Idea

Business Plan Preparation

Domain Expertise

Commitment and Risk

Responsibilities

Each category is then given a value on a scale of 0 to 10 and the value is multiplied by the founder's score to come up with a weighted score. An example of this method is illustrated on Appendix L.

The Grunt Fund method is described in the book *Slicing Pie* by Mike Moyers as well as online.[77] This method applies pre-assigned values or weights to enumerated inputs and provides an equity split, calculated in excel, at any given time based on the relevant weights.[78] Each founder, investor, and early employee keeps track of the hours, items, and money put toward the startup and utilizes Moyer's formulae to calculate the value of the contribution. Each person accumulates equity in a grunt fund and those who devote more time to the startup accumulate ownership faster, even if they initially came to the table with less money or experience. The split continuously changes until some point when we take a snapshot and lock the relative percentages in place. That point is usually a funding event, since the investors will not want the uncertainty of dynamic splits.

Several other equity split calculators can be found online.[79]

The Royse 10,000 Startups Subjective Method. My favorite system, of course, is the subjective method. Not all companies are created equally and not all factors should apply with the same weight to all companies. My subjective method identifies what is important at the outset – team, tech, IP, expertise, etc. – and ball parks a cap table based on what I have seen in the market over the past 40 years. It's not perfect but I find it to be as good as any other method.

Couples Therapy. Finally if all else fails, you might seek out mediation or, as I call it, couples therapy for founders. This system relies mostly on someone getting worn down by talk until they agree to something. If you think I am kidding, you haven't lived. Third party resolution tends to only be useful for companies that have been around long enough to have built some value because it can be expensive.

Additional Bites at the Apple. It is important to keep in mind that a typical startup will have numerous opportunities to correct its equity split mistakes during its life. If it goes out for funding, the VCs will have a view on what makes sense and will suggest a re-alignment. Given the long time period from formation to exit, it is likely that people will depart and join the company, resulting in a reshuffling of the economic deck at several points before exit. So, while getting the split right from the start is important, we can still make it work even if the original allocation was not optimal.

Chapter Twenty-five

Class F Super Voting Stock and Series FF Founders Stock

Class F common stock[80] and Series FF preferred stock, as they are commonly referred to, provide founders with two additional, yet distinct, capital structure choices to consider. These relatively creative types of stock have their advantages and disadvantages.

<u>Class F Common Stock</u>. Class F common stock is a special type of common stock that is designed to protect founders who fear losing control of their companies to investors. Class F stock has two fundamental features. First, holders of Class F stock obtain preferential voting rights over the common stock. For example, in contrast to Class A common stock – one vote per share – Class F holders are entitled to more than one vote per share. Class F stockholders may also have the right to elect one or more Class F Directors, whose interests are presumably aligned with the Class F holders.

Second, protective provisions provide that certain fundamental actions cannot be taken without the consent of a majority of Class F votes. For example, more than 50 percent of the Class F votes may be required to alter the company's bylaws in a way that might dilute the Class F stock's voting power, declare a dividend, or approve a merger. In other words, these provisions ensure that the founders retain control. Aside from these features, Class F stock and the classic common stock participate equally in distributions and other economic rights. Furthermore, Class F stock is convertible into Class A common stock whenever the holder wishes, whenever the holder dies, or when it is transferred to a person other than another Class F holder.

Class F stock is designed to protect founders. Of course, if investors are unwilling to accept Class F terms, having Class F stock is essentially meaningless. Although this option may make sense for those experienced or serial entrepreneurs who have plenty of negotiating power, newer entrepreneurs should think carefully before utilizing this type of stock.

Series FF Preferred Stock. Class F common stock should not be confused with Series FF preferred stock. Series FF stock is designed to permit its holders to cash out a portion of their stock, yet still keep some skin in the game. In other words, Series FF preferred stock allows founders who want (or find themselves needing) extra cash to liquidate a *small* portion of their stock in connection with or immediately prior to outside investment.

Series FF stock operates as follows. It is typically issued to the founders upon incorporation or immediately prior to a Series A financing round. At the option of the shareholder, these shares are convertible into a later series of preferred stock. For example, when an investor buys a future series of preferred stock, the Series FF shares can be converted into that type of preferred stock and sold to the investor. In addition, Series FF stock is convertible into common stock at the option of the shareholder.

Absent Series FF stock (or something like it), a founder who wants to get liquidity in a financing has some tax issues. First, if the company uses some of the proceeds of the financing to redeem some of the founder's common stock, the value at which that stock is redeemed may impact the pricing of the company's stock options (and not in a good way). For example, if the company is pricing its options at $0.10 per share and a founder sells common stock to the company at $0.50 per share as a means to get some liquidity, that sale may result in the IRS requiring a higher option price than the previous $0.10 per share (remember, options must be granted at no less than fair market value under Code section 409A). If we hold our noses and argue that the fair market of the common is really $0.10 notwithstanding the $0.50 per share that the founder received, the IRS might then treat the difference as compensation income (taxable at ordinary income tax rates and subject to tax withholding) instead of favorable capital gains rates.

Does FF stock avoid this tax problem? The IRS may argue that the Series FF stock was sold at less than its value to the founders thereby creating ordinary income at issuance or that the arrangement is economically identical to a redemption of the founder's common shares at a premium.[81] Also, the presence of Series FF stock in the cap table signals to investors that the founders want liquidity. Although this is precisely the point of Series FF stock, investors may not want founders to cash out, even in part, in a financing. I usually recommend avoiding this concept, especially since there are other ways of achieving liquidity. Although I advise against it, it must be stressed that I describe Series FF and Class F to illustrate the many possible capital structure choices.

Chapter Twenty-six

Cap Table Equity

Dead on Arrival contains an extensive discussion of the items that appear on a cap table and will not be repeated here; however, a summary is useful. A typical pre-funding cap table will contain a listing of all of the equity instruments issued by the company, such as:

Common Stock

Options

Warrants

Convertibles

The following is a discussion of what this means and why it is important.

Common Stock.

Common stock may be thought of as the residuary ownership – it is what is left over after the creditors and preferences on preferred stock, if any, are paid. It is the currency used to pay service providers, including founders and optionees. Because it is the residuary, it is priced cheap. That is a good thing since the value of stock granted to service providers for services is taxable. In addition, in the case of a sale of stock to a service provider, the difference between the value of the stock and its cost is taxable income to the service provider.

Many founders (and their lawyers) are under the mistaken impression that there is a magical kind of stock called founders' stock that transcends all these pesky tax rules and is never taxed. If you have not heard any anecdotal evidence to the contrary, it is only because startups are rarely audited by the IRS.

Founders' stock refers to the common stock that is initially issued to the company's founders or organizers. The issuance of founders' stock is generally nontaxable either because its value is equal to the small amount of cash that the founders pay for it or because the founders contribute property for their stock in a tax free transaction under Section 351 of the Internal Revenue Code.[82]

Some companies will add founders (or other shareholders) at some point after formation and will naturally assume that the new founders' shares can be received tax free since the founders received their shares tax free. This may or may not work and a review of the tax rules is helpful to understanding why.

When a service provider (including a founder) buys stock in a corporation, the difference between what he or she pays for the stock and its value is taxable as compensation to the service provider. Most founders are service providers and, thus, will recognize income equal to the difference between cost and value on incorporation. However, upon formation, the founders may take the position that there is no difference since the value of the stock is equal to the small amount of cash that they contribute to cover formation costs. That probably works at the very beginning of a company's life; however, most companies will then move quickly to entering into supplier and customer contracts, building technology assets, contracting with employees and other service providers, and so forth. That activity creates value which will cause the value of the stock to correspondingly increase. Thus, the tax-free issuance of founders' stock for nominal cash only works at the very early stages of the company's formation.

Suppose, instead, that the founders deferred the decision to incorporate until *after* they have created technology, hired contractors, and generally created value. Can they still incorporate tax free? The answer is yes, under Section 351.

Generally, the exchange of assets for stock is a taxable transaction. Section 351 of the Internal Revenue Code allows a tax free incorporation when a person or group of persons exchanges property for stock and, immediately after the exchange, owns more than 80 percent of the company's stock. In the typical case, the founders as a group will own 100 percent of the stock after the initial issuance and thus meet the requirements of the statute. This does not work, however, when a founder comes along after the initial issuance and contributes property for stock unless he or she (and other transferors who are part of a plan) will own more than 80 percent after that issuance.

In addition, the founder must contribute property to the corporation in exchange for stock in order to obtain tax-free treatment. The term property is quite broadly defined to include legally protectable know-how and secret processes. A letter of intent, for example, has been held to be property in a related context[83] because the parties viewed it as having value. A grant of nonexclusive patent rights to a subsidiary was also held to be property.[84] Broad does not mean unlimited, however, and there comes a point where the rights granted do not rise to the level of property. In that case, they may be more service related. In other words, if the thing being contributed is so unripe as to not constitute property, the stock received in return may be granted for the services that will be rendered to make it property. In that case, the value of the stock would be taxable.

One very common mistake that companies make is to misunderstand what the term "value" means for tax purposes. Imagine this scenario: You are an early-stage startup. You bought your shares in the company for $0.0001 per share or less. Since then, you have had no revenue but you have taken money from angels against a convertible note or SAFE (see below). No stock has been sold or options granted. In other words, there has been no priced round and no independent valuation. A new team member comes along and you want to sell him stock for $0.0001 per share.

Can you do it?

Let's thicken the plot. You ask your friends in the startup community and they seem to think it's OK. The hotshots on Quora say it is just fine because you are worth very little at this point. You ask a VC what your common stock is worth and he tells you hardly anything. Even your CPA is willing to sign the returns that treat your common stock as being worth $0.0001 per share.

Now what do we think?

The answer is: Welcome to Silicon Valley. That transaction is done every day despite the fact that there is close to a 100% chance that the IRS would challenge it if it were ever audited. If you doubt it, hire a professional appraiser and see if they come back with a 409A valuation of the company of $0.0001 per share. Not likely.

So how is it that companies will grant stock at $0.0001 when we all know a professional 409A valuation (which are notorious for undervaluing stock) will result in a much higher value?

The real, unspoken reason is a variation on the dumb agent rule. The dumb agent rule is a maxim of tax law that posits an IRS agent is not likely to discover a taxable transaction on audit if it is too complicated or because it is hidden in documents. This particular application of the dumb agent rule holds that the IRS will not challenge a valuation because it is so factual and speculative. That works great... until it doesn't. The problem with that approach is that the IRS is not your biggest problem in that scenario. The VCs are not even your problem because they have shown time and again that they are willing to close one eye and look the other way on this issue. Your bigger problem is the accounting firm that will conduct due diligence if your company is acquired before the statute of limitations runs (generally 3 years for federal purposes). They will likely take the most conservative approach, assume the worst, and either adjust your valuation or establish an escrow or holdback to hedge the risk. If you were sufficiently feckless on this issue, it might even tank your deal. I have seen it happen more than once.

The case of the careful angel. My promising agtech client attracted the interest of a wealthy and very well-known Silicon Valley angel. The founder, after bringing on his marquee investor, was able to recruit more talent. He went about offering cheap stock to his new hires, since they had not yet done a priced round or obtained a 409A valuation. The angel insisted that the company price the stock at a reasonable value and that the new talent pay for it even if the company should have to loan them the money to buy the stock. The angel knew what the founder did not – that this company was poised for a quick exit and a public company acquirer would not take any tax risk. The angel turned out to be right. He did have an exit path in mind and the buyer had no tolerance at all for fast and loose tax planning. With the angel's guidance, the company sailed through due diligence for a relatively painless close.

Had we followed the dumb agent rule, we would have had a valuation hit, a tax escrow, or a holdback. You can read about those cases in *Dead on Arrival*. Like I said, it's not a problem until it's a problem.

<u>Options</u>

As discussed above, an option must be granted at a fair market value strike price. Because of the potentially large tax exposure, almost all venture-backed companies will obtain a professional valuation to support their option price, as all companies should.

More often, in a start-up company environment, problems arise in connection with a promise of an option grant at a certain price. An option is not granted until it is *formally* granted, meaning that necessary corporate action has been taken, so an offer letter promising to make a grant does not result in a completed grant that locks in the strike price. That price will be measured not at the date of the offer letter but at the date of grant. Backdating is not allowed.

As noted above, the spread in an NSO is taxed at ordinary rates on exercise and any gain attributable to appreciation in the option stock after the exercise will be taxable at capital gains rates if the one-year holding period for long-term capital gains purposes is met. Because exercise closes the compensation element in the option, many employees are tempted to exercise their option early and exercise for non-vested shares if possible. This works fine for an NSO on stock that later appreciates. If, however, the option shares decrease in value, the employee will be out of pocket for the exercise price of the option shares.

Many employees believe that they should always exercise early to start the holding period and lock in this favorable capital gains tax treatment. This is not always a great solution, as a lot of Silicon Valley executives discovered during the dot-com days of the late 1990s. Here is why. An executive would exercise an option at a time that the value of the stock exceeded the exercise price of the option (while it was "in the money") and its value seemed to be going higher. Sometimes, the exercise price and the spread (the excess of the value of the stock over the exercise price of the option) would both be substantial, resulting in a large payment as well as a large tax bill on exercise.

Sometimes, the executive would pay for the stock with a promissory note and basically bet that he or she could pay the note with the proceeds of a later sale of the stock on exit. Then, the value of the stock would fall to an amount below the original exercise price and the executive would sell the stock or claim a worthless stock deduction.

The problem, as many found out, was that the income on exercise was ordinary income, taxable immediately at high rates. The loss on the later sale was capital, deductible only against $3,000 per year of ordinary income plus capital gains. The result would be a large economic loss but very little tax deduction. I saw more than one executive whose tax liability—as a result of exercise—exceeded his or her net worth. As you can imagine, many employees have been surprised at how the tax law works in this scenario but Silicon Valley executives do not engender much sympathy in Congress.

To put real numbers to it, suppose you have an NSO to acquire $1,000,000 worth of stock for an exercise price of $200,000. You exercise the option to lock in your ability to get capital gains treatment on the appreciation in value. You will have $800,000 of taxable gain on exercise. Then, suppose the value of the stock drops and you sell the stock in a later year for $200,000. You paid $200,000 for your shares and you received $200,000. How much did you make?

Assuming you are taxed at a rate of 35 percent, you lost a little less than $280,000. How? Taxable gain on exercise: $800,000 times tax rate of 35 percent = $280,000. Deductible loss on sale: $3,000.

And if the stock had decreased even more you would have lost that much more of the exercise price. The unused capital losses can be carried over and used to offset later year capital gains plus $3,000 per year of ordinary income. Unless there are substantial later year gains, the present value of those losses will be much less than the tax cost. Even if the taxpayer does have capital gains that can be reduced by the capital losses, the result is uneven because the income is taxed at 35 percent but the losses offset income that would be taxed at the 20 percent capital gains rate. This is why exercise is often a risky strategy as a tax matter.

<u>Options and Independent Contractors</u>. Typically, an option expires upon or soon after the termination of employment of the optionee since an

objective of an option plan is to entice employees to stay until exit. When an option is allowed to sit unexercised after an employee leaves, an overhang is created.[85] This overhang can wreak havoc with a capitalization table if it gets too large since it makes it hard to determine the fully diluted capitalization[86] of the company. For example, for purposes of valuing a company, an investor will assume that all options reserved under a plan will be exercised; however, everyone knows that employees will leave employment and let their options lapse unexercised so that they are returned to the pool and can be used for further grants. If a substantial amount of options will not expire until some date that is far out in the future, it is more difficult for an investor to anticipate how many shares will be outstanding on an exit.

With employees, the date of termination is not hard to determine. For independent contractors, however, it is not always clear when they have terminated service since their service may be only periodic. A well-advised company will clarify in writing when that termination has occurred, either by designating in the plan documents what events are deemed to be a termination of service or by expressly terminating service in writing.

<u>Notice on Termination</u>. As mentioned, options lapse automatically if not exercised within a certain period of time after termination of service. Formal notice of the fact that an option is about to lapse is generally not required to be given. However, although no option plan will obligate an employer to notify an employee of an option lapse, the cautious company will, as a matter of course, notify terminated employees in advance—in writing—of the lapse of their options.

<u>Magic Backdating Ink</u>. As noted above, options must be granted at fair market value, meaning that the exercise price of an option must be fair market value of the stock at the date of grant or the employee will have immediate income, penalties, and interest.[87] For as long as I can remember, clients have asked me if they can paper (or prepare a document evidencing) an option grant that had been promised long before. I have always discouraged this practice but the practice was widespread for private companies prior to 2002.

Here is how it works. Suppose the CEO tells you on Friday that he is going to recommend that your company grant you a stock option. The stock is trading at twenty dollars on Friday. On the following Monday, the board approves the stock option grant but the value has gone up to twenty-two dollars by then. Now your option price has increased to twenty-two dollars and you have to pay an extra two dollars per share to exercise. "Can't we just pretend that it was issued last Friday?" you might ask, since that is when it was promised. In fact, as long as we are pretending, why can't we pretend that it was issued last Tuesday, when the price was eighteen dollars? And thus, we start sliding down the slippery backdating slope. A 2000 e-mail among officials at one Silicon Valley tech company referred to this ability to leave dates open while we wait and see as magic backdating ink.[88]

As a tax and accounting matter, backdating results in the optionee paying less than fair market value at grant. In other words if the stock is worth more on the actual date of grant than on the pretend date of grant, the optionee will have paid less than fair market value for the stock. If the company does not record that expense because it is clinging to the fiction that the grant occurred when the stock was worth less, its financial statements will not accurately reflect the size of the stock option expense. Thus, income will be overstated and the investors will have been given false financial information. Silicon Valley executives have been criminally convicted for making it falsely appear that options had been granted at a lower price on an earlier date.

Summary. Options are a great tool for rewarding employees and service providers but they are fraught with potential problems for the company that is not well advised. My top ten most frequent option problems to watch for are as follows:

No professional valuation, resulting in potential taxes and penalties

No written plan or grant documents

Backdated grant documents

Lack of 83(b) elections on early exercises

ISO exercises resulting in alternative minimum tax

Grants to non-individuals under a Rule 701 plan

Lack of securities law filings or compliance

Excessive overhang

Extended exercise periods

Large grants to high-level employees

<u>Preferred Stock</u>

Preferred stock is what your company will sell to investors to raise money. The stock is called preferred because it has some sort of liquidation and dividend preference meaning that, on sale of the company, the preferred stockholders will be paid before the common stockholders. If there is not enough money to pay everyone, the preferred stockholders will take all the proceeds. The amount of this liquidation preference is negotiated and may be participating or nonparticipating. Participating preferred stock gets its money back *and* shares in sales proceeds based on its percentage ownership. Nonparticipating preferred stock only gets its money back (or a multiple of its money) and does not share in the upside beyond that. Preferred stock is also usually convertible into common stock at some agreed-upon ratio (usually 1:1) so that nonparticipating preferred stock will convert if the percentage of the company allocable to a share of stock exceeds its liquidation preference. Investors will also negotiate a host of other protective provisions (see below).

Although preferred stock has rights that the common stock does not, there are good reasons why the common stockholders would want the company to issue preferred stock instead of common stock to investors. From the company's standpoint, it receives more dollars for each share of preferred stock than it would receive from the sale of an equal amount of common stock. From the investor's standpoint, they will be protected on the downside by the liquidation preferences.

Preferred stock is not always the answer. Sometimes, other types of securities make more sense. Mistakes around preferred stock come in two varieties—companies issue it when they should not or do not issue it when they should.

<u>When a company should not issue preferred stock but does</u>. The sale of preferred stock necessarily requires a company to value its stock. When dealing with institutional or sophisticated investors who are investing enough money to conduct extensive due diligence, a priced round can be justified. With smaller numbers, however, the compliance costs might inhibit arriving at an accurate valuation. If, as a result, the company is valued too high, the next round will be a down round, possibly requiring antidilution adjustments

that further reduce the founders' percentage interests. If the value is too low, the founders will have given up too much in the first preferred stock round and will lose control that much more quickly. My rule of thumb is that if a company cannot raise at least $1 million in its financing round, I do not recommend the use of preferred stock. Does that mean the company should sell common stock to raise money? Absolutely not, for the reasons discussed below.

<u>When a company should issue preferred stock but does not</u>. The flip side of the company that is too early to issue preferred stock is the company that should sell preferred stock but instead sells common stock. If there is only one thing in this chapter that you should remember, it is that you never sell common stock to raise money. Common stock should be issued to founders, issued on exercise of options, or sold to C-level executives. Common stock must be cheap. If the value of the common stock is too high, the option price must be high and the company's options (which must have a fair-market-value exercise price) will not be attractive to optionees. Selling common stock to raise money will necessarily result in a higher common stock price. If it does not, that will mean that the common stock is being priced too cheap and the founders are giving up too much of the company for the initial sale of stock.

So if a company that needs less than $1 million cannot sell preferred stock or common stock, what can it do? The answer is convertibles.

Warrants and Convertibles

Convertible debt solves the problem of the company's current need for cash when it is not in a position to sell preferred stock. As noted above, the investor in a note gets the security of debt (which must be repaid before the equity gets a return) and need not gamble on a valuation. The company gets its investment without having to set a valuation. Both parties avoid a long and costly negotiation over equity terms.

Sometimes, but not often, the debt is secured. Usually it carries a higher than market interest rate. Since many technology companies do not have much in the way of hard assets to offer as security, the debt holder is really taking an equity risk despite the security interest it might take in technology. To reward the debt holder for investing early, before the company's larger preferred stock round, the debt holder will be allowed to convert at a discount or will be given warrant coverage (or both).

The discount means that the debt will convert at a lower price than the preferred stock price. A typical discount can range from ten to thirty percent depending on market conditions and the particular company. For example, a twenty percent discount would mean that each eighty dollars of debt would convert into one hundred dollars' worth of preferred stock when the company does its financing. Alternatively, the investor could have warrant coverage. Twenty percent warrant coverage, for example, would mean that (in addition to converting its debt) the investor would have the right to buy twenty dollars' worth of preferred stock for each one hundred dollars of debt that it holds.[89] If the warrant strike price is nominal (one cent per share, for example), warrant coverage could be similar to a discount with more paperwork. Sometimes, investors get both.

Over the last few years, more and more convertible debt instruments have included a price cap. Many investors have had the unpleasant experience of investing in a company's convertible debt and then watching the company use its investment dollars to increase its value, which, of course, increases the price per share at which their debt would convert to equity. In a sense, the terms of traditional convertible debt place the debt holders and the company at cross purposes—the debt holders would like a low valuation at the equity financing stage while the company seeks to maximize value.

In fact, there are stories in the Silicon Valley of debt holders convincing later investors not to invest at high values because of the potential dilution they would suffer. The perceived answer to the debt holder's dilemma is a price cap. A cap means that the debt will convert at the lesser of a discount to the price offered in the next equity financing or a price per share determined as if the company were worth X dollars. In that scenario, X is some reasonable estimate of the value at the next financing. The cap should be higher than the current perceived valuation since it is a downside protection device and not intended to be a proxy for valuation.

Similarly, the sophisticated investor will ask that they receive an equity return in the event of a sale before a financing. In other words, the investor will receive some multiple of their investment upon a sale of the company (unless the debt has converted to equity).

There are a couple of traps in this. First, the discount should be market and not more than that. Market may depend on how hard it is for the company to raise money. As stated, 20 percent is typical but it could be much higher if the company has no other options. Second, whatever the discount, it is coming out of the founders' hides and not the Series A investors'.[90] While it might seem like the eventual Series A investors are being forced to carve out a piece of what they are getting at a cheap price, in fact, the Series A investors will take the effect of debt conversion into account to ensure that they end up with whatever percent of the company they desire. In other words, regardless of the size of the discount to the debt holders, the later investor will decide what percent of the company it needs for its investment and it will simply price the preferred stock at whatever price it takes to get to that result.

Finally—and this is a big trap—an S corporation is limited in its ability to issue convertible debt. As noted earlier, an S corporation can only have one class of stock and will often issue convertible debt in order to avoid having to issue preferred stock (the issuance of which would terminate its S election). That all works fine unless the debt converts to common stock at a discount because, if the debt is not convertible at fair market value, it may be treated as stock. If the convertible debt holder is not a US individual and the debt is treated as stock for tax purposes, the corporation may be treated as having a disqualified shareholder. And finally, even if the debt is convertible to common stock and is held by a US individual, the debt might be treated as stock that does not share in distributions, thus creating the prohibited second class of stock. This is tricky stuff and requires counsel from someone who understands S corporations. Losing an S election is an expensive mistake to make.

Convertible Equity

As is apparent, convertible debt suffers from the is-it-debt-or-equity problem. The investor is taking equity risk and expects to get equity in the company. Rarely does a startup company convertible debt investor just want his money back plus interest. Because of the above valuation and administrative issues, the investor is forced into a debt instrument when he really wants equity. That structure is in some ways advantageous (compared to equity) for the investor and not so much for the company. For example, debt pays interest; equity does not. Debt ranks ahead of equity in priority of payment. This latter factor can be significant as I have seen more than one debt investor end up with the company to the exclusion of equity investors (and even junior or later debt holders). Debt must have a term, usually within a year or two, at which time the debt comes due and must be repaid. Finally, if the debt converts to equity at a discount, the debt holder is getting a liquidation preference that he did not pay for ($0.20 for each $1 invested if the debt is issued at a 20% discount), although that may seem fair compensation for getting in early.

<u>Enter convertible equity.</u>

The concept behind convertible equity (a misnomer as it may not be equity at all) is that the investor buys a right that converts to equity in the first equity round. The most prevalent convertible equity instrument is the cleverly named SAFE - Simple Agreement for Future Equity. Under a SAFE, the investor will contribute cash to an early-stage company now and receive stock later on the occurrence of a triggering event described in the SAFE. Although the SAFE is not a debt instrument, it is an alternative to convertible notes and referenced on the company's cap table like any other convertible security. The SAFE benefits both companies and investors since it avoids the requirements of debt instruments such as term, interest accrual, and maturity dates. Moreover, a standardized SAFE can significantly reduce the transaction costs of negotiating as the only item typically negotiated with a SAFE is the valuation cap and possibly a discount rate. The SAFE is discussed below in Chapter 25.

<u>Phantom Stock, SARs and Virtual Stock</u>

The Silicon Valley was built on equity compensation (stock for sweat). For many years, we had it pretty good out on the West Coast. Options could be granted at artificially low prices and, so long as the value was not too far off, the regulators accepted the board's good-faith determination of value. No more! Internal Revenue Code Section 409A requires a company to be correct in its option valuation and, if it is wrong, the result is immediate taxation, a 20 percent penalty and interest, plus state taxes, if applicable.[91] Since the only way to know for sure that you are right about the price is to obtain an expensive professional valuation, many companies are rethinking the value of an option plan.

The problem is exacerbated in the case of an S corporation since the exercise of an option on S corporation stock could result in a loss of the S election if the optionee is not a qualified S corporation shareholder. LLCs do not have that problem but they have other issues. In particular, the exercise of an option on an interest in an LLC that is taxed as a partnership requires complicated accounting entries that, as a practical matter, most companies will not bother with or understand. The exercising optionee of an LLC option will become a member of the LLC and receive the IRS Form 1065, Schedule K-1, which will require the optionee to pay tax on their share of the income of the LLC, whether he or she receives it or not. That may not be the great result everyone intended.

For those reasons, S corporations and LLCs have long used phantom stock, options, or LLC interests to reward and motivate employees. The phantom plan comes in two basic flavors. Under one system, a company promises to reserve a portion of the proceeds of a sale or exit for distribution to holders of phantom stock units. That amount, whatever it is, is then divided by the number of units in the plan. Each holder of a unit then shares in the proceeds of the sale based on his or her relative number of units. A more typical scheme is to pay each phantom unit the same amount that a share of stock would be entitled to on a sale or exit. In either case, those units can be made subject to vesting or can be granted in tranches. The only catch is that the unit holder must usually be employed at the date of the liquidity event (such as a sale of the company). In this way, a phantom unit in a privately held company mimics an option.

Options are often cashed out at exit (and not exercised) and expire if not exercised within a short period of time after termination of employment. Most options on private company stock expire unexercised, meaning that typically the only employees who cash out of options are those who are employed when the liquidity event happens. Of course, unlike most phantom plan unit holders, an option holder has the ability to terminate employment, exercise the option, and hold the stock until a sale of the company. That does happen sometimes. I know people who have gotten rich that way.

The downside is that phantom units are not stock—even though they are stock-like—so holders do not vote or otherwise share in current earnings, although they could be drafted to share in current distributions, and often are. Phantom units typically expire if the employee leaves before an exit, unlike stock. Most significantly, there is no possibility for capital gains tax treatment with a phantom unit. It is compensation, taxed at the highest federal and state rates (plus payroll taxes). A grant of stock, by comparison, can potentially qualify for low capital gains tax rates.

The benefit of the phantom stock plan is simplicity. In fact, it is so simple that there are really only a few ways that a company could screw it up. One is to not think through how proceeds are divided up on exit. Importantly, the proceeds to be divided must be proceeds *net* of liabilities. So if a company ends up getting sold for liability assumption and there is nothing left over for the shareholders, there should also be nothing for the optionees. Always split net.

Second, the amount to be divided should be based on the total number of units reserved under the plan, not the total issued. For example, if the company reserves 10 percent of the net proceeds of a sale for distribution under the plan and if there is only one unit holder at the time of the exit—and he or she has been granted 10 percent of the units in the plan—he or she should get 1 percent and not 10 percent of the net proceeds of the sale. Sounds simple but companies regularly get this wrong because they assume that they will eventually issue all the units but then fail to do so.

Finally, it is pretty easy to inadvertently end up within the penalty provisions of Code Section 409A. The easiest way for management to run afoul of Section 409A is to allow unit holders to keep their units long after departing, which converts the plan into a deferred compensation plan under 409A. If the plan then does not comply with 409A, the result will be a tax disaster.

The Polka King.

Finally, we close this chapter with a cautionary tale. The story of Jan Lewan, the Polka King of Pennsylvania, has been re-enacted on the television show *American Greed*, a documentary, and in a Hollywood movie starring Jack Black.[92] The Polka King sold millions of dollars' worth of 12 percent promissory notes to his friends and fans. Some of those sales were to Pennsylvania residents in violation of state securities law requirements. When the state of Pennsylvania learned that he had sold unregistered securities, Jan was warned to stop, but he persisted. Jan was eventually arrested for money laundering and securities fraud and sentenced to prison, where he was stabbed in the neck by a cellmate and almost died. Jan's wife also divorced him while he was in prison. I like to think that if only he had seen a lawyer and had not tried to do it all himself, he could have avoided these problems. Think about that the next time you go online, download a SAFE, and sell it to your neighbor to raise money, all without any legal advice because it seems so easy.

Chapter Twenty-seven

SAFEs

When *Dead on Arrival* was published, simple agreements for future equity (SAFEs) were just beginning to become popular and the book spent about a paragraph or two talking about them. SAFEs are now pervasive in the pre-seed (and even seed) startup world and a lot has happened. In particular, SAFEs are neither simple nor are they equity and they certainly are not safe.

Before the SAFE, when a startup needed money but was too early to have a credible valuation, they would sell convertible debt or debt with warrants. Convertible debt (or debt with warrants) solved that problem. The company would get the cash and the investor would get stock down the road at a discount to a professional investor's (the VC's) valuation. Both parties should be happy. As discussed above, the debt form did not fit the equity reality of a pre-seed investment since the investor was not expecting debt risk or debt returns. The SAFE can be thought of as a convertible debt without the debt features, such as interest, a repayment obligation, or a minimum financing threshold for conversion.

In the case of either convertible debt or convertible equity, the more well considered agreements provide that the instrument converts into shadow preferred in the Series A financing, which has all the rights and privileges of the preferred stock except that the liquidation privilege is based on the amount paid rather than the price per share of the preferred stock. In other words, if $.80 of SAFE converts into $1 of preferred (a 20% discount), the liquidation preference for the SAFE stock should be $.80 per share, not $1.00.

Unfortunately, anyone can go online and download a SAFE template and sell SAFEs with or without legal advice. However, any founder who wants to sell SAFEs to raise money should be aware of a few things.

<u>A SAFE is a security</u>. This means that the sale of the SAFE must comply with applicable securities laws. The penalties for failing to comply include rescission, disgorgement, personal liability, and sometimes criminal penalties.

It is a rare founder who can manage the federal and state securities law exemptions from registration without a lawyer.

You may recall from *Dead on Arrival* that every sale of securities must either be registered or exempt. Attached as Appendix M Overview of Securities Law Exemptions is a handy summary of the securities law exemptions from registration. Each state may also have its own rules.

There is a huge difference between a pre-money SAFE and a post-money SAFE. A pre-money SAFE is based on the valuation cap immediately before the SAFE converts to stock; a post-money SAFE sets the value cap after the conversion. Here is an example of what I mean. Assume a company has the following simple cap table:

Founders	4,000,000	100%
Stock Pool	0	0%
Total	4,000,000	100%

If the Company sells $1,000,000 of equity with a $4,000,000 *pre*-money valuation, the investor will take 20 percent of the capitalization ($1,000,000/$5,000,000). If the Company sells $1,000,000 of equity with a $4,000,000 *post*-money valuation, the investor will take 25 percent of the capitalization ($1,000,000/$4,000,000).

If you are a founder, you will give up less equity using pre-money SAFEs than with post-money SAFEs.

In addition, if the Company sells additional SAFEs or grants options, in the pre-money scenario, the investor and founder both share that dilution. In the post-money scenario, only the founder is diluted. The one advantage of a post-money SAFE, often touted by investors, is that the parties have a little bit more certainty over how much of their company they have sold in a post-money world, since the percentage is fixed. With a pre-money SAFE, the parties will not know how much they have sold until closing because the SAFE is always being diluted. That is an odd argument since the percentage at which the pre-money SAFE can convert into will always go down (not up) as new securities are issued. It would be more accurate to say that we cannot say how much of your company you have sold with pre-money SAFEs, but we can estimate the percentage the post-money SAFE investor will own. And that brings me to my next point. But first, Appendix N SAFE has a handy chart of the differences between the pre- and post-money SAFEs.

Keep track of how much of your company you have committed to SAFE holders. It is very easy to sell off more of your company than you expected through SAFEs. I have seen many founders get to their SAFE conversion event (a Series A round) only to find out that they have given too much of the company away to the SAFE investors. In some cases, I have seen the Series A investors walk away from the deal because there is not enough equity left for the founders after accounting for the SAFE stock. Learn excel, keep a spreadsheet handy, and run pro forma cap tables showing what will happen if you do a financing at various valuations. Commercial cap table technology providers may be able to run these numbers for you.

Give your SAFE investors pro rata rights. A pro rata right (or right to maintain) is a right of the investor to purchase more stock if the company raises another round. Sometimes it is in the SAFE itself and sometimes it is in a side letter. In the old days, pro rata rights were less of an issue since angels were not expected to be a perpetual funding source. These days, with SAFE rounds getting larger and later and angels having more money to invest, pro rata rights are seen at the SAFE stage more often. In general, sophisticated investors will demand pro rata rights and will be very offended if they do not get them. Unsophisticated investors might not think of it. My view is that you should take care of the people who bet on your start-up early. Give them the pro rata rights.

However, don't forget to do the math. In your pro formas, what happens if everyone always exercises their pro rata? Will there be enough equity left for new investors and do you care where the money comes from? The answer is yes, you should care. More on that later.

Finally – Investor Rights. SAFEs are being used more and more as a proxy for priced rounds. As this happens, investors will be asking for the rights that you might expect to see in a preferred stock financing. After pro rata rights, the next shoe to drop will be a control issue, often expressed as a board seat or position as a board observer. See the discussion below about boards for more on this topic.

SAFE Summary. To summarize, here is what you should focus on when issuing SAFEs:

Pre or post-money. If you are a founder, you will likely give up less equity with a pre money SAFE.

Discount rate. This is the discount to the price per share of the stock sold in the next financing. It is usually 20 percent but can vary.

Valuation cap. This is the safety valve that ensures the investor gets some benefit from the low valuation tied to investing early. The cap should be what you think the company will be worth at the next round.

Change of Control ("CoC"). The SAFE can convert to common stock at the cap if there is a sale before a financing. The SAFE could also be redeemed at face value or a multiple thereof prior to and in preference to the equity in a CoC.

Pro rata rights. This is the investors' right to maintain their percentage interest in the company after the next financing.

MFN. A most favored nations clause ensures the investor gets the benefit of any more favorable rights negotiated after the date of the SAFE.

Other rights. Sometimes SAFE holders get board seats, board observer rights, reports, and inspection rights.

Chapter Twenty-eight
Angels and Devils

As you know by now, an angel is early-stage individual investor.[93] This chapter adds a few words of advice for those of you who will be seeking angel money.

As a startup, you will likely need angel money before you get to the VCs. In fact, you will want angel money first because you want to stage your financings. That is, you want to take as little money as possible early when your valuation is low and when you will suffer the least dilution.

By the time you get to an angel you should be at the proof of concept stage. Your friends and family will have relied on a whiteboard or a power point to get you launched but an angel needs to see more. Lately, angels in my neighborhood have gotten so spoiled that some will want to see traction (see below) before they will talk to you but, as a general rule, plan on at least having a proof of concept.

Proof of concept generally means an exercise that tests a design idea or assumption and demonstrates functionality. People sometimes equate proof of concept with a prototype but it is not the same thing. A prototype is a model of the product. Proof of concept shows that a product or feature can be developed. A prototype shows how it will be developed.[94]

We need to add one more definition here. In recent years, angels have been demanding more than proof of concept or a prototype. They may want to see a minimum viable product or MVP. If all this jargon is starting to seem silly, hang in there. You will want to be familiar with these terms when you are asked about them even if the angel isn't quite sure himself what he means. The term MVP probably comes from the Lean Startup methodology[95] and means, just as it sounds, a version of a product with just enough features to work. Early customers can then validate the idea and provide feedback for future product development. These days, angels want to see that.

Assuming you have your proof of concept, prototype, or MVP, depending on which buzz word your angel likes best, you should then consider how much angel money you should take. Here are some rules of thumb. You want to take enough money to get you to the next valuation point. That usually means traction, which means sales, revenue, or, most importantly, users who will ideally (but not necessarily) pay you for what you have built. Thus, you should fire up your excel program and project out what it will take to get into the market. That is how much money to take.

You should also give yourself enough time to get to the next valuation point. That should be a year to 2 years (18 months may be ideal). One of the best and worst things about angel money, however, is that the nature of the securities sold need not require one big closing. Thus, if you run out of time and runway before you get to MVP, or whatever, you can keep selling more SAFEs and raising more money until you do. That's one of the best things about angel money. That is also one of the worst things about angel money because, if you are too far off on your projections, you may end up giving up too much of your company by the time you get to the VC.

And, of course, there are potential legal issues in this scenario. One potential problem that comes up when you miss the mark with an angel is twofold. First, what exactly did your projections tell the angel? As a matter of securities law, you are allowed to make forward looking statements, which are merely predictions or projections of expectations or possibilities.[96] If you give your angels a set of disclosures, including risk factors, you should include a form of a disclaimer that states that any forward-looking statement is only true at the time it was written and you have no obligation to update those statements if things change. A form of disclaimer is attached as Appendix O Forward Looking Statements. I suggest that you add that to your investor materials. You also may want to attach a standard set of risk factors, an example of which is attached as Appendix P Risk Factors.

By the way, the safe harbor for forward looking statements is not as expansive as you might expect. The statute has some detailed exclusions from the safe harbor for what statements may be said and who may say them. For a startup company, the most relevant exclusions are for issuers who, during the previous 3 years, have been convicted of a felony or been subject to certain securities law related judicial or administrative decrees.[97]

Secondly, if you do oversell your company at the angel level, the temptation is almost irresistible to tank the company and start over. I suggest that you try very hard to resist that temptation lest you draw a fiduciary duty claim from some angry investors.

Assuming you have done all of the above right, who should you accept as your angel? It is important to get this right because, contrary to what you might think, you typically do not have the right to buy out an investor if you decide that you do not like them. If they buy into your company, you are stuck with them. You might ask for some sort of call or buyback right but since the value in a startup is usually at the exit and not at some midpoint, no sophisticated investor will limit their return like that. You are stuck with them until the end absent a mutual agreement to the contrary.

One of the great spaghetti westerns of all time is Sergio Leone's *The Good, the Bad and the Ugly*. If you have not seen it, you should stop reading this book and Netflix it now. I saw it in 1969 and have been wondering since then which character was good, bad, or ugly, since they all seemed pretty flawed. I do not want you wondering what kind of angel you have, so here are some tips.

The Good: smart money is better than dumb money. You would rather have a smart angel than a dumb one. By smart, I mean someone who gets what you are doing and can add something other than just money to the equation. Ideally, your angel will have connections to talent, other angels and, eventually, venture capitalists. Smart angels will become advisors to the company and possibly even take a board seat. They will be there for you when you need follow on or more angel money and they will help you negotiate with the VCs because their ox is likely getting gored as much as yours at that point. The best angels will have experience in your market. They may have been entrepreneurs themselves and seek to change the world with your idea as much as you do. You will know these angels by reputation (see discussion of reputation below) and you will get clues as to who they are in the due diligence process. The smart angel will ask all the right questions. Because they have done their due diligence at the outset, they will not be surprised at your results or put off by setbacks. Get yourself a good, smart angel.

The Bad: whiners, control freaks and ankle biters. The thing that makes a whiner bad is the distraction they cause. Rather than giving you advice you can use, they will blame you for everything that doesn't go well or, worse, give you bad and unwanted advice. You can spot a bad angel by (i) reputation, (ii) inexperience – who have they invested in before? - and (iii) lack of diligence. Again, if an angel does not ask questions or rely on someone credible who did, that is a big warning sign because they may complain if you do not hit your projections. They may pester you for details while you are trying to run your business. You may have to deal with their constant complaints if you do not meet the forward-looking statements described above.

A control freak can even be worse. They are frustrated businessmen who will tell you how to run your business and expect you to blindly follow their advice. They want more meetings than they need and constant updates. They don't trust you and never should have been let into your round.

In modern slang, an ankle biter is a small dog who tends to be a tough, feisty little beast who is often touchy and quarrelsome.[98] I use the term to describe an investor who, although they did not invest much, have a lot to say about it. They are a lot like the whiner. They may constantly be asking for reassurance or often offering criticisms. Because their investments are so small, you may not see the urgency in dealing with them and the issue is merely one of distraction. When an ankle biter's investment gets to be large, they drop into my next category.

The Ugly: adversarial, confrontational, and litigious angels. The truly ugly angels are the ones that will damage you or your company. They may be all of the bad listed above, but they will also discourage later angels, disparage you in public, and, in the worst case, sue you.

A lawsuit may be a death knell for a startup. Few investors want to fund a defense, so it is a real threat. Many of my clients have received letters from litigators that are quick to point out the damage that will be done by their mere assertion in court of their claim. It is a threat that cannot be taken lightly not only for the company, but also for you as a founder, since a fiduciary claim or a securities fraud claim will follow you for years, maybe forever. You must avoid these people like Covid.

Fortunately, there is a way to screen ugly angels out. First, you can do background checks with permission. Secondly, you can search the court records for prior lawsuits. Thirdly, you should take note of who their advisors are – especially their lawyers. Finally, who else have they invested in and how did it turn out? This is discussed more below.

Chapter Twenty-nine
Fake it 'Til You Make It

I first met Liz Holmes, the founder of Theranos, at a political fundraiser held at a private residence in Palo Alto. She was not wearing a turtleneck and was not using that weirdly deep voice (you know the one). She told me that she was a startup founder and she seemed to be much like most of the startup founders I was used to seeing every day. She told me that she was the founder of Theranos, a health care and life sciences company with the mission of revolutionizing medical laboratory testing through innovative methods for drawing blood, testing blood, and interpreting patient data.

As everyone knows by now, Theranos is claimed to have exaggerated its claims as to the viability of its technology. As of this writing, Liz Holmes and Ramesh "Sunny" Balwani are being tried for conspiracy and wire fraud, based on allegations that Holmes and Balwani engaged in a scheme to defraud investors, doctors, and patients. The government claimed that they promoted their blood testing laboratory services even though they knew Theranos was not capable of consistently producing accurate and reliable results for certain blood tests. It was further alleged that the tests performed on Theranos technology were likely to contain inaccurate and unreliable results.[99]

In some ways, Theranos is not much different from a lot of companies that I see pitching to investors in Silicon Valley. "Fake it 'til you make it" is not just a mantra but a way of life for some entrepreneurs. But for the grace of God go they. In fact, the investment community almost expects exaggeration, hyperbole, and embellishment. They do not, however, expect to be lied to and you need to understand the difference in practice and in law.

Fraud generally consists of nine elements: (1) a representation of fact; (2) falsity; (3) materiality; (4) knowledge of its falsity or ignorance of its truth; (5) the intent that it be acted on; (6) an injured party's ignorance of the falsity; (7) the injured party's reliance on the representation; (8) the party's right to rely on the representation; and (9) proximate injury.[100] Fraud is a misrepresentation of a material fact used to induce someone to do something. That is much different than an opinion that no reasonable person would believe is an objective fact, often referred to as puffing. Misrepresentations generally, whether they be fraudulent, negligent, or innocent, only apply to statements of fact. All three types of misrepresentation are actionable and all can be avoided by not misrepresenting facts. Use your common sense.

Securities fraud is different. Securities fraud describes several causes of action, some of which are for other forms of misrepresentation.[101] When lawyers talk about securities fraud, we usually mean Rule 10b-5 under the Securities Act of 1933 (the "33 Act"). The '33 Act prohibits (1) schemes or artifices to defraud, (2) false statements of fact or omissions that make truthful affirmative statements misleading, and (3) acts or practices that operate as frauds or deceits.[102] These claims can be brought by private investors, the SEC, or both because the '33 Act authorizes what we call a private right of action. In addition, as Liz and Sunny have learned, the Department of Justice can base a criminal complaint on securities fraud.[103] Much has been written about what constitutes fraud and in what context. We could spend many pages dancing on the head of that pin trying to define just exactly how culpable you have to be and what mental state is required. I am not here to do that. Instead, I want to give you some practical advice on how to avoid becoming an accidental expert in securities fraud claims.

First, never fudge a fact. Never make up a number or lie about having a customer. While the line between fact and opinion or fraud and puffing may become blurry, you will avoid that issue by over disclosing. When in doubt, disclose.

Second, if you would rather your investor not know about it, it is probably material. If you don't want them to know about that harassment claim, it is probably material. If you don't want them to know about that ex-founder's claim to equity, it is probably material. You get the idea.

Third, do not omit material facts. Sophisticated investors will ask for a representation that you have disclosed all material facts. The rest should be given that courtesy. Again, if you end up arguing over this in court, you have already lost. When in doubt, disclose.

Finally, I have no legal basis for this next recommendation, other than almost 40 years of watching people decide whether to forgive human folly or punish it. Be transparent. Communicate with your investors. Don't hold back. As noted above, anyone with $2,500 can file a lawsuit. You do not want to poke that bull. Angels know that you are wildly optimistic and capable of suspending reality. They likely don't believe all of what you say anyway – don't give them a reason to make a claim out of it.

In sum, if you follow my rules, you should not end up like Theranos.

Chapter Thirty

Are You Ready for Venture Capital?

Venture capital tales

A dorm room startup. Alexandria grew up in a foreign country but worked hard enough in school that she was able to get into Stanford. In her senior year, she and some friends had an idea for a gig economy platform company. Her relatives were her first investors by giving her a modest sum to do some early development work. She was fortunate to know a local angel (the Valley is lousy with them) who fronted the development costs in exchange for a SAFE. The angel also provided business advice and support by helping them allocate equity, introducing a corporate and IP lawyer, refining the business plan, and getting them the advisors that would connect them with their first customers. Importantly, the angel also introduced AlexandriaCo to a group of venture capitalists who were impressed with the team, the pedigree, the tech, and the opportunity. They funded the company and it was able to scale quickly. It did two more rounds before exiting.

A serial entrepreneur. Alex was one of Alexandria's co-founders. He left the company earlier than Alexandria and went to work immediately on some new ideas that he had been thinking about. He had established connections with the VCs in Alexandria's company and had proven himself to be a solid performer. As soon as he got some traction, he went back to the same group of VCs, who funded his company as well.

A great referral. Beta was a friend of Alex and Alexandria from their days at Stanford and they hung out at the same startup events in San Francisco and Palo Alto. Beta did not have any connections within the VC community but did manage to get his startup to a small amount of revenue and assembled a strong team of co-founders, advisors, and partners. When the time was right, Alex introduced Beta to the VCs who had invested in his startup. One of the investors liked it and the introduction led to his series A round.

A great networker. Charlie didn't know Alex, Alexandria, or Beta and did not attend Stanford. Also, his company developed a healthtech solution and was not in the space in which Alexandria's investors invested. Without that personal introduction, Charlie sent his PowerPoint to every VC on Sand Hill Road, with no response. Undeterred, Charlie found out where some VCs would be speaking and caught the ear of one smaller fund manager after a digital health event. That connection led to a small round, which led to a larger round, and then to later VC rounds.

Those stories may sound like fairy tales but I have seen all of these scenarios play out many times over. Venture capital is a $200 billion per year industry with up to half of that amount managed or invested in Silicon Valley, by some estimates. As such, founders from around the world will often end up in Palo Alto to take their shot at startup fortune and fame.

There are plenty of good books written by VCs on how great they are but when it comes to advice on how founders should approach venture capital … not so much. I typically represent startup founders. I keep my friends close. I also represent some venture capital funds. I keep my enemies closer. This chapter is not about what a great bunch of guys and gals the VC community is. This chapter is about how you should deal with them.

First, do you want venture capital? Before you answer, understand that venture is the most expensive money in America. VCs expect a return that would make a loan shark envious. It is only suitable for companies that have no cheaper options, like debt. Rarely do I see a company that can borrow money take venture, unless there is some strategic advantage to it. VCs expect outsized returns because they take outsized risk. Are you too risky for debt or other forms of funding?

Second, does venture capital want you? At a high level, you will need to show three things to even get in the door with a VC: market, ability to scale, and explosive growth potential. In a nutshell, you have to be able to show that you can turn their investment of a small fortune into a large fortune.

To get a sense as to why that is so, you need to know a little bit about VC economics. First, as Bob Dylan says, we all got to serve someone, and it is no different with VCs. They operate funds or pooled investment vehicles. The pooled funds are from their investors who are often large institutions who expect (or hope for) a 20 to 30 percent return, which works out to 2 ½ to 3 times their investment during the life of the fund. Put a pin in that number for now.

The fund's managers and general partner will take 2 to 2.5 percent of the total committed capital every year off the top as a management fee. This is said to be necessary to cover overhead, like rent and salaries, but over ten years (a realistic life of a fund), by my expert calculations, that could add up to 20 to 25 percent. Again, by my expert calculations, that's a lot.

One of my VC clients once told me that nobody gets rich off of management fees. Ten years later, he looks like he has gotten pretty rich off of management fees.

On top of the management fees for overhead and expenses, the general partner will take a carry or carried interest. I call her a general partner because many or most funds are organized as limited partnerships, mostly for legacy reasons (limited partnership have been around a long time). In a limited partnership, the investors are limited partners and the management is the general partner. Many funds are organized as limited liability companies (LLCs), in which case management is called a manager. In either case, the GP or the manager will likely be a separate entity that has its own set of constituents splitting up the carry.

The carry is the share of the profits and gains from the fund's investments. There are many ways that carry gets calculated and when but, for now, just know that it is usually 20 percent. Thus, a typical fund should, over the life of the fund, pay the management fee, return the LPs' investments, pay a preferred return, pay a 20 percent carry, and triple the LPs' money. That is a heavy lift. But it gets worse.

VCs make risky investments so a typical VC fund will expect to lose money on half their investments. Another 20 percent to 30 percent will return one to two times their money. That means the rest must be home runs. They are expected to return 10 times to 100 times the VC's money.

Finally, you should keep in mind that a VC can only place so many bets. They must manage their investments. In fact, the regulatory category that allows VCs to fashion their economics requires that they pursue a venture capital strategy, which anticipates some level of participation in management.

That takes time and that is a limited resource. Thus, the VC must really believe that you are the wunderkind that is going to get them past the management fee, the preferred return, and the carry and give their LPs a VC sized return. Do you feel lucky? Well, do you?

So, at a high level, you have to be a company that can meet those expectations. More importantly, you have to be able to convince a VC that you are a company that can meet those expectations.

Third, is there a Company/VC fit? As noted, a gating item for a VC is that you must be in a market that can produce a large business. It need not be a market that currently exists. In fact, some of the largest markets could not have been conceived of until someone convinced us that we really like sharing rides or staying in people's homes or having our food delivered or whatever. Are you in a market that can support a big company?

Do you have some unfair competitive advantage? Why you? Why now? Do you need the VC's cash to be the first mover or the first to market?

Similarly, how do you know that there is what we call product market fit? That means how do you know people are going to buy your product? The best way of knowing is by showing that someone has paid you for it. That is a form of traction, a word you will hear often in the VC community. It's not only a good thing to have traction. It is usually essential to raise money at that level.

What does the long term look like? Most VCs that I know hate paying taxes and, by extension, hate it when their portfolio companies pay taxes. Instead, they would rather see you plow that money back into the business, scale, and do it quickly. That is long term thinking, not short-term profits. With IPOs being fewer and taking longer these days, you have to be in it for the long term. As an example, Zipcar, mentioned earlier, was founded in early 2000 but did not IPO until 2011 or merge until 2013. That is a typical time horizon these days.

Fourth, are you the right team? I know you think you are as unique as a snowflake and have no competitors, but that is unlikely. When the VC looks at you, they are not only evaluating your idea, they are considering whether you have the chops to pull it off. And they are not making that judgment in a vacuum. Consider that even if they like your idea, they might find someone else with more pedigree, better credentials, or more relevant experience. Team is so important. There is no room for charity.

Finally, what is it you are trying to do? What problem are you solving? What pain point are you addressing? Do you offer a nice to have or must have solution? Are you a vitamin pill or an aspirin? You will hear all of these phrases and more. Be prepared and come armed with a real problem to solve. The world will not likely fund many more pet rocks.

Chapter Thirty-one

Picking a VC

Once you know you are VC material, the next question should be which VC is right for you. There are a few things you should know about approaching a VC.

VCs develop reputations like anyone else. If your VC prospect does not work and play well with others, that may show up in a quick Internet search. Some VCs are known for firing founders early and often. Some are known for being uncooperative with other investors. Some make lousy board members.

Ryan Caldbeck encountered a difficult VC in his company, CircleUp. After the company had bought out the investor, Ryan sent the VC a long letter offering feedback and stating: "I'm sure we both regret working together. Looking back, I think if we had met in person before [your] original investment ... we all would have realized this wasn't a fit."

Not many founders will share their criticisms of a VC in a noisy Medium post, but a bit of diligence is due when taking money. Ryan was lucky to be in a position to buy his investor out and to have an investor who was willing to go. That does not always happen and there is no easy way to get rid of an investor once you take their money. You should consider it a marriage with no divorce. If things don't work out, the company's death may be the only way to end the relationship and that will hurt you more than it will hurt them.

If you do not have the good luck to find a Medium post about your potential investor and, even if you do, talking to the founders they have backed is a great way to get a sense of how the VC operates. Are they hands on? Helpful or obstructionist? Importantly, you should check the public records, in particular the court filings. The VC will likely be running a background check on you. You should do the same thing and if you find that the VC tends to be in court a lot, that is an issue. If you find that they have been sued by their founders or have sued their founders when things didn't go their way, that is an issue. I personally check the court docket for every person I do business with and, while it may seem odd for a lawyer to say this, I will not do business with a litigious party. Again, anyone with $2,500 can file a complaint and disrupt your life. There are penalties for frivolous pleading but the bar for filing is extremely low. You do not want to do business with those people.

When I started practicing law in Fargo, North Dakota in the mid-1980s, I had a client who maintained his competitive advantage by using me to whittle down everyone he did business with. We would demand and get concessions because the alternative was an expensive lawsuit. We were acting within our legal rights and it didn't occur to me that we were doing anything wrong until one day he turned our strategy against me. My bill had gotten old and large and rather than pay it, he offered to pay half of it, or we could litigate over it. He threatened to raise spurious claims about the quality of the work, maybe counter claim, or maybe complain to the bar. Of course, I would have prevailed in all of those cases, but you cannot purge the stigma of a claim any more than you can unring a bell. I learned how it felt to be on the receiving end of a legal, but unjust, process. I no longer do business with people like that, and neither should you.

Once you have determined that your VC has a good reputation, you should consider how likely it is that you will close. As a practical matter, it is rare for a VC not to close once they have gone to the trouble of giving you a term sheet. Rare, but not nonexistent. I have had deals crater many times in due diligence. On one occasion, a Singapore VC backed out of a deal on the day that we were schedule to sign. After months of negotiation, as we were awaiting signature pages, we instead got an email that said that they had changed their mind. Reputable VCs will not do that to you and my experience is that the larger and more established the VC, the simpler and cleaner the term sheet and the quicker you will get to a close. They do not want to fool around.

Before you approach a VC, you want to know that they invest at your stage, at your size and in your sector – the three S's. Don't waste your time (and your one shot) asking for seed money from a late-stage fund unless they are known to make seed investments to secure a spot in the later stage round.

How big is the fund? How committed is it? In other words, does it have money available for follow on rounds, also known as dry powder? And where are they in their fund's life? If they are close to the end of their 7- to 10-year term, will they be forcing an exit before you want to exit? And if they are well into their term, how likely is it that there will be a fund 2 to support later rounds? All of this should be on your checklist.

Chapter Thirty-two
Getting a Meeting with a VC

Getting a meeting with a VC may be the hardest part of the entire process. Resist the temptation to email your 50-page pitch deck to every VC you can find online. No one is going to read it. Instead, you should seek a warm introduction. A warm introduction means something. It is not just an introduction. It is an endorsement. The introducer is effectively vouching for you. The closer the introducer is to you, the better your chances.

Step 1 is to find someone in your network who can make that intro. The step before step 1 is to establish a network. In the pre-COVID days, that meant that you would come to Silicon Valley, attend events, meet people, and follow up with coffee meetings. In smaller markets, like Los Angeles, people do lunch. In Silicon Valley, there are not enough lunches in a week to meet all the people you want in your network, so we do coffee. That's why southern Californians are fatter and northern Californians are more wired.

I grew up close to the junction of the Heart and Missouri Rivers in western North Dakota. During the summers, you would find me by sunup walking the long dirt road to one of those rivers carrying an old fishing pole. Halfway through one long unfruitful day sitting on the riverbank, waiting for a bite, an old man in a small boat motored by me. "Any luck?" he asked. "No" I told him. "I've been here all day and ain't had a bite."

"Son," he said. "The first rule of fishing is that you got to fish where the fish are."

So, with that sage piece of advice, let's go fishing.

Startup Events

Idea to IPO is one of the largest startup meetup organizations in the world, with chapters throughout the world. The organization hosts meetings every week that consist of panels and presentations. Since COVID, their meetings are entirely virtual, meaning that you can access the presenters from anywhere in the world. The VCs who participate in Idea to IPO panels are remarkably approachable and there is usually no cost to participate and interact with them. And, as a frequent presenter, I must add that the content is awesome.[104]

Idea to IPO is just one of many similar events in the Silicon Valley and around the world. The important thing to keep in mind is that you need to fish where the fish are. Given that a disproportionately large percentage of VCs are located in the Silicon Valley, you should get dialed into this community.

Pitch Events

There are some great organizations for establishing connections. KC Wisdom's Pitch Globally is one of the most successful super connector event platforms in the Silicon Valley.[105] Pitch Globally has a surprisingly high success rate when it comes to matching startups with money, probably due to the sheer force of will of its founder, Kaustav Chaudhuri (aka KC Wisdom). Pitch Globally is not the only game in town, of course. There are, in fact, too many to mention including the ones that I organize and host through the Royse Innovation Network.[106]

Fortunately, the SEC has given us favorable guidance on whether a pitch event is a public solicitation. In 2015, the SEC stated that an invite only demo day would not constitute a general solicitation. A public demo day would also not be a general solicitation if the company is not offering a potential investment opportunity to the audience. That is, of course, a factual determination but I regularly advise companies to avoid the whole issue by either (i) not pitching at public events (where anyone can join, more common now on Zoom) or (ii) not saying anything that looks like you are trying to raise money. In other words, you can talk about the team, the product, how great you are, and how you will change the world but do not say you are offering investors an opportunity, you are valued at X, or here are our financials, etc.

More recently, the SEC has loosened up a bit. In late 2020, the SEC issued a final rule under which certain demo day communications will not be deemed general solicitations or general advertising provided certain conditions are satisfied, including limitations on the sponsor's activities, a requirement that the advertising for the event not reference any specific offering of securities by the issuer, and limits on the information conveyed at the event regarding the offering of securities by or on behalf of the issuer. The communications must be made in connection with a seminar or meeting sponsored by a college, university, or other institution of higher education, state or local government, or instrumentality of a state or local government, or a non-profit or an angel investor group, incubator, or accelerator.

To qualify, a sponsor would not be permitted to:

Make investment recommendations or provide investment advice to attendees of the event;

Engage in any investment negotiations between the issuer and investors attending the event;

Charge attendees of the event any fees, other than reasonable administrative fees;

Receive any compensation for making introductions between event attendees and issuers or for investment negotiations between the parties; or

Receive any compensation with respect to the event that would require it to register as a broker or dealer or as an investment adviser.

Under this rule, the company will be allowed to disclose that it is in the process of offering or planning to offer securities, the type and amount of securities being offered, the intended use of the proceeds and the unsubscribed amount.[107]

Angel Groups

The traditional wisdom is that you can do a pre-seed round based on a PowerPoint deck (after all, you are taking money from friends and family), a seed round based on a beta version of your product or proof of concept, and a Series A round based on traction (users, sales or revenue). To get to the VCs, most companies will have to have raised some early money. Hopefully, that early money will provide a pathway to later money. A good angel will provide that connection and a good way to meet angels is by pitching to them through an angel group.

The concept of an angel group is that you may present your idea to a relatively forgiving group of rich people. If they like it, they may invest, either individually or as a group. The difference between a pitch to an angel group and a pitch event is that, with an angel group, you have a curated audience of investors rather than voyeurs, at least theoretically. They may or may not give you money, but they certainly will give you feedback and, the more you pitch, the better you will get at it. Most importantly, you may establish a relationship with a connector for later money.

Some of my favorite Angel groups include Peter Kuo's Venture Capital Roundtable,[108] David Cao's F50,[109] the Band of Angels,[110] Sand Hill Angels,[111] Kieretsu Forum,[112] Tiger 21[113] JFE Network[114] and many, many more. There are, of course, some of the large events that you can easily find online but if the goal is to establish a network, less may be more.

Some of these groups are harder to get into than others. Most are free but some charge to pitch. The pay to play events are controversial but, my view, as a professional service provider myself, is that I do not begrudge anyone for charging for the value they add, provided that they add value. If your entrance fee gets you funded, it will be money well spent.

For purposes of the securities law exemption for angel groups, the SEC has its own definition of what is and what is not an angel group. The term angel investor group means a group: (A) of accredited investors; (B) that holds regular meetings and has written processes and procedures for making investment decisions, either individually or among the membership of the group as a whole; and (C) is neither associated nor affiliated with brokers, dealers or investment advisers.[115]

Professional Service Providers

I cannot recall the last full day I went without someone asking me for an introduction to an investor. Sometimes I make those introductions; usually I do not. When I do, I really have to believe that there is a good fit. You can make my job easier by helping me know if there is a good fit. Are you in an industry or market that is of interest to a particular VC? Are you at the stage at which they invest? Do you have all the right metrics? I am not going to shotgun scatter your pitch deck to my network. If I did that once, no VC would ever open my emails again.

Having said that, your lawyer can be a great source of intros since we all know and deal with VCs all day every day. Leverage that relationship well and carefully.

Other Founders

The best referral source is another founder. If the ABC VC has invested in your buddy's company and they are in your space, nothing beats the warm introduction given by that founder. It almost guarantees you a meeting.

The power of weak ties

Contrary to conventional wisdom, not all relationships have to be strong. If you have the right idea at the right time, a weak tie may work just as well. After all, the VC doesn't want you to be his best friend. She wants you to be her best investment and that doesn't depend on who you know. If only there were a huge public database of all the VCs with their bios and history and something about what they do. And if only it were searchable. Luckily, there is such a thing, and it is called LinkedIn. Here's how you leverage it.

Do an industry and geography search of all the VCs in your area. A lot of fake VCs will pop up (there are more sellers than buyers in this business) but that is just noise.

Enter some additional search terms for your domain like agtech or fintech. You may have to upgrade your account to do this.

See how you are connected to that person or who you know who is connected. Make that connection your best friend.

Ask your friend to make the intro. As simple, intuitive, and easy as that sounds, few do it right. Use the technology.

The Executive Summary

I don't like to start with a pitch deck. Due to our short attention spans, people don't often get far without their minds wandering unless they are focused on something relevant. I expect most VCs are also like that. I also expect that if they have to read several pages of pitch before they realize the company is not in their space, they will regret wasting the time and as a result may not even start.

I prefer a one (maybe two) page executive summary. The executive summary should be a *Dragnet* piece ("Just the facts, ma'am"). Strip out all of the hyperbole and boil it down to the following:

The product or industry: What problem are you solving and what is your solution? If the VC never invests in adtech, he will want to know immediately if you are an adtech company.

The team: Who are you? Why are you the right team to execute on your solution? This is your chance to make a good first impression.

Market size: As discussed, is this a big enough opportunity to move the needle for the VC?

Technology and IP protection: What is your tech and why is it awesome? If you have intellectual property protection (patents, trademarks, etc.) say so here.

Financials: How much have you raised so far? How much do you think you need? Include a short line with financial projections.

Notice that your executive summary does not mention valuation. It does not state that you are selling x percent of the company for y dollars. VCs will view that as a rookie mistake and will automatically heavily discount whatever number you use. Leave valuation out of it. The VC will tell you what they think you are worth.

A sample of my template for an executive summary is attached as Appendix Q Executive Summary.

<u>A word about looky loos</u>

A looky loo is a person who views something for sale with no genuine intention of making a purchase. Some investors are like that. They only want to know what you are up to. Perhaps they have invested in a competitor. The honest ones will tell you that upfront. The rest will let you give them your whole pitch and see what information they can take from it. Don't fall for that.

And don't think you can protect yourself with a non-disclosure agreement ("NDA"). Most VCs will not sign one and will be very offended that you even had the gall to ask. They might even think that you must be a rube to suggest it. After all, they are pitched ideas all day long. The last thing they need is some disgruntled founder suing them for trade secret theft. The industry will not accept an NDA in this context.

That isn't to say you can never get an NDA. Once you are into due diligence and are disclosing the secret sauce, then it is appropriate to ask for an NDA. Of course, at that point you should have competent legal counsel to guide you.

More importantly, and this might sound like an odd thing for a lawyer to say, but an NDA is just paper. All the paper in the world will do you little good if your adversary is a deep pocketed, well-funded, malevolent actor.

Finally, as I heard one VC respond when asked to sign an NDA, "no one is going to steal your stupid idea." What he meant by that is that ideas, even ones as good as yours, are probably out there in the ether already and it will be the execution and not the idea that gives it value.

Chapter Thirty-three

The First Meeting, and the Next One

Many years ago, I broke all my rules about eating my own dog food and co-founded a company with a client. We were in a hot space, had some real tech, and ended up in a conference room with a first tier VC on Sand Hill Road. My co-founder pulled out his pitch deck and made it to slide 2 before the VC jumped in and went right to the very heart of our biggest problem. I still do not know how he got there so quickly. My co-founder stammered a bit and said that he would get to that, but he wanted to follow his presentation first. A short, uncomfortable conversation ensued. The VC did not want to see a show. He wanted answers and he had no patience for a presentation. Not getting them, he looked at his watch, stood up and said that he had seen enough. His parting comment to my co-founder was "you don't have this figured out yet" and to me "and you … you're just a lawyer."

Guilty as charged. The whole meeting lasted less than 15 minutes but was a valuable lesson in meetings. It is not a presentation or a lecture or even a friendly discussion. The lesson is that once you have that meeting, you need to persuade the investor on their timetable. It is what famed Silicon Valley venture capitalist Bill Reichert calls Getting to Wow.[116] Bill suggests that founders be clear, credible, and compelling. He offers a four-step framework to wow investors. The framework is comprised of the following:

Context: State what it is that you do better than anyone else in simple, easy to understand words.

Benefit: Clarify your unique benefit or advantage.

Differentiation: Clarify how you are different from the competition and the alternatives.

Close: Call to action. Wrap up with something that gets your listener to actively engage.[117]

The framework is elegant in its simplicity. It often seems that the best companies are based on ideas that, in hindsight, seem obvious once they unfold. The best pitchmen can share that vision and paint that picture. The more quickly you can do that, the better.

The objective of your first meeting with a VC is to get a second meeting. You will not likely get to yes in one meeting, especially if you are dealing with more junior people. You are trying to recruit your VC to be your champion so that he can talk his partners, investment committee, or whoever to take the next steps with you.

While the VC is evaluating your company, you should be evaluating them. As mentioned above, you should find out what their process is. Will they have numerous meetings to get to a term sheet? Will they decide quickly? Will it take weeks and months? The reason you want to know is that ideally you want to have more than one term sheet. Since term sheets almost always come with a no shop clause and a short fuse, you want to have them at the same time.

A no shop clause means that once you sign a term sheet with a VC you will not engage in discussions with another VC for a period of time, usually 90 days, sufficient to get the deal closed. The no shop takes you off the market, so you do not want to sign one unless you know you have the best deal. Given that you will only have a few days to accept a term sheet, you would like them to come in at about the same time. Because different VCs have different processes, it will be easier to orchestrate the receipt of term sheets if you know their timing.

Earlier I said that you do not want to mention valuation. The VC will tell you what you are worth. That is usually true but not always. Once in a while the VC will want you to put an offer on the table. Then what?

In that event, and it does sometimes happen, you should have a number in mind and be prepared to back it up. Keep in mind that this is a negotiation and whatever number you come up with will be challenged. You just need some support for your number.

Over the years, I have chronicled numerous different ways that I have seen VCs peg a value to a company. They are summarized on Appendix R Valuation Methods. None of these are scientific, are not professional valuations by any means, and would never stand up for 409A purposes. However, they give you something to stand on, especially if you can find three that converge on a number that you like.

Valuation is a negotiation, as is the amount of funding that you think you need. Many founders make the mistake of thinking that valuation is the only issue to consider when evaluating a VC's offer. As discussed in the next chapter, it is only one piece of the puzzle.

Finally, when you do present, you will likely use visual aids such as a slide deck. So much has been written about pitch decks that I will not repeat it here. Appendix S Pitch Decks has a summary of some good resources. Don't be afraid to ask for help. There are many good pitch coaches that can give you some pointers.

From a legal standpoint, you should not do a few things. We have already spoken about the importance of being truthful and transparent. If things go sideways, your pitch deck may be Exhibit A in the fraud case against you. If so, you will want the jury to see the big forward looking statement disclaimer that we spoke about earlier. You also do not want the jury to see any obvious lies. You do not want incomplete information. If you do not have a customer, you cannot say that you do. Verbal encouragement is not a purchase order or a sale, but I have seen entrepreneurs represent it that way. Do not do that. If it is a nonbinding letter of intent, you cannot say that you made a sale or have a contract. Again, although it detracts from the Steven Jobsian simplicity of your beautiful graphical representations, the more accurate, factual detail you include, the less likely it is that you will get sued.

On that point, at the early stage you are likely keeping your own books. Unless you are a CPA, I can promise you that they are wrong. When you do present your QuickBooks numbers, unless a CPA has compiled them (and even then, maybe), you should note that they are not GAAP and, if they are not consistent with past historical practice, you should say that too. GAAP means generally accepted accounting principles and it has a very specific meaning in the law. I would argue that no investor can assume you are giving them GAAP financials, but I don't want you to have to argue when you can just tell them up front. This is especially true since many engineers I have met think they can figure out GAAP. I am a CPA myself (California, non-attest) and I can promise you that your large engineer's brain is no substitute for accounting practice. And, of all the things you can get wrong, a financial misrepresentation is a very bad one.

Granted, we are going to clean all of this up and absolve you from your presentation sins in the definitive documents. These documents will carefully define what representations and warranties are being relied on, but more and more investors are investing based on inadequate documents (such as the SAFE templates that can be easily downloaded) and sometimes these things slip through the cracks.

Not to beat a dead pitchdeck, but here is a summary of a typical conversation between founder and investor on this point:

Founder: We project $1,000,000 in revenues this year based on our customer base.

Investor: You have POs for $1 million?

Founder: Yes, we have commitments from Google, Facebook and Apple.

Investor: That's impressive! You have signed orders for $1 million.

Founder: Well, no, not exactly, we have their interest in placing that much in orders from us. And we are confident that they will.

Investor: So, you have nothing signed but they say they might buy some products?

Founder: Yeah something like that...

If the investor had not kept asking question, the founder would have hung himself with these representations and sloppy language. It might have been fixed later in the agreements but, if not, he has a problem. Here is how this conversation should go:

Founder: We hope to generate $1 million in revenue this year.

Investor: You have POs for $1 million?

Founder: No, but we have received verbal interest from Google, Facebook and Apple and if we can close on 50 percent of our approaches, we can hit that revenue number.

Just keep in mind that honesty is always the best policy even when dealing with VCs. The next big issue with pitches and meetings is that you do not inadvertently fail to meet securities law exemptions. As noted above and in the appendices, when selling securities to a VC, you will likely be relying on a private placement exemption from registration under one of the safe harbors of Regulation D. In particular, you will likely be relying on Rule 506(b), which allows you to sell securities to accredited investors (the VC will be accredited) but you cannot use general solicitation in doing so.[118] As long as you are sitting at the marble desk pitching in the confines of a VC's conference room to a defined group of people, you are not violating the no solicitation rule. If you are on a Zoom call pitching your company to that same group, you are not soliciting. What if you do end up soliciting, possibly by broadcasting on your web page?

The penalty for violating the no solicitation rule is that the issuer cannot rely on

Rule 506(b) and would instead be stuck with 506(c), a rule that does allow public solicitation. The catch, however, is that the company would then have to verify that all of its investors in the 506(c) offering were indeed accredited.

But surely there are crisp, clear rules on how to verify someone, right? Oh, if only it were that simple. The relevant regulations set forth a factual test and require the issuer to take reasonable steps to verify the purchasers' accredited investor status. This means things like reviewing bank statements, tax returns, etc. to prove that the investor has the income or net worth needed to satisfy the exemptions. You can also get a statement of a lawyer, banker, or CPA attesting to the net worth or income of the investor, but many investors will be put off by having to incur that additional level of expense and bureaucracy. The good news is that many third-party services can handle this function for you, so failing to meet the 506(b) exemption may not be the death penalty for early-stage companies that it once was – except in one specific common case.

The 506(b) exemption allows participation of up to 35 unaccredited investors. Companies regularly use this exemption to let their employees, friends, family, and other early supporters into a round. The 506(c) exemption contains no such carve-out for unaccredited investors. Thus, if a company has taken money from an unaccredited investor and then publicly solicits, it has violated the securities laws. This generally means that the investor can rescind the transaction and get their money back. Also, the SEC can impose penalties for violations of the securities laws and regularly does so. SEC remedies may include cease-and-desist orders and injunctions (court orders prohibiting further actions) and monetary penalties. An individual who participates in the violation may be prohibited from acting as a corporate director or officer.

Fortunately, if a company has messed this up, there is a way to fix it. A company can conduct what is known as a rescission offer. Think of it as a do over. The company must go back to all of its investors and let them know that there was a screw up and that they have the right to rescind their purchase of securities and get their money back. The unaccredited investors in this case, of course, must be given their money back in order for the company to rely on 506(c). If the investors do not opt to rescind, they participate in the new and compliant offering. Usually, few investors opt to take return of their money.[119]

In a rescission offer scenario, the company must make a very full disclosure. In addition, many states have specific laws relating to rescission offers that must be consulted.[120]

The text of 506(b) and 506(c) are set forth in the Appendix T Rule 506 of Regulation D.

Chapter Thirty-four

Term Sheets

Deals do not start with binding documents; they start with non-binding term sheets that summarize the terms of a proposed transaction. The term sheet is the VC's written (but mostly non-binding) indication of their intention to invest in a company and will summarize the major terms of the proposed investment.

Let's assume that you have received a term sheet. Maybe you have received more than one. Now the fun begins. What can you expect to see in that term sheet? What should you fight for and what should you accept?

Delaware. If you are not already a Delaware corporation, you will be one by the time of closing. See Chapter 2 for a discussion of the reasons why.

Security Offered. You will be selling preferred stock and the first VC round will be Series A Preferred. Before that you may have sold stock designated as series seed preferred. Each series is generally tied to a letter of the alphabet and there is some meaning attached to the lettering. The conventional wisdom is that you seek Series A after you have traction and B after you have shown you can scale. Thus, a company might be reluctant to call their round Series B if they are not quite there yet. The naming can get to be downright ridiculous. I have seen the first preferred call Pre-Series A, when there wasn't sufficient traction and, more commonly, A-1, A-2, A-3, etc. when there is a new preferred but not enough money in the deal for a new B round, the difference between the new series being the price of the preferred stock. Let's just say there is more art than science in naming the preferred. We will assume you are starting with Series A Preferred Stock. The preferred stock will be convertible into common stock so that the investor can share pro rata in the proceeds of the sale along with the common (see below).

Valuation. Valuation is the first thing that will jump out at you, but may not be the most important factor. It may show up as a price per share or by reference to a method of determination. The National Venture Capital

Association (NVCA) standard form term sheet uses a formula and expresses it on a pre-money basis as follows:

Pre-Money Valuation:	The price per share of the Series A Preferred (the "Original Purchase Price") shall be the price determined on the basis of a fully-diluted pre-money valuation of $[_____] (which pre-money valuation shall include an [unallocated and uncommitted] employee option pool representing [__]% of the fullydiluted post-money capitalization) and a fullydiluted post-money valuation of $[_____].[121]

By the way, the NVCA forms have become very standard in venture deals. They are a good place to start, but keep in mind that they tend to be investor friendly, probably because they are the National *Venture Capital Association* forms. When you deviate from them, you may hear from investor counsel "but that's not what the NVCA form says," so you should have good reasons for doing so.

The price per share and valuation will determine how much of your company you are selling in the first round. Most first rounds will be between 20 percent and 40 percent. You should not give up control in Series A but you might in Series B. That will become important when we get to the management and voting provisions.

Option Reserve. Notice, in the standard language above, that the company, at closing, will have a new employee option pool based on a percentage of the post-money capitalization. This is another way the investor gets you. The investor is basically saying that they are taking a certain percentage post-money so the increase in the option pool will dilute the founders, not the VC. In in our example above we had the following pre-money cap table:

Founders	4,000,000	100%
Stock Pool	0	0%
Total	4,000,000	100%

If the investor is investing $1 million on a $4 million pre money ($5 million post-money) and wants an unallocated (meaning new) option pool of 20 percent, the company's cap table will look roughly more like this after the closing:

Founders	4,000,000	60%
Stock Pool	1,300,000	20%
Investor	1,300,000	20%

The term sheet will clarify (and be more precise) but the essential point is that the founder doesn't stay at 80% after giving up 20% of the company. The founder gets diluted for the option pool.

Liquidation Preference and Participation. The liquidation preference puts the "preferred" in preferred stock. It is what the VCs get that you (the common stockholder) do not and what justifies the huge price difference between the common stock that you sold to your investors and what the VCs are buying. A liquidation preference is the investor's right to receive their money back first and in preference to another class of stock in the event of a liquidation. A liquidation generally refers to a sale but also includes a winding up of the company where it distributes all its assets to its shareholders.

There can be multiple liquidation preferences. A 1X liquidation preference means that the VC gets one times her money in preference to the more junior stock, a 2X preference means two times, and so on.

The liquidation preference and the concept of participation go hand in hand. Participation refers to the right of the preferred to share in the proceeds of a sale along with common stockholders based on their percentage of stock ownership. Non-participating stock does not participate – it just takes its liquidation preference and calls it a day (unless it converts, see below).

Participation was once common in the Valley. Not so much anymore. Most Series A deals are non-participating, in which the investor can take their company back on exit, convert to common, or take the greater of the two. When preferred stock is participating, it is usually capped at some multiple of the investment.

In the case of non-participating preferred, the VC will take the greater of the preference or their pro rate percentage. For example, if the VC invests

$1 million in nonparticipating preferred on a $4 million pre-money valuation, they have 20 percent of the company ($1 million divided by $5 million). If the company is then sold for $10 million, they will convert to common stock and take their 20 percent because 20 percent of $10 million is $2 million, which is greater than their $1 million liquidation preference.

Participating preferred can be tricky, even if capped, and will require the founder to do some what-if calculations. This is where valuation may not be the most important issue. For example, a participation right will quickly eat up a valuation premium. This is not an accident. You can bet that the VCs have modeled what they expect your exit to be and what they will take away. You should be doing the same thing. I have seen many founders end up working for the VCs with no chance of clearing the preferences (a hack for that is described later in this book).

Dividends. The terms of the preferred stock will also grant the investor a preferential right to dividends, meaning that the investor gets their dividend before the common does. Because startups rarely pay dividends – if they had cash flow for dividends they would be talking to lenders and not VCs – the VCs will usually toss you a bone and make their dividend preference non-cumulative and payable when, as, and if declared by the board, which is VC-speak for never.

A cumulative dividend means that if the dividend is declared but unpaid, it rolls over or accumulates and gets paid the next year that dividends are paid. A noncumulative dividend goes away if not paid. The dividend rate can be as simple as the same amount as is paid on the common stock but is usually expressed as a percentage of the investment. This is much different than private equity deals so, if you are from that world, prepare for this difference.

Board Representation. As mentioned earlier, your VC will take a board seat. If you have one VC in your round, you might give up one seat. You (the founder) would take one and the third would be an industry luminary that you both like or, sometimes, someone selected by the common stockholders. If the round is big enough as a percentage of the company and there are multiple VCs, you may end up giving up 2 seats. Because you want an odd number of board members, not an even one, you will now have a 5-member board. That is as big a board as I like to see. Beyond that it gets clunky, but boards do definitely grow beyond 5.

The mechanism for board representation is a voting agreement, whereby each stockholder agrees to vote their shares to elect a party's designee to the board. Board members will demand and should receive indemnification. Indemnification means that the company will cover the costs, expenses, and any loss that a director suffers if he is sued as a result of being a director, for example, by a shareholder. By the time a company is sued, there may not be much company left so the indemnity should be backed by directors and officers (D&O) insurance. It is only the most feckless investor who will sit on a board without insurance, especially in a litigious state like California.

Interestingly, the investor is likely covered by his venture fund's insurance policy. Nevertheless, she will want the company to obtain its own policy on the investor both to fill gaps in coverage and also to keep the claims off of their insurer's loss run. If the VC's insurance company pays a claim, that will be reflected in the VC's premiums. If the company's insurer pays, then maybe not.

Protective Provisions. Because the VC will not have voting control of the company, they want to ensure that they have a veto right over certain actions that might affect their interests. These are the protective provisions of the term sheet. They will generally provide that so long as the VC owns a certain amount of stock, the company cannot take certain actions. Here are a few standard asks:

sell, liquidate, dissolve or wind up the Company;

amend the company's charter or bylaws in a manner adverse to the Series A Preferred Stock;

> create a new class of securities unless it is junior to the Series A Preferred with respect to its rights, preferences and privileges;

> increase the number of shares of Series A Preferred;

> redeem stock or pay any dividends prior to the Series A Preferred; and

> increase the board.

Beyond the above, terms that are frequently requested and sometimes negotiated include:

adopt or amend a stock option plan;

grant shares under the stock plan;

borrow money in excess of certain amounts; and

create or dispose of a subsidiary.

The consent of the preferred stockholders may also be required for the creation of digital tokens, cryptocurrency, or other blockchain-based assets.

Sometimes, a compromise to some of the above provisions is an agreement that a certain board member or number of directors must vote in favor of a provision.

Transfer Restrictions. Your company should already have a well drafted right of first refusal prohibiting the founders from selling their shares. The VC will impose a whole new set of restrictions.

Your existing right of first refusal ("ROFR") will be replaced by a new ROFR that grants, first, to the company and then, to the investors, a right to buy your shares if you should ever try to sell them. In addition, a co-sale right will provide that, should the company and the investor not buy the founder's shares under the ROFR, the investor may participate in the sale. In other words, the investor will be allowed to sell shares in the founder's sale. This is also known as a tag-along or take-me-along right.

The flip side of a co-sale right is a drag-along right which is, as it sounds, a right by the investor to force a founder to sell in a sale that they orchestrate and for which they secure shareholder approval. A drag along is an attempted waiver of a shareholder's right to dissent to a sale or merger of a company and be paid the appraised value of their shares. It is not at all certain that it works but it is very common (if not universal) in VC deals.[122]

Tags and drags will sometimes pop up at founder stage before there are any investors, but most well advised companies will not expend the resources on a set of agreements that are going to be replaced at financing stage.

The VC's View of Founder Vesting.

Earlier in this book, we discussed vesting. As noted, the standard for most startups is 3 to 5 years of vesting but, as a founder, you should not get too attached to the idea that you will be fully vested in 3 to 5 years. If you get venture funding, the VCs will almost always unvest your shares and start the clock ticking all over again. That being the case, why do we start with 3 to 5 year vesting instead of 8 to 10 year?

The 3 to 5 year vesting schedule is a fossil. It is an artifact of an earlier time, before Enron, Sarbanes Oxley, and Dodd Frank, when companies could and would access the public markets much earlier in their lives. Twenty years ago, most of my clients were planning on going public next year. It didn't matter how far along they were. It was always next year. That year was likely within 4 years of their start. These days, if a company goes public at all, it will be 10 years out on average. The recent trend of SPAC (Special Purpose Acquisition Company) financing might change that for many companies but, for now, you can assume (on average) a long haul until pay day.

Even though liquidity horizons have expanded, vesting periods have not. Instead, VCs require founders to unvest and start over to give them more runway to exit. Vesting is the golden handcuff that keeps founders engaged in their companies until there is an exit. In the case of an exit by sale or merger, unvested shares reduce the cost of the exit to the investors because the acquiror need not give up more new unvested shares to the service providers to keep them bound to the company post-merger. If they do have to give up new shares to founders, that will leave less for investors. Investors do not want to lose exit value, especially when that problem can be fixed with the stroke of a pen. Plan to have unvested shares for at least 8 years.

<u>Pro Rata and Similar Rights</u>. Pro rata rights are also called a right to maintain, right to participate, and pre-emptive rights (although that is not quite technically correct) and they are very important to an investor. The basic idea is that investors have a right to buy enough stock in the next round to keep their same percentage ownership. Usually only major investors will get these rights because of the administrative hassle of sending notices, dealing with over allotments, etc. You may have given pro rata rights to early SAFE holders as part of their deal and the VCs may attempt to negotiate that away.

It might be hard to imagine now but the hot companies will be over sold because everyone knows that they are hot. A VC will look very silly if they are aced out of a later round in a company that they invested in. My most successful client companies have been the ones that would not let their lawyer invest because there was so much demand from other investors. Generally, however, the upstanding, honest, and reputable VCs will let valued early supporters, like company counsel, who took a risk on a fledgling startup, into the round.

On that point, keep in mind that everything is on the table when the VCs get involved. Many companies and early investors try to hard wire immutable terms into a company's structure and they will eventually find out that everything is negotiable when faced with the question of "do you want my money?" So, keep in mind that pro rata, much like vesting, share splits, compensation, etc. is all on the table or, as one VC so eloquently put it to me, "We are gonna' make a pancake out of this cap table."

Information and Reporting. For larger rounds, prepare to be audited and you will be surprised by how much that costs. VCs are nothing if not good bureaucrats and they do not like to be subject to criticism by their LPs. One way to ensure that they will not be subject to criticism is to make sure that they have engaged professional counsel, including auditors, to make sure they have good numbers.

There are other good reasons for audits. Your company will become an easier acquisition target if it has audited statements, especially if it is acquired by a public company. The auditors will pick up things that may have been missed in diligence and will have recommendations on how to tighten up the ship.

You can expect to be required to report to your investors on a regular basis and that includes annual, quarterly, and, possibly, monthly financial statements. You will also be preparing an operating budget and keeping the cap table current. These reporting rights are usually only reserved for major investors due to the hassle factor.

Redemption Rights

Sometimes VCs will request a right to force the company to buy their shares at the original purchase price. The right, when given, is usually reserved for major investors, exercisable after a period of time (like 5 years), and may occur in annual portions. It is a harsh provision and I always push back on this one. Here is why.

As a practical matter, a VC will not exercise her redemption right unless something is very wrong at the company. If things are going well, they will ride the wave to exit. If things are not going well, the company will not be able to redeem the shares anyway and will have converted the stockholder to a creditor. Recall that creditors can sue on their debt and get paid ahead of any equity. The VC does not want to sue, however. Nor does she want your company or its assets. She wants you to sell and, by exercising a redemption right, she can force you to sell to pay the redemption price.

Conversion

Conversion refers to the exchange of the preferred stock for shares of common stock in an initial public offering or other events. Initially, preferred stock will usually convert to common on a 1 to 1 basis (meaning 1 share of common for every share of preferred) but that number can be adjusted (see below). The stock will automatically convert on a public offering of a certain size and will often convert with the consent of some type of majority of the preferred stock or at the option of some holders.

You might wonder why the preferred stock would ever convert to common before an exit or IPO. After all, you will not know if the exit value exceeds the preferences in advance of an exit. The answer is that sometimes a company must do a recapitalization in order to attract new capital. A recap may involve a forced (by majority vote of the preferred) conversion of shares to common so that there is room in the cap table for a new class of preferred. This happens more often than you might think.

Anti-Dilution Protection

The preferred stock will preserve its right to a certain percentage of the company through its conversion right. If the company's stock should increase, the conversion ratio or conversion price would also have to change to ensure that the preferred stock maintains the same percentage on conversion. That is protection from dilution in ownership, or anti-dilution protection.

There are two kinds of anti-dilution protection: adjustments for stock splits, stock dividends, and the like; and price based anti-dilution. In the former case if the company splits its stock (meaning divides the shares into a larger number), the conversion price of the preferred stock should also adjust so that the investor's percentage is not also split. A stock dividend (a dividend paid in shares) has the same effect as a stock split and will also result in an adjustment to the conversion price.

Price based anti-dilution is triggered when stock is sold at a price less than the price paid by the current preferred stockholders. There are generally three kinds of price based anti-dilution protection: full ratchet, broad based weighted average, and narrow based weighted average. Full ratchet means that if shares are sold at a lower price than the preferred stock price, the conversion ratio will adjust proportionately so that the investor gets the benefit of the lower price, as if they bought at that price. This can be especially harsh on the founders when the company does a down round (a sale of securities at a lower valuation than the last valuation) and is usually only seen in troubled companies.

Weighted average anti-dilution is much more common and calculates the anti-dilution adjustments under a formula. The number of shares that would have been issued to the new investors if they would have paid the same price as the earlier investors is compared to the number of shares actually issued to the new investors at the lower price. Broad based weighted average anti-dilution uses the fully diluted capitalization of the company. Narrow based weighted average anti-dilution uses only the outstanding shares of stock. Broad based weighted average anti-dilution is almost always used.

Pay to Play. A pay to play provision mean that an investor must partic-ipate in a later down round by buying their pro rata share of new securities or face some form of punitive treatment, such as their shares converting to common stock on a very unfavorable basis. Pay to play can be painful but I have seen it save companies. One of my clients, in particular, exercised its rights and did a pay to play round and later went public. They never would have survived without the new money from the investors who, understand-ably, needed more incentive to gamble on a down round. Although it is fun to talk about, pay to play is rarely seen in VC financings these days.

Registration Rights. The VCs will always ask for the right to register their shares with the SEC so that they may sell into the public markets. Every venture deal has registration rights but, in all of my years of practice, not only have I never seen anyone exercise a registration right, I have never even heard of anyone doing so. Nevertheless, they are always in the term sheet.

There are three kinds of registration rights: demand, S-3, and piggyback. A demand registration right allows a holder to request one or more registrations of their shares at a certain minimum aggregate offering price. A right to an S-3 registration means that the holders can require the company to register on Form S-3 if available. SEC Form S-3 is a simplified filing that is sometimes used after an IPO. Piggyback registration rights allow an investor the right to register her stock when either the company or another investor initiates a registration.

Registration rights are usually limited to major investors for the reasons discussed above. Sometimes the founders can include themselves in the group that gets registration rights, but my view is why bother, since it is so unlikely that they will be exercised.

Expenses. The Company can be expected to pay the expenses of the investor, including due diligence costs and their legal fees. The best you can do on this point is to try to cap the fees at some reasonable amount in the $30,000 to $50,000 range. Depending on how due diligence goes and how reasonable the parties are, the company's fees range from $15,000 to $50,000. That is a wide range but most VC preferred stock deals come in at about $35,000 of fees on each side, which may be one reason why SAFEs are so popular.

Non-Binding. The term sheet will always be non-binding, except for the no-shop (discussed above), confidentiality provisions, and the parties' good faith obligations to work toward a close. The no-shop will usually require the company to refrain from soliciting other investment and notify the investors of any inquiries by any other interested investors. The confidentiality clause will prohibit disclosure of the term sheet to anyone other than persons who have a need to know, such as employees, stockholders, members of the board, accountants, attorneys, and other investors.

The good faith obligation to work toward a close is a sleeper. You may be thinking that, because the term sheet is non-binding, you can walk away at any time. It doesn't quite work that way. The obligation to negotiate in good faith, while a very fuzzy sounding standard, has some real teeth to it, even if the term sheet does not specifically call it out. The founder that changes his mind could find himself in a lawsuit for bad faith refusal to negotiate.

If that seems unlikely, you might ask Venture Associates Corporation, who signed a nonbinding letter of intent with Zenith Data Systems Corporation proposing terms for the acquisition of certain assets. The letter stated that it was not a binding obligation on either party but was subject to execution of a definitive purchase agreement. However, the parties agreed to negotiate in good faith to enter into a definitive purchase agreement. The Seventh Circuit Court of Appeals found that the letter of intent was a binding agreement to negotiate in good faith toward the formation of a contract of sale.[123] The Delaware Supreme Court came to a similar conclusion in the case of a non-binding letter of intent to consummate a merger.[124]

We need not forge new pathways in the law here, as there is an easy way around this issue. The term sheet can expire at the end of a certain time period - win, lose, or draw. It's not a perfect solution as a party can always claim that another party acted in bad faith just to run out the clock, but it is better than saying nothing about it.

PART 4: PLANNING AND STRATEGY

...most overnight successes took a long time.
Steve Jobs

Chapter Thirty-five

Financially Troubled Startups

"I have learned fifty thousand ways it cannot be
done, and therefore I am fifty thousand times
nearer the final successful experiment."
—Thomas Edison

Startups operate in a funnel. There is no ceiling on how high they can go. There is also no floor. The previous chapters were about the lofty heights of the funnel. This chapter is about the bottomless pit.

First of all, you should know that your startup is likely to fail. I know that you do not think so. Like the contestants on American Idol, every single founder believes they will be the next Kelly Clarkson. If that sounds like you, then you should think of me as your own private Simon Cowell.

According to the Small Business Administration (SBA), in 2019, the failure rate of startups was around 90 percent. Of those, 21.5 percent of startups failed in the first year, 30 percent in the second year, 50 percent in the fifth year and 70 percent in their tenth year. I think the SBA numbers might be a little optimistic but, clearly, failure is the price of innovation.

I hosted a panel a while ago for one of the pitch groups mentioned above. Our topic was doing business in Asia and funding companies with Asian markets. In explaining the difference between the Silicon Valley and Asia, one of the entrepreneurs who I had invited to the panel, commented:

"I have lost more than $100 million of investor money in my career. If I lived in Japan, I might have to drive a sword through my heart or something. In Silicon Valley, that is viewed as valuable experience."

As jarring as that statement is, there is a powerful lesson in it. First, that the Silicon Valley is forgiving. Second, people lose a lot of money here and live to fight again! I want you to live to fight again, so here is my advice:

Protect the Business

> "When the going gets tough ...
> c'mon man, you know the thing."
> —Joe Biden

Pivot.

A pivot is when a company discovers that what it was doing isn't working and decides to do something else. The company shifts its business strategy based on market feedback or changes its business model.

A startup named Gigya famously pivoted in 2009. Gigya sold products for MySpace and Friendster; however, Facebook was taking over the market. The CEO realized that radical change was needed. They convinced their existing investors to extend their last round so that they could put R&D dollars into a new product that worked with Facebook instead of competing with it. The strategy was successful. The company survived and was eventually acquired by SAP for $350 million.[125]

The Valley is full of stories like Gigya's. They could fill a book in their own right. Often overlooked, however, are the legal strategies necessary to pull off a successful pivot.

A pivot is a big deal, so the board should carefully consider the issue and document it. As noted above, the board is generally protected from the adverse consequences of its decision by the business judgement rule, but the board must still consider its duty of care. A meeting is advisable, with a record that the issue was thoroughly discussed and the issues vetted, with the help of professionals if necessary.

Obviously, the investors may not understand a pivot. They invested in a company that makes gadgets and now you are making widgets? Were you always planning on making widgets and, if so, why am I just now hearing about this? As noted above, transparency is key, since once an investor gets it in his head that you have deceived him, it may take a court to convince him otherwise. Many shareholder lawsuits start with a failure to communicate.[126]

You should consider how the pivot will affect existing contracts with vendors, suppliers, customers, consultants, and employees. Will it require the company to breach its obligations and, if so, what is the expected cost of that?

Some more arcane issues that should be run by counsel are licensure, regulatory and trade. If the company has foreign investors, it may not be allowed to enter the new business.[127] A pivot can be as legally complex as starting a new business in some ways.

Play offense.

Out of chaos comes opportunity. In 2020, the Covid shutdowns threatened to close every restaurant in the country. Anjou Ahlborn Kay and Sebastiaan van de Rijt, co-founders of the Bamboo Asia chain of restaurants, had just recently opened their Oakland location when they were ordered to shut down. Even in normal times, 60 percent of restaurants don't make it past their first year and 80 percent go out of business within five years.[128] In 2020, half of all restaurants closed permanently. In 2020, restaurant reservations were down 57 percent from the same period in 2019.[129] Bamboo Asia, however, is doing fine and will likely even return dividends to its investors.

Instead of shutting down, Bamboo Asia doubled down. It implemented a novel new way of delivering meal kits to its patrons. People were stuck at home but still wanted fine dining on demand. Having prepared food delivered just wasn't the same since high end meals do not travel well. The ingredients had to be kept separate until the meal was prepared at the customer's home. The problem to solve, as Anjou describes it, was threefold. They wanted to provide a safe environment, they wanted to do it economically, and they wanted something that would support the community.

Bamboo Asia's idea was to prepare the ingredients but keep them separate and let the customer do the final assembly. A customer would order a meal online and it would be delivered cold. The customer would then combine the ingredients and heat. In that way, the quality of the meal would be preserved.

Meal kits were almost unknown in the restaurant industry before Covid, but the kits were so popular that Bamboo Asia started using their online delivery platform for other restaurants and other meals. "Why dine out when you can feast in?" Sebastiaan says, giving rise to the new platform

– Feastin – which became a new company that independently services restaurants throughout the Bay Area. That is an example of playing offense in the face of a crisis.

Protect the Founders

Protecting the business is important but it is more important not to do so at the expense of the founders. Some of the most famous entrepreneurs in the world failed before succeeding; some failed many times. Evan Williams joined a podcasting platform called Odeo, which was driven out of business by iTunes after raising a Series A round.[130] Williams went on to co-found Twitter. Reid Hoffman, one of the founders of LinkedIn, failed first and fast with SocialNet – a slightly scattered online dating and social networking site.[131] A hedge fund started by Peter Thiel, one of the co-founders of PayPal, lost money in stock, currencies, and oil.[132] I could go on and on, but you get the idea.

The one thing that all of these failures had in common is that they did not let the failure of the idea bring them down personally. They were able to live to fight another day and form a later successful company. This chapter focuses on those legal strategies.

Personal Liability. First and foremost, I want you to avoid any personal liability for any debts of your startup. The risks of the business should stay with the business. Here are the key takeaways.

Personal guarantees and co-obligors. In 2020, the nation was reeling from the effects of the state ordered shutdown of many businesses. My restaurant clients suffered because they were not allowed to do business. My heavily leveraged landlord clients suffered because they could not collect rent. Lawsuits have started and more will ensure. Many business owners signed personal guarantees of their leases. Many borrowers financed their businesses with recourse debt. This means that they must step up and pay the leases or the loans personally if their companies do not.

A personal guaranty is often demanded by vendors for new businesses that have no credit history. The person who promises to answer for the debt (the guarantor) might also pledge their assets such as checking accounts, savings accounts, cars, and real estate. The guarantor is said to have secondary liability, meaning that the guarantor must pay the debt only if the debtor does not. This differs from a co-obligor's obligation, which is primary, meaning that the debtor need not proceed against any other party before suing the co-obligor.

Generally, in states such as California, a guarantee must be in writing and must be supported by consideration. The concept of consideration means that the parties engaged in a bargained for exchange or that the party giving the guarantee received something in exchange. Do not confuse consideration for value. For example, the loan that your company received is probably good consideration to support a guarantee even though you may have gotten no value out of it. Some consideration substitutes include reasonable reliance and promissory estoppel.

Since the guarantor is somewhat at the mercy of the creditor, state law provides many protections to guarantors. For example, they may be able to assert any defenses that the primary obligor has or may have a defense because the creditor did not proceed against the primary obligor or did so in a way that increased the risk to the guarantor, for example, by not seizing collateral or acting soon enough. State law may allow a guarantor to waive those defenses and well drafted guarantees will always have the waiver language.[133] Nevertheless, there are defenses to guarantees. One article discusses 24 separate defenses that guarantors may have.[134] To paraphrase, there must be 50 ways to lose your liability (or at least 24).

Real estate lending is a world unto itself. Many states, such as California, have one form of action or anti-deficiency laws designed to protect a borrower from a deficiency.[135] California case law might extend those protections to sham guarantees or guarantees that are in reality primary obligations.[136] This area is highly specialized and requires the assistance of an experienced real estate or banking attorney.

Sometimes a party will guarantee a debt for tax purposes. It was widely reported that Donald Trump guaranteed $400 million of debt, allowing him to claim tax losses. You can read my musing about how he did it in Appendix U *Donald Trump's Billion Dollar Loss: Good Tax Planning or Dubious Trick?*[137]

The best defense to a guarantee, however, is to not guarantee a corporate debt in the first place. Like Donald Trump, one of my real estate developer clients similarly built his real estate empire largely on debt. We will call him Carl and his story started in the 1960s when he jumped a freighter out of Baltimore at the age of 15. Having the right appetite for risk, he went from real estate brokerage to development and recently passed away with a substantial net worth. One of his later projects hit hard times during the Great Recession.[138] When the bankers came to refinance, they did not ask for a personal guaranty, much to my surprise. When I asked Carl about it, he told me that he had them seal trained to not ever even mention the words guarantee or they would lose his business forever. I like that term "seal trained" but I like the fact that he was able to stay off the debt even more. At the end of the day, the failed projects did not affect his successful projects one little bit, and he died a wealthy man.

Recourse and Nonrecourse Debt. Closely related to the concept of a personal guarantee is the idea of recourse debt. A recourse debt means that the creditor may proceed against the personal assets of the obligor. A non-recourse debt means that they may only proceed against a certain source, usually the asset securing the debt. For example, a piece of real estate financed with non-recourse debt means that the creditor may only proceed against the real estate.

But read the fine print. Nonrecourse debt will often have bad boy carve-outs. This means that in the case of some types of enumerated misconduct by the borrower, the debt becomes recourse. For example, if the borrower lied on the loan application, they may suddenly find themselves liable for millions of dollars of debt that they did not expect. Other carve-outs may include filing bankruptcy, diverting cash from operations, or transferring assets.

Beyond bad boy carve-outs and guarantees, the possibilities are only limited by the imaginations of hungry creditors. Recourse liability or guarantees can spring into existence, they can be stacked and limited to a certain tier of debt or a percentage of debt, and they can come in and out of existence based on various factors. They can be secured (although there are potential UCC and bankruptcy law issues with that). This is another area that can become exceedingly complex quickly. I suggest that you do not dabble and call a lawyer if you decide to get creative with recourse and guarantees. There are sometimes good tax reasons for financing projects, especially real estate projects, held in entities with non-recourse debt.[139]

COD Income. How unfortunate it would be to negotiate a settlement with your creditors only to be wiped out by taxes on that settlement. That is exactly what often happens to the uninformed. As a general rule, forgiveness or cancellation of debt is a taxable event to the extent of the cancelled debt.[140] Thus, if you owe your creditor $1,000,000 and settle that debt for $100,000, you have taxable income of $900,000. The rules are subtle and complex and cancellation of indebtedness ("COD") income can be triggered in cases in which you might not expect. Fortunately, there are exceptions. Here are a few:

COD income is excluded from gross income when the discharge of indebtedness is granted in a bankruptcy case or when the discharge of indebtedness is granted by a court order or in a court-approved plan.[141] Bankruptcy might seem a little extreme so, fortunately, another exception applies when the taxpayer is insolvent (outside of bankruptcy).[142] Insolvency means that your liabilities exceed the fair market value of your assets, determined immediately before the debt discharge, and including the debt to be discharged.[143] An insolvent taxpayer can exclude COD income up the amount of their insolvency but must then reduce other tax attributes, such as NOLs and tax basis.[144] Other exceptions include debt forgiveness arising from qualified farm indebtedness, qualified real property indebtedness, certain reductions of purchase price, certain student loans, and COD in connection with the contribution of debt to the capital of a corporation by a shareholder. This is technical. The rules contain traps for the uninformed and planning opportunities for the rest of us.

Payroll Taxes. This is the main gotcha' that surprises companies and their management. Employers are required to file returns, withhold federal income and other payroll taxes from an employee's wages, and deposit and pay those taxes to the United States.[145] The typical scenario includes a cash starved company paying more demanding creditors (landlords, payroll, vendors, etc.) with the idea that they will get the tax payments caught up later. That is an extremely dangerous strategy that often does not end well.

Because the taxes are held in a special trust fund for the United States, the IRS calls them trust fund taxes and views the fund as their money, which is held by the employer for them in trust. If the employer does not make the deposits, they may be subject to civil and criminal penalties and interest. Worse, the officers and other responsible persons can also be held liable for the tax personally.[146] This is not merely a theoretical liability; the IRS is very aggressive about chasing business owners for unpaid payroll taxes.

In deciding whether a person is responsible for payroll taxes, the IRS takes the position that responsibility is a matter of status, duty, and authority,[147] and looks to the extent to which a person exercises control over the finances of the employer, such as office or other position of authority held, authority to sign checks or disburse funds, ownership interest, ability to hire or fire employees, and ability to determine who is paid and when.

As a practical matter, the IRS goes after everyone in sight, including officers, directors, stockholders, members, trustees, personal representatives, employees, lenders, creditors, accountants, and even attorneys (yikes!).[148] I have even seen the IRS pursue bookkeepers who were able to counter sign checks.

The take-away for you as an entrepreneur is to not use payroll taxes as a source of financing. Never get behind in the payment of payroll taxes and, if you are in a situation where you must prefer creditors, and have a choice, it might make sense to pay the payroll taxes before paying debts for which you are not personally liable (although see below on fiduciary duties).

Piercing the corporate veil. Piercing the corporate veil is a phrase that is often used to describe a scenario in which courts ignore the liability shield of a corporation (or LLC) and hold its shareholders, members, directors, and others personally liable for the corporation's debts. Whenever a company fails, you may hear a creditor's lawyer threaten to pierce the veil and go after its owners. I hear that threat from litigators often in these cases, as if veil piercing were the natural consequence of a failed company.

In fact, it is not so easy. To put it in perspective, I have formed thousands of new companies over the past almost 40 years. Most of them are no longer in business. If the startup statistics are accurate, most of them went out of business leaving some hapless creditor holding the bag. That translates to thousands of unpaid creditors and thousands of potential veil piercing claims. In all that time, I have had a grand total of exactly *zero* individuals get tagged with veil piercing liability. All of those individuals, however, were well advised.

The reason is because courts have a strong presumption against piercing the corporate veil and will only do so if there has been serious misconduct. Limited liability is extremely important as it encourages development of public markets for stock and, thus, helps make possible the liquidity and diversification that investors receive from those markets.[149]

That is not to say that it cannot happen. If the misconduct involves intermingling of personal and corporate assets, failing to adequately capitalize the corporation, failing to follow formalities, or using the corporation to fraudulently escape liability, the veil may be pierced. Courts often recite other facts but, for the most part, will typically follow the money in these cases, so financial formalities are important. The biggest (and wholly avoidable) mistake companies make in this regard is to commingle funds. The Company needs its own bank account, to be used for its own expenses (and nothing else).

Managers of an LLC may likewise be liable for the debts, obligations, and other liabilities of the company due to a failure to respect the company's separate identity; however, personal liability will not be imposed for failure to follow corporate formalities in an LLC. Instead, the alter ego doctrine is usually applied where there is a: (1) failure to complete formation of the company; (2) failure to properly capitalize the company; (3) use of company assets for personal use; and/or (4) commingling of company funds with personal funds.

Since the law of piercing the corporate veil varies from state to state, local advice is prudent. The bottom line is that if you incur liability under this doctrine, you haven't been paying attention.

Fraudulent Transfers. The year 2020 will long be remembered for a worldwide pandemic, a hotly contested Presidential election, riots and strife, the rise of the Black Lives Matter movement, the worst fires and most powerful hurricanes in US history, and, of course, the Tiger King. The Tiger King was a documentary chronicling the rise and fall of zookeeper Joe Exotic. In the end,

Joe Exotic lost a trademark infringement lawsuit to his arch enemy Carole Baskin. To avoid the claims of Baskin and other creditors, a court found that Exotic fraudulently transferred a zoo property to his mother.[150] Exotic's mother admitted that the property was transferred to her to remove it from the reach of creditors and, for her trouble, she too became a defendant.[151]

Joe might be exotic but he is not very original or very bright. His story is one that plays out regularly for troubled companies as follows: debtor gets into financial trouble and transfers his property to a relative to keep his or her creditors from getting at it. The creditor finds out about it and sues the relative. Gee, thanks son.

Courts will readily undo transfers that place a debtor's assets beyond the reach of his or her creditors. Generally, fraudulent (or avoidable) transfer laws permit creditors to void a debtor's transaction when a debtor engages in a transaction with the actual intent to hinder, delay, or defraud any creditor or when a debtor makes a transfer without receiving reasonably equivalent value and, as a result, is unable to pay its debts. In that case, a court may undo the transfer, prohibit (enjoin) further transfers by the debtor or the transferee, prevent the debtor from transferring any remaining assets, or appoint a receiver to take charge of the transferred asset.[152]

It is important to note that a transfer is voidable regardless of when the creditor's claim arose if the transfer is made with actual intent to hinder, delay or defraud, without a reasonably equivalent value in exchange, and the debtor either was engaged or was about to engage in a business or a transaction for which the remaining assets of the debtor were unreasonably small in relation to the business or transaction or intended to incur debts beyond the debtor's ability to pay as they became due. A transfer is also voidable as to a creditor whose claim arose before the transfer if the debtor made the transfer (or incurred the obligation) without receiving a reasonably equivalent value in exchange and the debtor was insolvent or became insolvent as a result of the transfer. That is pretty dense, but the general idea is that you cannot give your property away to avoid creditor claims.

Bankruptcy courts have their own version of fraudulent conveyances. A debtor who engages in a fraudulent conveyance risks having his or her bankruptcy case dismissed as well as other creditor remedies.[153] Bankruptcy law also allows a court or trustee to recover certain preferences in payment of a previously incurred (as opposed to current) debt made while the debtor was insolvent (meaning its assets are less than its liabilities).[154]

Also, most states criminalize unlawfully disposing of assets or property in order to avoid having to use that property to pay back a debt.[155] It may be a rare and soulless prosecutor who will prosecute a case like that, but I have seen it happen.

Contract Fraud. Here is another sleeper issue. In *The Sopranos*, Tony Soprano's old high school buddy, Davey Scatino, who runs a sporting goods store, loses forty boxes of ziti ($40,000) at Tony's card game. In order to collect the gambling debt, Tony and his gang take over the sporting goods store, cause Davey to purchase merchandise on credit, and then take the goods for themselves. Eventually, Davey gets sued for fraud. "You're doing a good job," says Tony. Ironically, the episode is called, "The Happy Wanderer." [156]

Could that really happen? Where is the fraud in a simple breach of a promise to pay for sporting goods? And why does it matter?

A person commits fraud when they make a knowingly false statement that deceives another person into signing a contract.[157] The fraudulent actor can be personally liable in damages to the defrauded party. Thus, unlike a breach of contract claim, in which the company may be liable for breach, a fraud claim may be brought against the individual actor personally; thus, it is important to avoid giving a creditor a fraud claim. A court could also award exemplary or punitive damages in a fraud claim to punish bad conduct.[158]

The difference between a fraud and contract claim is subtle but significant. Consider the CEO who says to a creditor, "Company promises to pay" vs. "Company has enough money to pay" when it clearly does not. The former case involves failed expectations whereas the latter involves dishonesty. The first is opinion driven while the latter is fact driven.

Closely related to fraud are the torts of deceit and misrepresentation, which can be intentional (fraud) or negligent.[159] Many states, such as California impose an implied covenant of good faith and fair dealing between contracting parties, which assumes that parties intend to honor their word and not attempt to avoid their obligations. Bad faith involves intentional dishonesty, such as entering into an agreement with no intention of fulfilling the obligations. There are as many examples of bad faith as there are ways to mislead someone and, as a result, it comes up often in disputes. When a client asks how to avoid being sued for violating the implied covenant of good faith and fair dealing, I generally tell them to act in good faith and deal fairly. Another good defensive approach is to have extensive disclosures and acknowledgements in your documents to counter any claims of false representation. I usually get accused of over lawyering when I suggest that, but, at least for Delaware contracts, that is a powerful defense.[160]

Securities Fraud (or Seller Beware). The bar for proving common law or civil fraud is pretty high. Not only must it be proven by clear and convincing evidence, but the plaintiff also has the difficult task of getting inside the head of the defendant and proving a bad intent. Securities fraud differs from common law fraud in that it is prescribed by statute and can generally be thought of as deceptive practices that induce investors to purchase securities on the basis of false information in violation of securities laws. That misrepresentation can include an omission of a material fact.

In the case of a failed company, the stockholders, having equity, are paid last, after the creditors. They will be the persons who are most likely damaged. All else being equal, sophisticated investors understand the risks and are less likely to pursue a company and its promoters for their losses. They are also afforded less protection under the securities laws as they are better able to protect their own interests. Unsophisticated investors, however, in my experience, will squawk the loudest.

The best way to protect yourself from a personal fraud claim is to be scrupulously honest in your disclosures. The second-best way is to over disclose in writing so that it cannot be said that you misrepresented something. Memories fade and circumstances change and years from now, when a claim comes up, your written record may be the only way to know what representations were actually given. Thus, I like to see extensive written disclosures of material facts.

Fiduciary Claims. Directors and officers owe fiduciary duties to their shareholders, including a duty of care and a duty of loyalty. If a company is insolvent, however, the assets are not sufficient to return anything to the equity holders. If there is nothing left for the equity, the actions of management affect only the company's creditors. Under the trust fund doctrine, directors owe a duty to act in the creditors' interests when a corporation is insolvent.[161] The doctrine varies from state to state but many jurisdictions hold that directors and officers of an insolvent corporation owe creditors a fiduciary duty to maintain the assets of the corporation. In that case, management has a whole new set of potential plaintiffs to worry about.

This issue comes up when the company (and its management) decides to prefer one creditor or group of creditors over another. To prefer a creditor is to pick and choose – to pay one and not the other when there are not enough funds to go around. That might be viewed by a creditor as a breach of duty. In California, directors of an insolvent corporation may be held liable for breaching fiduciary duties to creditors if they prefer alternate creditors. However, they will generally be protected by the business judgment rule if their decision to prefer certain creditors is made in good faith and does not involve a conflict of interest. Directors must be especially careful if the creditor is also a member of management or there is otherwise a conflict of interest.[162]

D&O Insurance. Directors and officers (D&O) liability insurance protects the directors and officers if they are sued by employees, vendors, competitors, investors, customers, and other parties for wrongful acts in managing a company. The insurance should cover legal fees, settlements, and other costs as well as any underlying damages claims.

After the company is gone and the creditors are seeking the deep pockets of its promoters, D&O insurance is essential to guard against liability. No person should ever be a director of any company, public or private, without insurance.

D&O insurance works in conjunction with an indemnification agreement, which indemnifies a person for losses due to their role in the company. The company's charter and bylaws will usually provide that the corporation will indemnify directors and officers if they act in good faith in a manner reasonably believed to be in (or not opposed to) the best interests of the corporation and have no reasonable cause to believe that his or her conduct is unlawful.[163] Notwithstanding the provisions contained in the company's governing documents, management will want a separate indemnification agreement to spell out the process of indemnity. For example, the indemnification agreement will cover things such as the applicable standard of care, advancement of expenses, who can select the indemnitee's lawyer, and how decisions to indemnify are made. A sample indemnification agreement is attached as Appendix V Indemnification Agreement.

Improper Distributions. A financially troubled company should not be making distributions to its shareholders. California law, for example, imposes personal liability on directors for authorizing a shareholder distribution that would render the corporation insolvent. Once corporate dissolution proceedings have commenced, there cannot be a distribution to shareholders unless there is payment or adequate provision for payment of all known liabilities of the corporation.[164] Similarly, the law prohibits the making of loans to officers or directors or guaranteeing their obligations without prior disclosure and approval of a majority of shareholders.[165] California rules limit the amount that a corporation can distribute to shareholders based on a retained earnings or asset test.[166]

Wages. Some states, such as California, impose civil penalties and criminal sanctions for an employer's failure to pay the wages owed to employees, including vacation pay and benefits.[167] A company's agent, manager, or officer might also incur personal liability if he or she willfully refuses to pay wages, if the corporation has the ability to pay. The risk of personal liability for directors and officers is greatest in circumstances where they continue to let employees work after the point in time when they know that the company does not have sufficient funds to pay the employees' accrued wages. Officers and directors may be liable for such wages on a fraud or intentional misrepresentation theory similar to that discussed above in connection with potential liability to trade creditors. Briefly stated, by continuing to employ the employees, the corporate management—in the person of the officers and the board of directors—is making an implicit representation that it intends to and has the ability to pay the employees their compensation. If corporate management knows that it does not have the ability to pay the employees' compensation, its implicit representation is knowingly false. The employees may be deemed to have relied on that false representation to their detriment. Thus, officers and directors could be found liable for fraud or intentional misrepresentation and the measure of damages would presumably be the unpaid wages. There is even a potential for criminal liability for failure to pay wages.[168]

ERISA Liability. ERISA (the Employee Retirement Income Security Act of 1974) is the federal law that applies to employment benefit plans, such as your 401(k).[169] A startup's benefit plan will often designate a member of the company's management as the plan administrator, plan trustee, or member of an administrative committee. Even if it does not, a manager might perform a function that ERISA deems a fiduciary function, such as discretionary authority or control over the management of the plan or any authority or control over management or disposition of the plan assets. A fiduciary might be personally liable to make good on any losses to the plan.

Not every act by an officer, director or manager affecting a benefit plan is a fiduciary act. The law distinguishes between purely corporate functions and fiduciary functions. Unfortunately, it is not always clear where company functions end and fiduciary functions begin. Liability may attach where monies withheld from an employee's paychecks for contributions to the pension fund are deposited into the company's general account but not paid over to the pension fund. In such circumstances, the U.S. Department of Labor (DOL) and the pension trustee may argue that, when management fails to timely segregate the employees' contributions from the corporation's assets, they became fiduciaries under ERISA.

Other Personal Liabilities. There are many other ways an individual could become liable for the debts of an insolvent company. By way of example, that could include the following:

State taxes. Some states impose officer and director liability for willful failure to pay some taxes;[170]

Bad checks and credit cards. Individuals who sign bad checks may incur criminal as well as civil liability.[171] Credit card debt may be backed by individual guarantees.

Statutory or regulatory. Statutes or regulations may impose liability on management. One example is the Comprehensive Environmental Response, Compensation, and Liability Act ("CERCLA"), which relates to hazardous wastes. CERCLA allows the government to recoup clean-up costs from potentially responsible parties. The definition of a potentially responsible party is broad and may include corporate officers and directors.

A summary of possible corporate liabilities is attached as Appendix W Individual Liability for Managers/Directors and Officers.

Tying it All Together. Obviously, there are many ways that a founder may have personal liability when a company fails. Here are some rules of thumb when shutting down a company that has more debt than assets.

If the founder is personally liable for a debt, he or she should consider paying those debts first. A creditor might seek a return of those amounts to the company or its creditors, but management is generally entitled to rely on the business judgement rule, except in the case of a conflict. Since trust fund taxes are not treated as owned by the company, paying those first is probably a safe bet. Paying other debts for which a founder is personally liable might be a bit more uncertain and may be thought of as a tradeoff between a *possible* creditor claim versus a *certain* cost. Laws vary from state to state and legal counsel should be consulted.

If the risk is too great and the founder does not want the potential cost and expense of being sued, there is a safer way out.

Bankruptcy

My client was a manufacturer of a little electronic doohickey[172] that had an application (at the time) in millions of electronic devices made for the consumer market. When they agreed to sell the line to one of the largest consumer electronics companies in the world (BigCo), I suggested that we limit our liability for damages, given that our doohickey was so important to the buyer. My client did not take my suggestion because management did not want to risk losing such a big and important contract. They just wanted to sign, and sign they did (against my advice). Soon after the announcement of the sale, a patent popped up that took my client's former doohickey off the market. Soon after that, we received a demand letter from BigCo asking for damages. The damages were not the millions that they paid us. Oh, no. The damage demand was for the billions of dollars they would have made if we had owned our product. The company's next stop was the United States Federal Bankruptcy Court.

Think of bankruptcy as a break glass emergency measure. If there are no other options, there is bankruptcy, which allows a debtor to conduct an orderly liquidation or reorganize its affairs. Bankruptcy can also be used to settle equity squabbles.

The Bankruptcy Code[173] is organized in chapters. Its principal chapters are 7, 11, 12, 13 and 15. A Chapter 7 bankruptcy is a liquidation proceeding available to consumers and businesses. Those assets of a debtor that are not exempt from creditors are collected and sold and the proceeds distributed to creditors. A debtor can obtain a complete discharge from debt under Chapter 7 except for certain debts. Chapter 11 bankruptcy provides a procedure by which an individual or a business can reorganize its debts while continuing to operate. The vast majority of Chapter 11 cases are filed by businesses. The debtor, often with participation from creditors, creates a plan of reorganization under which to repay part or all of its debts. Chapter 12 allows a family farmer or a fisherman to file for bankruptcy, reorganize its business affairs, repay all or part of its debts, and continue operating. Chapter 13 is used primarily by individuals to reorganize their financial affairs under a repayment plan that must be completed within three or five years. To be eligible for Chapter 13 relief, a consumer must have regular income and may not have more than a certain amount of debt, as set forth in the Bankruptcy Code.

The Bankruptcy Code enjoins or automatically stays any action to collect pre-petition debts owed to creditors, such as commencing or continuing a lawsuit, entering or enforcing a judgment, terminating contracts, or taking any other action to enforce payment. A creditor may seek relief from the automatic stay from the Bankruptcy Court to collect its debt but is otherwise prohibited from taking collection activities.

Debtors must file detailed schedules of assets and liabilities and financial affairs. The Bankruptcy Code sets forth priorities of payment or entitlement to payment by types of creditors or claims. Secured creditors, administrative claims (costs associated with the administration of the bankruptcy estate), certain employee wage and benefit contribution claims, tax claims, and others may be paid before other debts. Debtors have the right to assume or reject executory contracts and leases (contracts in which both parties owe performance to the other). If a debtor rejects an executory contract, the non-debtor party has a general unsecured claim for damages arising from its breach of contract.

Creditors register their claims with the bankruptcy estate by filing a proof of claim. A debtor in bankruptcy can sell all of its assets free of liens. This is one of the main reasons for filing and provides a quick way to sell a business before it loses value.

The debtor will file a plan of reorganization, which describes how it will reorganize and pay its debts. The plan must be confirmed by the Bankruptcy Court.

There are two important avoidance provisions in the Bankruptcy Code. One allows the debtor to recover preference payments to non-insiders that were made within 90 days prior to filing. The time period is one year (instead of 90 days) for insiders. A preference is a payment on account of antecedent debt, which allows the creditor to receive more than it would in a Chapter 7 liquidation.[174] The second provision applies to fraudulent transfers under which a debtor can recover certain types of payments made to non-insiders within one year prior to bankruptcy and two years prior to bankruptcy with respect to insiders.

Bankruptcy can be a good option for a company that could reorganize if it had a little breathing room. It can also be used by nervous founders who would like the protection of a court to decide how its assets are divided up. However, bankruptcy is expensive and absent the foregoing objectives, most corporations simply dissolve under state law and leave the creditors where they are (unpaid).

A bankruptcy need not be the sad event it implies. I represented the creditor group of a company that acquired a hotel right before 9/11. Talk about bad timing. Tourism dropped and the hotel descended into creditor claims, squabbling owners, and bad management. My creditor group seized managerial control and filed for bankruptcy protection over the anguished objections of some of the stakeholders. Under our guidance, we found an experienced hotel manager and, with some bankruptcy protected funding and a little time, eventually put the hotel back in the black. By the end of the proceeding, every single creditor was paid in full and the hotel still operates profitably today. The system worked exactly as it was designed.

A smaller company that cannot afford a long-drawn-out bankruptcy might also need court or statutory protection to help them wind up or reorganize. There is a cheaper option for them, which is discussed next.

Assignment for the Benefit of Creditors (ABC)

As an alternative to a bankruptcy, a troubled or distressed company might enter into an ABC transaction. Compared to a bankruptcy, an ABC may be cheaper, faster, and more flexible.

An ABC is a state proceeding that allows a company to quietly transfer its assets to a new entity free of its unsecured debt and limit the potential liability of its management. Procedurally, a distressed company (assignor) assigns all its assets to a party (assignee) who will conduct the liquidation for the benefit of the assignor's creditors. The assignee liquidates the property and distributes the proceeds to the assignor's creditors. The assignee will run a sale process that is designed to obtain market value for the business.

When an ABC is used to sell a business, the ABC allows a sale of the business as a going concern, which is more valuable than selling off individual assets. The ABC allows a buyer to avoid (or at least minimize) claims that the assets were acquired as part of a fraudulent transfer or that they are subject to successor liability for claims against the distressed company.

Often, the ABC is prepackaged, allowing the purchaser of the business to acquire the ongoing business free of the former owner's unsecured debt. The purchaser is often the secured creditor or management of the distressed company.

The ABC is good but not perfect. In California, there is no court order approving the sale transaction, so a creditor could attack the transaction. Unlike a bankruptcy sale, assets are not sold free and clear of liens (unless the secured creditor will be paid in full from sale proceeds) and there is no automatic stay.[175]

Friendly Foreclosures

Finally, an extremely cash strapped company that wants to shed its unsecured creditors and start over might consider a friendly foreclosure or private sale. This is the cheapest but riskiest approach.

In the foreclosure scenario, a secured lender can take possession of the collateral and sell it in a commercially reasonable manner.[176] The secured lender would advertise or solicit the sale of the collateral. Upon completion of the sale, the buyer would take whatever rights the debtor had in the collateral and the foreclosing party's security interest would be discharged. The process is relatively quick and easy and requires no court intervention.

A major disadvantage for the buyer is the possibility of successor liability. A buyer of assets is generally not liable for the debts of a seller unless the buyer agreed to assume the liabilities, there was a *de facto* merger of the buyer and the seller, the buyer is a mere continuation of the seller, or the sale was intended to avoid the seller's liabilities and defraud its creditors. The mere continuation exception prevents the owners or managers of the seller from simply walking across the street, setting up a new company and buying all the old company's assets for less than the company's debts. The possibility of a fraudulent conveyance (or avoidable transfer) action against the buyer makes this approach very risky since, if the reorganized company is successful, the old company's creditors may be back to claim that the company was sold for too little.

Chapter Thirty-six

Happy Endings: Mergers, Acquisitions and Sales

"All entities move and nothing remains still."—Plato
"Nothing is permanent but change."—Heraclitus

In March of 2006, I took a deep breath, signed a 5-year lease for 2500 square feet in Palo Alto and launched the Royse Law Firm. It started with exactly one employee – me. My vision was to deliver a fully integrated solution that considered both legal and tax issues for corporations and their shareholders. It was my view that the law firms in Palo Alto had not done a good job of considering the interests of all the stakeholders in a company. The large corporate firms were good at company corporate matters but, as to the individual interests of the shareholders, not so much. I ran into Larry Sonsini, the founder of the well-known Silicon Valley law firm Wilson Sonsini Goodrich & Rosati, at a wedding and ran my idea past him. He agreed that there was a place in this Valley for a business tax lawyer so, despite the naysayers, I knew I was on to something.

Over the next 10 years we grew rapidly, expanding our ranks from just me to 27 lawyers. And then, it just stopped. Were we to be a victim of the rule of 30?

The rule of 30 is the odd phenomenon that law firms tend to hit 30 lawyers, then either merge or dissolve. For some reason, we could not bust past 30 lawyers – 27 was the maximum load that I could manage without running into quality control issues. We had hit a plateau. We had stalled. It was time to change.

"Now is the time to start thinking about your exit," according to the book *Finish Big*.[177] You should do so even if you think you will never sell because, one way or another, you will eventually leave the business. Considering an exit will lead to better business practices and force a founder to consider what they want from the business.

An exit usually means an IPO or a sale. Since Enron, Worldcom, Dodd Frank, and Sarbanes Oxley, very few of my clients go public anymore. Almost all of my successful clients will exit via an acquisition or sale. This chapter contains a few tips for making sure you have a successful exit.

Structure. We have come full circle. We discussed choice of entity in the first chapter of this book and here we are again in this chapter. As noted, the choice of entity determines whether you pay one level or two levels of tax on a sale of your company. If only it were that simple. Most of the companies that I work with are C corporations because that is what the VCs will demand. If you do not have that limitation, the analysis becomes a bit more involved. Here are the considerations.

Taxable Sales. Asset sales have the advantage that the buyer need not take all of the unknown liabilities of the selling company. The buyer also obtains a cost basis in the acquired assets, which can be depreciated or amortized and reduce its taxable income in the future. The difficulty is that a company may have contracts that are hard to transfer. It may (and probably does) have contracts that may not be assigned without the consent of the counter party. Sales tax might apply to the sale of assets that would not apply if the acquiror were to buy interests in the company to be sold (the "target"). Moreover, it is hard to catch all of the assets of a company in an asset sale – it seems there is always some piece of IP that is forgotten. The bigger issue is income tax.

Passthroughs. S corporations and LLCs taxed as partnerships are subject to one level of tax and, since the 2017 Tax Cuts and Jobs Act, might qualify for a 20 percent deduction (the "199A Deduction").[178] The 199A Deduction can disappear with the stroke of a Congressional pen and is subject to many limitations but, if it applies, the effective maximum federal rate of income tax on sales gains can be pushed down to less than 30 percent on income and 23.8 percent on capital gains. That is pretty attractive in the case of a cash sale of assets.

In the case of a cash sale of stock of an S corporation, provided that the one year capital gains holding period is met, the top federal rate would be 23.8 percent (20% capital gains plus 3.8% net investment income tax). That's even more attractive to a seller but what about the buyer? Do they want stock or assets?

If tax were the only issue, the buyer would always want to acquire assets because assets can be expensed, depreciated, or amortized while stock cannot. However, as discussed below, a stock sale is easier for everyone as a legal matter than an asset sale. This creates a tension between buyer and seller, as the seller wants to sell stock and the buyer wants to buy assets. Fortunately, in the case of an S corporation (not a C corporation), there is an app for that. It is called a Section 338(h)(10) election, or a Section 336(e) election in some cases, and allows the parties to treat a stock sale as an asset sale for tax purposes.[179] That gives the buyer a fair market value basis in depreciable or amortizable assets while having the convenience of acquiring stock. To give it perspective, I have sold dozens of S corporations and I can count on one hand the number who have not made a Section 338(h)(10) or Section 336(e) election.

C Corporations. A C corporation is a state law corporation that has not elected to be taxed as a passthrough under the special rules of Subchapter S of the Internal Revenue Code. A C corporation is subject to two levels of tax on its earnings – once at the corporate level and again at the shareholder level when those earnings are distributed. Thus, when a C corporation sells its assets and distributes the proceeds (or liquidates), it has the double tax problem. As noted above, however, the buyer gets a fair market value depreciable basis in an asset sale. An asset sale is bad for the seller but good for the buyer and C corporations may not use Sections 338(h)(10) or 336(e) to reduce their taxes.

At the shareholder level, the federal income tax rate on a stock sale drops to 23.8 percent if the sellers have held their stock for one year as a capital asset and possibly zero if the stock is qualified small business stock ("QSBS"). See Chapter 1 for a discussion of QSBS. This difference increases the tax tension between stock and asset sales even more.

Non-Taxable Acquisitions. Depending on the form of consideration paid for the target company in an acquisition, the transaction may be tax free to the selling shareholders to the extent of acquiror stock received in the transaction. These transactions are referred to as tax-free reorganizations and take one of the following forms:

Type A merger.[180]
Type B stock for stock exchange.[181]
Type C stock for assets exchange.[182]
Triangular or subsidiary mergers.[183]

Appendix X Tax Free Reorganizations summarizes the various types of tax-free reorganizations.

In a Type A merger, the target company merges with and into the acquiror under state law and the shareholders of target receive acquiror stock and/or other consideration in exchange for shares of the target. Because a merger only needs majority approval of target shareholders, many deals are done this way instead of as a stock sale to avoid having to obtain the unanimous consent of the selling shareholders. Provided that a high enough percentage of the consideration consists of acquiror stock, the selling share-holders will not be taxed on the receipt of that stock.[184]

In a Type B reorganization, the target shareholders exchange their stock for voting stock in the acquirer. The acquirer must have control (80% by vote and value) of the target immediately after the acquisition.[185] B reorganizations are rare because even $1 of non-stock consideration will cause the transaction to fail to meet the requirements of a B reorganization.

In a Type C reorganization, the acquirer acquires substantially all of the properties of the target corporation solely in exchange for all or a part of its voting stock. The terms "solely" and "substantially all" are terms of art and do not exactly mean solely or substantially all.[186] In effect, the target company would sell all of its assets to the acquirer in exchange for voting stock and then liquidate, distributing the voting stock of acquiror to its shareholders. The parties will structure a transaction this way if the target has assets or liabilities that the acquirer does not want to acquire.

In a forward triangular (or subsidiary) merger, the acquiror uses stock of its parent to acquire substantially all of the assets of the target corporation. The target merges with and into the acquirer. In a reverse triangular merger, the target survives (much like a stock for stock deal). While they might seem similar, the requirements to qualify as tax-free under each type differs.[187] Type B and Type C reorganizations can also be structured as triangular reorganizations. Most deals are done this way to isolate the target's business and liabilities in a bankruptcy remote subsidiary.

Price and Payment Terms

The merger or purchase consideration can consist of acquiror stock, cash, deferred payments, or contingent consideration (earnouts).

Acquiror Stock can be problematic when the target has unaccredited investors since an acquisition using acquiror stock is a securities offering that must be registered or exempt. Companies that resisted the temptation to sell stock to unaccredited investors will have more flexibility when it comes time for an exit since they can be acquired under an accredited investor only Reg D offering. The other, often overlooked, practice when issuing acquiror stock is that the sellers of the target are, in effect, making an investment in the acquiror and should conduct the same due diligence as if they were buying its stock. In the case of a public reporting company, that information may be readily available from the SEC. In the case of privately held companies, the target will have to conduct its own diligence.

Deferred payments and notes raise similar issues. The notes themselves may be securities requiring exemption. The seller would be a lender and its due diligence should extend to ensuring that the buyer can pay the bill. If there is any doubt (and even if there is not), the payment can be secured by the stock or assets sold so that if the buyer defaults, the sellers can foreclose and get the company back (or what is left of it).

Earnouts are a special case. An earnout is a useful device to bridge the gap when a seller and buyer cannot agree on the value of a company. The buyer will pay a fixed amount and also a contingent amount based on the future, post-close performance of the target. The contingent portion of the consideration is called an earnout and can be based on gross revenue, gross profit, net income, or any other measure that the parties agree on. If the company hits its targets, the seller gets paid more. That is how it works in theory.

In practice, an earnout is often a way for (depending on your perspective) a seller to increase the price or a buyer to decrease it. For that reason, lawyers sometimes refer to earnouts as "never earned, always paid" or "never paid, always earned," depending on who we represent. As you might suspect, the chances of litigation over an earnout are high.

Having said that, I see an earnout in most of the deals I do. Given that we are probably stuck with the earnout, the best we can do as seller's counsel is to build in as much protection as possible. The seller will want the buyer to promise to support the acquired business, not take it apart, and not fire people or burden it with overhead that may affect the calculation. Sometimes a seller gets those promises; most of the time they do not.

The Professional Buyer

Know who you are dealing with, whether it be a financier, co-founder, or especially an acquiror. Clients often believe they can rely on a lawyer and a document to protect them from unscrupulous actors. I tell them that a document is just paper. Yes, they might acquire some legal rights but will they be in a position to enforce those rights against a large and well-funded buyer? More significantly, it is not possible to anticipate all the issues that might arise or all the ways that parties might disagree. I often see pages and pages of detailed verbiage around contractual obligations and I am reminded of the principle of relative ambiguity. Every refinement, clarification, and definition raises new ambiguities. Even the meaning of the word "is" can be ambiguous, according to Bill Clinton.

The professional buyer knows this and will use it to negotiate a reduction in the price. They will either find problems in due diligence or try to shift post-closing business risks to the seller. The professional buyer believes they create value by taking it away from the seller, fairly or not. Beware the professional buyer.

There are ways to know who you are doing business with. If the buyer is publicly traded, a seller can review their public filings with SEC. Those filings will reveal material contracts and litigation. The filings will reveal what their other acquisitions looked like. They may have been fairly even handed or one sided. Their litigation docket might disclose that they have sued sellers for breach of warranties or have been sued for failing to honor their agreements. The identity of their lawyers is significant since you are known by the company that you keep. Consider carefully whether you want to do business with litigious parties or companies that hire opportunistic lawyers who might view their value add as taking unreasonable positions and forcing you to fight your way back to the middle.

<u>Negotiation</u>

I stared at my speaker phone. On the phone were 12 lawyers from a large New York City law firm. This was our introductory call and they were already being demanding and confrontational. We were engaged in barnyard negotiation. They peck at me, I peck back, and we get nowhere. My client was aghast at how unfriendly his deal had suddenly become. "Don't worry," I told him, "It's all just an act."

The next day we started again. However, this time they were not confrontational. They were technical. They argued that certain fine and arcane legal points required certain issues to be resolved their way. I know a thing or two about the law, however, and their ploy did not work.

The third day, they simply argued, *ad nauseam*. I set a record that day for my longest conference call. We started at 6:00 a.m. and ended sometime after midnight but they did not wear us down. Excellent pain management skills might be my only athletic talent.

The fourth day, they were our best buddies. It was more of a "can't we all just get along approach." Yes, we can but that doesn't mean we concede to unreasonable positions.

Such is the M&A dance in the hands of a master. They will simply try different approaches until they find the one that works for them.

Selling a business is not like selling a house. There is no pre-printed form where we can just check the boxes among a small list of market conditions. "Market" is a relative term and what is market for one deal is irrelevant for the next. Anyone who tells you differently is trying to persuade you to give up something that you should not. When a lawyer argues for a term because it is market, it is because (i) the lawyer is inexperienced and doesn't know any better or (ii) they have no real arguments.

As a general rule, lawyers tend to be lousy negotiators. Litigators get paid to litigate, not negotiate and see no reason to do so because in the back of their mind they believe there is a judge that can settle any dispute for them.

Business lawyers are better at it, but many suffer from the out-of-sight, out-of-mind problem. Most lawyers will find a style that fits them. For example, the lawyer that has always been able to get results mostly by being good at establishing rapport may be a little light on strategic thinking. Similarly, the brilliant strategist may not be able to communicate as effectively as she should. For these people, adding a few techniques to what-has-always-worked will often have exponential results.

STRATEGY

It is somewhat surprising how often parties walk into a meeting with very little forethought as to what they expect to happen. To give the process some structure, every plan should start with three questions: who am I dealing with, what do I want, and how will I get it?

"Who am I dealing with?" The "who am I dealing with" question may be the most overlooked part of the strategic process. It is often said that a person cannot *not* communicate and one of the most telling communications is the identity of the person your counter party assigned to your negotiation. In one case, I suspected that a company being sold might have shorted my shareholder client by some unknown amount. When my information request letter to the company was answered by the head of litigation at one of the largest law firms in the world, I knew we had a very large claim. You can't not communicate.

"What do I want?" Modern psychology teaches us that the mind doesn't do very well with ambiguous goals. Going into a negotiation with the goal of getting as much as you can is almost always bound to render a dissatisfactory result. Setting a range of acceptable outcomes in advance is a far better idea. It also tells you when to stop negotiating and take the deal. I failed to follow my own advice in one case of a founder dispute. We put an offer out before internally defining our bottom line. Surprisingly, the other founder immediately accepted our proposal. The relative ease in which we obtained our first concession caused my client to start asking for more since we had not really determined what an acceptable outcome would be. We did not get more but he did drag the matter out longer than necessary and created unnecessary

ill will. We had achieved our goal and should have simply taken the money and closed.

"How do I get it?" The rest of this section answers this question.

RAPPORT

Everyone knows the importance of establishing rapport. Rapport implies trust, cooperation, and a desire to reach a resolution. People are more likely to concede points to people that they like and trust. They are more likely to offer up compromises and solutions. Some people are naturals at it; the rest of us will have to learn it, and those who understand rapport will find that better results are easier to come by.

Although there are naturals in the field, rapport is a skill that can be learned. The field of neuro-linguistic programming ("NLP"), for example, has developed sophisticated tools and techniques to maintain rapport in a wide variety of settings.

PREPARATION

In the information age, no one need ever go into a negotiation without knowing quite a lot about the opposing party. A quick Google search can result in documents, SEC filings, financials, litigation history, news items, and biographical information from which you can anticipate the opposing party's hot buttons, priorities, personality, reputation, and objectives. If knowledge is power, anyone with an Internet connection can be powerful.

PERSONALITY TYPES

Psychologists have devised numerous personality tests that are useful in negotiation. The DISC method places people into four categories. If we know which category a person is in, theoretically, we can then predict how they will respond to different approaches. The "D" for example (dominant) will demand concessions rather than explaining the rationale for their positions. Donald Trump is a classic D type. My experience is that most attorneys are type D type negotiators and D types only respect other D types. That is why most negotiations start out a bit on the confrontational side.

An "I" (Influencer) will take a more cooperative yet active approach, looking for win-win solutions (if there is such a thing). An I type can negotiate with everyone, works best with other I's, and feels frustrated with D types.

The S (Steady) and C (Compliant) categories refer to more passive participants who will either be overly accommodating in trying to reach agreement or stubbornly refuse to move from a position. If you are negotiating with an S or a C, be prepared to adapt. If you are an S or a C, get over it.

BE FLEXIBLE

Skilled negotiators know that they have to try things. A skilled negotiator will draw out the style of an opposing party by mixing up their approach until something works. For example, they may start out being aggressive and borderline obnoxious. If that doesn't work, they may switch to a more cooperative style of interaction. Everyone should be prepared to try different approaches and, if you should find yourself feeling like you are dealing with a Sybil set of personalities across the table, you are likely being tested.

GAME THEORY

The movie *Little Big Man* depicts a suspicious Custer questioning a scout played by Dustin Hoffman (who he suspects of attempting to betray him) as to whether he should lead his troops into the Little Big Horn Valley. Custer says, "You want me to think that you don't want me to go down there but the subtle truth is you really don't want me to go down there." We all know what happened next.

Custer's last stand, nuclear deterrence, battlefield strategies, and the prisoner's dilemma are all examples that negotiators should be familiar with. Some models assume that the players act perfectly rationally and have a known (if not identical) amount of knowledge. One problem with these models, however, is that rarely does anyone act with similar knowledge and even more rarely do they act perfectly rationally, especially when the outcomes are weighted solely by monetary values. Game theory is, nevertheless, an important arrow for the strategist's quiver.

PERSUASION THEORY

An unskilled persuader will rarely get what they want. A good persuader will often get what they want. A highly skilled persuader will often get what they want and make everyone feel good about it. One of the easiest ways to do this is to make sure that the opposing party thinks it was their idea. It is difficult for the human mind to reject an idea that it thinks it came up with and even more difficult to accept an idea that someone else is trying to impose on it.

There is no single set of skills that can define a negotiator. Instead, there are numerous aspects to a negotiation. Because of our natural tendency to stick with what we know best, many negotiators will rely on only one or two skills. Like the fisherman that picks the right times, the right places, and the right baits to catch more fish, acquiring and combining some of the above skills can have exponential results.

CALIBRATED QUESTIONS

We can learn from the super high stakes negotiators when it comes to tools and techniques. In his book *Never Split the Difference*,[188] FBI hostage negotiator Chris Voss describes an extremely effective technique. When a hostage taker made an unreasonable demand, the negotiator replied "How am I supposed to do that?" Surprisingly, the hostage taker then reduced his demand to something more realistic. In that case, the negotiator used a calibrated question, which frames the conversation but makes the counterparty believe that they are in charge. "How are we supposed to do that" is my favorite calibrated question, but other effective ones include:

What about this is important to you?

How can I help to make this better for us?

How would you like me to proceed?

What is it that brought us into this situation?

How can we solve this problem?

What are we trying to accomplish here?

LITIGATION

Attorneys are often inclined to get what they want with a hammer of litigation. Previously, I believed that if we ended up in litigation, it was because we failed at negotiating. Litigation dramatically increases everyone's cost, time, and effort and there is the possibility that you might lose. Litigation may also open a Pandora's box of new and unknown counter claims. Often it feels like the lawyers are the only winners in litigation.

My view on the topic has since evolved and I now see litigation as a card that may have to be played but should be done at the right point in the negotiation. Litigation raises the stakes, signals commitment, and requires parties to adhere to a schedule. Sometimes it is the only way to resolve a dispute. The parties may not be able to come to an agreement, but I have never seen a dispute that a judge could not resolve. Like nuclear weapons, we hope never to have to use litigators, but the parties need to know it is an option.

THIS STUFF WORKS

My client hated his co-founder and wanted out. The co-founder felt the same way but after months and years of negotiating, we were unable to agree on terms. If the price were high enough, my client would sell. If it were low enough, we would buy. Neither party would make an offer or agree to a blind option. See Appendix Y Blind Option for an example. It could be $3 million, $30 million, or something in between.

One day I received a call from the secretary for a very high powered anti-trust litigator for the largest firm in town summoning me to a meeting in their offices. The opposing party had hired him to represent his interest in our buy sell negotiation. This is the kind of lawyer who negotiates for billions of dollars – what is he doing in our little startup squabble? The opposing party decided to bring out the biggest gun he could find. He obviously was desperate to resolve the matter. You cannot not communicate.

When I arrived at the office, I was led to a humungous conference room, where they let me wait just long enough to let me know that this was their home turf. Opposing counsel eventually walked in with a team of lawyers and they all lined up on the other side of the table from me. He then spent the next ten minutes joking about his large conference room, telling me about his fancy vacation that he just returned from, and engaging in other small talk.

I did not say a word. Instead, here is what was going through my mind. First, I needed to know what value they placed on the business. If they offered us $5 million, we would sell. If less, we would want to buy.

Secondly, I knew I would be dealing with a D in the DISC types before I even arrived. Who in the world would a top litigator possibly respect? For someone like this, only a judge, and not just any judge. A Federal Appeals Court judge. Have you ever met a Federal Appeals Court judge? I have. They tend to be arrogant. [189] They tend to be all business. They tend to be direct and to the point. Think of the 2018 Justice Brett Kavanaugh Senate confirmation hearings. Judge Kavanaugh lectured and scolded his Senate questioners. And these were United States Senators!

When it finally came to be my turn to talk, I mimicked a federal judge. I did not make small talk. I did not comment on the room size. Instead, I positioned myself directly towards opposing counsel, looked him straight in the eye and said, "There have been some serious allegations in this case. There have been allegations of mismanagement. There have been allegations of oppression." All the while I tapped my finger on the table for emphasis as I made those statements, like I have seen judges do. Tap tap tap. I saw him nod in agreement slightly after the third question.

I continued, without interruption, "I don't know if your client wants to come to an agreement today. And it's probably not important that we settle today. And I don't know if it's important to you if we settle or if you will [pause] tell me. What you will offer to buy us out at [pause] is a number we will work towards as well as what we would offer." Tap tap tap.

The next words out of his mouth were "We would not be in interested in selling but we could buy at about $10 million."

Boom! We had our offer, and we moved quickly to a decision based on that number. He gave me everything we needed in that short exchange, and they overpaid us by about $5 million.

How did that happen? How did a top litigator give away the farm in such a short period of time? Well, let's break it down.

I followed a 3,2,1 pattern, often used in police interrogations. Three true statements, 2 suggestions, and 1 implied directive (or embedded command).

1. "There have been some serious allegations in this case." (true) Tap tap tap.
2. "There have been allegations of mismanagement." (true) Tap tap tap.
3. "There have been allegations of oppression." (true) Tap tap tap.

By the way, the tapping is what we call an anchor. I will come back to this later.

Next were two suggestions:

1. I don't know if your client wants to *come to an agreement today.*
2. And it's probably not important that *we settle today.*

Note that I preface these suggestions with softeners ("It's not important" and "I don't know") which tell the subconscious mind to be receptive to what I am about to say, because it doesn't really matter. This was a favorite tool of the famous psychologist Milton Erickson.

And finally, the command:

"And I don't know if it's important to you if we settle or if you will [pause] *tell me. What you will offer to buy us out at* [pause] is a number we will work towards as well as what we would offer…" Tap tap tap

First you will notice that it is a little bit of a confusing statement. Confusing language is good if you are speaking to the subconscious, because that allows it to fill in the blanks and make sense of the words. The brain seeks consistency, and a person loves to think it was their idea if they can find it. A top persuader will let you think it was your idea.

Secondly, the pauses are really oddly placed. The actual words do not command him to do anything. They just recite a bunch of stuff we already know. But the words between the pauses *"tell me. What you will offer to buy us out at"* are what I want his mind to hear.

And, by the way, the tap tap tap is the anchor that reminds him of a few seconds ago when he agreed with everything I was saying.

Now, I know what you are thinking. Is it really fair to use some advanced negotiation techniques in business, or in life generally for that matter? Isn't that a little manipulative? My answer is yes, it is manipulative and yes, it is fair.

Manipulation is simply getting someone to do what we want them to do. We all do it all day every day. Some of us are just better at it than others.

It was fair for two reasons. First, my clients' causes are just and they deserve to win. Secondly, I was dealing with a top professional. He does this for a living. He has a big conference room, tries billion dollar cases, and just took a fancy vacation. He told me so. I shed no tears for the gladiators when they lose.

<u>Pre-Transaction Planning</u>

The federal government and many states impose an estate tax or a death tax on decedents' estates. The estate tax is often viewed as a voluntary tax since it is so easy to plan out of. Startup entrepreneurs in particular are ideal candidates for estate planning since they hold assets that are expected (if all goes well) to appreciate wildly in the future. The tax laws change often but a few techniques and tricks seem to endure.

GRATs, GRUTs and GRITs. A grantor retained annuity trust ("GRAT") allows a stockholder to give property to children or trusts for children while retaining an annuity interest, the value of which reduces the taxable gift, sometimes to zero.[190] A stockholder establishes a GRAT by making an irrevocable donation into a trust. Each year, the trust pays back to the stockholder a specified percentage of the value of the stock given to the trust (this retained interest is called an "annuity"). The annuity payment is often made by transferring some of the same stock back to the shareholder, but this time at its then-current (and hopefully higher) value. A grantor retained unitrust ("GRUT") and a grantor retained income trust ("GRIT") are similar to the GRAT, except that the annual amount paid back to the stockholder is calculated differently. With any of these techniques, however, at the expiration of the trust term, the remaining trust principal is either distributed to beneficiaries or held and managed in further trust for the benefit of the stockholder's children or other predetermined beneficiaries.

These types of trusts are designed to save gift and estate taxes by reducing the value of the taxable gift to the discounted present value of the expected remainder, as prescribed by IRS regulations. For example, if a founder wants to gift $2 million worth of stock to a beneficiary, he or she could either make a direct gift and pay gift tax based on its $2 million value as of the date of gift, or he or she could make the gift through one of the foregoing types of trusts and pay tax on the current discounted value of a gift that passes at some point in the future (i.e., the present value).

Defective Grantor Trusts. Closely related to the GRAT is the concept of a defective grantor trust. This type of trust structure anticipates a sale of stock to a trust that is treated as owned by the grantor for income tax purposes (thus, it is referred to as "defective"—a misnomer). The trust, however, is respected for gift and estate tax purposes so the property is moved out of the grantor's taxable estate. Though often more effective than a GRAT, GRIT or GRUT and although founded on well-established statutory authority, legal precedents, and IRS rulings, the defective grantor trust technique is not specifically sanctioned by statute. Thus, as a tax matter, it can be viewed as a riskier technique.

Annual Exclusion Gifts. Finally, the law allows an annual exclusion from gift tax for gifts of up to certain amounts annually, per donee, per donor.[191] In addition, by electing gift splitting among spouses, a donor and his spouse can double or quadruple the gift without gift tax consequences.

With all of these techniques, the trick is that they are most effective when done early while valuations are low. Waiting until the eve of a deal to implement these strategies is better than not doing it at all but will not take full advantage of the lower valuations that can be supported early in a start-up company's life.

Asset Protection Planning. Related to pre transaction estate planning is the idea of asset protection planning. Just as you might transfer assets to avoid the IRS, you might also transfer assets to avoid future, unknown creditors. We live in a litigious society where disastrous liability lurks everywhere. You or your child gets into a car accident, you get dragged into a lawsuit, or you suffer a claim that exceeds your insurance limits. There are many cases of wealthy people being wiped out from a claim that they never saw coming. Asset protection planning is based on placing your assets beyond the reach of creditors before any of that happens. Importantly, under fraudulent conveyance laws, a court can set aside a transfer that is made too late, such as after a claim is made or (in some cases) foreseeable. I have seen many creditors and predators come out of the woodwork after an entrepreneur exits and suddenly has newfound wealth. Common asset protection techniques include trusts, ERISA benefit plans, and exempt asset planning.

Deal Process. This section describes the typical stages and steps in an acquisition.

The typical deal starts with a meeting. You might at that meeting disclose high level information about your business and its financial condition – enough for the potential buyer to make an offer. If you are using a broker, they would have done this for you. The goal at this stage is to get a written offer embodied in a letter of intent ("LOI").

The LOI will set a price and structure of the deal and serve as the outline for the binding purchase agreement (the "definitive agreement"). It is at that stage that you are able to do some negotiation and planning around the big issues – tax, security, targets, etc. The LOI will also usually have a no-shop provision meaning that once you sign it, you cannot talk to any other buyers. **You, as seller, will never have as much leverage in a deal as you do the moment before you sign the LOI**, which is one reason why, as seller's counsel, I try to make the LOI as detailed and specific as possible. The other reason is because, once you sign an LOI, you very much want the deal to close. If it does not, you will be viewed as damaged goods and it will be a long time before you are back on the market.

Upon the signing of the LOI, the buyer will have the chore of drafting a purchase agreement and starting due diligence. The due diligence will start with a due diligence list and at this point the seller can ask for a non-disclosure agreement. The results of due diligence will drive a lot of what is in the purchase agreement. For example, if a buyer finds problems in diligence, they may allocate the cost of those problems back to the seller rather than assuming them as business risk. It is often said that time kills deals, and a cratered transaction is much worse for a seller than a buyer. Consequently, the seller is usually pushing the buyer while the buyer is usually dragging their feet on the main agreement to give them time to conclude their diligence.

These days, almost all diligence is done through an electronic data room. Ideally, the seller's lawyers would have access to documents before the buyer does in order to resolve any issues before the buyer sees them and also to ensure that confidential or sensitive documents are not inadvertently disclosed. Mistakes are free if they are fixed before the buyer gets involved. They cost you credibility points (at least) if the buyer finds them.

Pro Tip – Get a Data Room. Because your company may eventually be facing an exit, liquidity event, or financing, you can anticipate that you will be engaged in due diligence at some point. You can greatly ease the process by setting up a data room early and storing all essential documents in that one online repository. My practice is to store company documents online from day one so that we are not scrambling when the term sheet arrives years later. The number of commercial data room service providers is too numerous to mention but do your research and read their privacy policies. You might be surprised. Some are more secure than others.

During due diligence, the buyer will usually draft and circulate a purchase or merger agreement. These tend to be heavily negotiated and take time. I often have sellers tell me they want to close within a week or two. That is never realistic and displays a lack of sophistication that you probably do not want to be displaying to your buyer at this point. If you do in fact close that quickly, you should keep a healthy reserve for litigation costs to defend the lawsuits that may result from a hasty and inadequate due diligence disclosure.

The definitive agreement could provide for a simultaneous sign and close or a deferred close. In a simultaneous sign and close, the parties sign the transaction documents and close at the same time. In a deferred close, the closing occurs sometime after the transaction documents are executed, usually to give the seller time to round up required votes, approvals, and consents and other matters.

Usually, a buyer will want the founders to stay with the buyer as an employee or consultant long enough to transition the company. The buyer will often ask a seller to vest into his or her deferred merger consideration to ensure their continued service (also known as a golden handcuff). The buyer will also ask for a non-compete or non-competition agreement from the sellers to protect the value of the goodwill that they are buying. In some states, like California, non-compete agreements are not enforceable except in the case of a sale of the goodwill of a business.[192] Non-competes are often heavily negotiated, both as to scope and term, as they will limit your ability to make a living in the future if things don't work out with the buyer.

And things often do not work out with the buyer. I always caution my selling entrepreneurs to expect to start feeling antsy anywhere from 6 months to a year into their job with corporate America. Many founders have never had a job and are not used to being told what to do, which is why the terms of the agreement vis a vis vesting, non-competes, and for-cause terminations are so important.

A for-cause termination means that, if the founder is fired for cause, then he loses unvested consideration and may suffer some other consequences. Cause is usually defined to mean various acts by the founder. The founder has to do something wrong to trigger a for cause termination. Similarly, if the founder leaves for good reason, implying that it was not his or her fault, he or she will get the benefit of the contract and not lose vesting. The definitions should be carefully considered, as they are often expansively drafted to give the buyer an out that the sellers might not have anticipated.

Deal Terms. If the LOI is the outline, the definitive agreement is the book. At the heart of the agreement will be an extensive set of representations and warranties. Most first-time founders are quite surprised at the breadth and length of the representations that they must make. You can expect to be representing to the buyers the absence of any problems, except as listed on an accompanying disclosure schedule. The representations will cover matters such as title, ownership and authority, and the absence of any undisclosed taxes, claims, litigation, and the like. To the extent the company cannot make a representation, it will carve that out on the disclosure schedule.

Although framed as a disclosure schedule, it is really a means of allocating risk more than disclosing. A lot of founders make the mistake of thinking that if they have disclosed a problem to a seller, they are free of it even if it is not scheduled. A non-scheduled disclosure might get you out of a fraud claim but is irrelevant to the allocation of costs and risks under the definitive agreement. If it isn't in writing, it didn't happen. That creates a lot of paper and a lot of work but that is how the process works.

The sellers will agree to indemnify the buyer for any breaches of the representations and warranties (and any other agreements and covenants under the definitive agreement) meaning that the sellers will pay the buyer for any losses they suffer if the reps and warranties are untrue. The seller, of course, does not want to spend the rest of his or her life looking over their shoulder hoping a claim does not come out of the woodwork so that indemnification obligation will be limited to a certain time period (from 6 months to two years usually). The seller also does not want to be wiped out by an indemnity claim so the indemnity will usually be limited to some percentage of the purchase price. Finally, the seller will not want to have to deal with small claims so the indemnity will have a basket or deductible that excludes small claims from the indemnity. A basket means that until claims exceed a certain amount, they will not form the basis of a claim but, once they do, the entire amount is indemnifiable. A deductible means that the first $X of claims will be excluded from indemnifiable losses.

Parties now regularly insure against breaches of reps and warranties, which changes the dynamic a bit and has taken a lot of pressure off negotiating the reps. Insurance protects both the buyer and seller against unknown liabilities.

Most deals also have a working capital adjustment. A company will often be priced and sold on a cash free/debt free basis and assume a certain level of working capital (usually based on a historical average to avoid a seller looting a company right before close). After close, the parties will determine the actual working capital and the price will be adjusted depending on the difference between the target amount and the actual amount of working capital. Disputes are settled by the accountants.

Accountants are super important to the deal given that so much is tied to GAAP (see above). If the sellers represent that the financials are GAAP, they had better be GAAP or the seller will have to pay. Surprisingly, even financial people (or people who think they are financial) do not seem to understand GAAP. A company absolutely needs a CPA to make this determination for them. I often have to remind clients that GAAP is a manmade construct that they will not likely simply intuit. Also, GAAP can mean different things to different companies, which is why it is helpful to specify whose GAAP we are talking about.

I recently helped one of my clients sell their energy tech company to a buyer who valued the company at a multiple of EBITDA, determined in accordance with GAAP. My clients kept their books themselves on QuickBooks and did not have a CPA based on the rationale of "who needs that unnecessary expense when we are so small and the accounting is so simple?" After close, it was discovered that ending inventory was mis-stated (under GAAP), meaning that the price would have been higher if the buyer had been given the right numbers. To add insult to injury, the buyer also made a negative working capital adjustment as a result of the mis-statement. The refusal to engage a CPA cost the sellers millions.

Sometimes, sales proceeds will be escrowed to satisfy representation and warranty claims; other times it will simply be held back. Escrows are expensive and whether one is used depends on the credit worthiness of the buyer. If there are disputes over the indemnity, and there often are, the agreement will provide for a dispute resolution mechanism.

The agreement will contain numerous other agreements, clauses, covenants and conditions, all of which are to be negotiated.

Acqui-hires. Facebook CEO Mark Zuckerberg once said, "Facebook has not once bought a company for the company itself. We buy companies to get excellent people."[193] We call that an acqui-hire – an acquisition of a company for its talent rather than for its products, services, or goodwill. The buyer might not even retain the target's existing products or continue its operations. Acqui-hires are common in industries in which talent is scarce. Because so much of the deal consideration is going to the talent and less is left over for the equity, investors might not be happy about an acqui-hire and it may raise fiduciary issues. In particular, management should consider its duty of care (did it follow a reasonable process to achieve the best value for the company's stockholders?) and duty of loyalty (was the decision based on the best interests of the corporation as opposed to the interests of the management?).

Fiduciary duties and *In re Trados*. The case of *In re Trados Inc. Stockholder Litigation* shows what can happen when a sale does not benefit all of the constituents of a company. In the *Trados* case, a venture-backed company was sold for $60 million. The preferred stockholders received $52 million, management received $8 million under a management incentive plan (the "MIP") and the holders of common stock received no payments in respect of their common shares. The common stockholders sued.

Directors are protected from such lawsuits by the business judgement rule, which is generally a high bar, but not when the directors are conflicted and cannot obtain a vote of a majority of disinterested directors. In this case the directors were conflicted and were alleged to have favored the interests of the preferred stockholders at the expense of the common stockholders. Because of the conflict, a more rigorous entire fairness standard was applied to the transaction. The court was critical of the process followed by the board but, at the end of the day, delivered a defense verdict on the basis that the amount received by the common stockholders – zero – was the value of their shares.[194]

Out of the ashes of *Trados* comes some valuable lessons for startup companies considering sale. Since many venture backed companies will be conflicted and unable to rely on the lax business judgement rule when it considers a sale, it should ensure that it meets the entire fairness standard. To do so, it should identify and consider all M&A or financing alternatives, using bankers and brokers to run a good process. The board minutes should reflect this careful consideration as well as disclosures of any conflicts. Independent committees may be appropriate. *Trados* also supports seeking the approval of the common stockholders to the adoption of a common stock carve-out or similar payment plan. At the end of the day, you want the exit to be a happy event.

Chapter Thirty-seven
A Closing Success Story

This book is a collection of success stories. I opened with some success stories and now close with one of the great success stories of the Silicon Valley.

I met Martin Babinec in 1991 at a Japan Society networking event in Berkeley, California. I was establishing my law practice and Martin was building his company. Trinet was then a small business with an uncertain future. Today it is a NASDAQ listed company with $4 billion of annual revenues.

Trinet provides outsourced human resources and benefits and allows companies to consolidate their purchasing power in the insurance markets to get better rates. Martin's bold idea was to allow many small companies to compete for benefits like big companies by adopting a co-employer arrangement. That may not seem like much of a stretch today but, at the time, the business model was novel and uncertain. Moreover, the Company succeeded because Martin decided to focus on the emerging growth companies that needed Trinet's service. Most of those companies were located in Silicon Valley, and that is where Martin established and built his business despite being from upstate New York. Trinet was much like its customers –early stage, thinly capitalized and risky.

Trinet started by offering a paper intensive service. The internet boom of the 1990's changed everything. Trinet was one of the first companies to move its solution to an online environment. Instead of being disrupted by the internet, Trinet was enabled by it.

Although he did not think of Trinet as a typical startup in 1991, Martin might have been the perfect startup founder. His story is instructive.

First, Martin was a hardworking marketer. The world does not beat a path to better mousetraps, they have to be sold. Successful founders know this and are willing to roll up their sleeves and do the sales and marketing needed to get traction. Even today in an age of social media, only so much of the marketing function can be outsourced. The founder must speak for the company.

In the early days, Martin built the company largely through referrals, which required time consuming networking. Business development is hard work and not all founders have the stomach for it. Martin did not shy away from the sales function.

Secondly, Trinet was an exercise in courage. Its solution was more innovative than you might think today. The idea of a co-employer was not well established in the law and was rife with potential issues around tax, liability, employment, benefits, and more. In addition, Trinet had to deal with all of the problems around delivering a service via the internet. Much like the rideshare and gig economy businesses that have come more recently, Trinet was an internet pioneer.

Trinet also saw the value in being in the right place and the right time. Although Martin is from Upstate New York, he launched and grew his company in the Silicon Valley because that is where his market – tech startups – was located. As Martin says in his book, *More Good Jobs*:

"…had I attempted to start Trinet in Upstate New York, I would have failed. Same guy, same idea, same starting knowledge and capital position – just a different location – and there was no doubt in my mind that the business wouldn't have succeeded."

How many founders have the commitment and vision to be willing to cross the country to make their company a success?

Martin exhibited the qualities of a great founder and leader – courage, commitment, perseverance, and vision – and followed a legal strategy for success. Early on, Trinet structured its novel and innovative solutions in compliance with the law, so that when it became big enough to exit, it survived the grueling due diligence review required to go public.

These days, Martin spends his time back in Upstate New York, mentoring startups and helping to develop the region. Martin describes his journey and provides his thoughts on building entrepreneurial ecosystems in his book – *More Good Jobs*[195].

Chapter Thirty-eight
Concluding Thoughts

I hope this book has shown you some startup successes that were helped, or at least not hindered, by sound legal, tax and business planning. My hope in writing this book is to give you a sense of the importance of good legal planning and make you are aware of the major legal issues facing your startup. If you have made it to the end of this book, you are well armed to achieve startup success.

Good luck.

APPENDICES

A. Entity Comparison Chart
B. QSBS
C. Delaware Tax Memo
D. Flip Transaction
E. FAQ Stock Option Plans
F. 351
G. Independent Contractor Guidelines
H. Buy Sell Questionnaire
I. Patent Process
J. Scoggins Partnership
K. Dynamic Split
L. Founder's Pie
M. Securities Exemptions
N. SAFE
O. Forward Looking Statements
P. Risk Factors
Q. Executive Summary
R. Valuation Methods
S. Pitch Decks
T. Rule 506
U. *Donald Trump's Billion Dollar Loss: Good Tax Planning or Dubious Trick?*
V. Indemnification Agreement
W. Individual Liability for Managers/Directors and Officers
X. Tax Free Reorganizations
Y. Blind Option

Appendix A

Entity Comparison Chart

ENTITY	LLC	S Corporation	C Corporation	Partnership
Liability for Entity Debts	Members have limited liability.	Shareholders' liability limited.	Shareholders' liability limited.	General partners have unlimited liability.
Participation in Management	Flexibly determined by Operating Agreement; LLC generally managed by "manager" or managing member.	Directors and officers have management duties; shareholders not entitled to participate in management.	Directors and officers have management duties; shareholders not entitled to participate in management.	General partners have right to manage, limited partners' rights restricted to preserve limited liability.
Transferability of Interests	Securities law restrictions on transfer. Operating Agreement may also restrict transfer. A member may assign right to distributions, but assignee becomes member as provided in Operating Agreement.	Securities law restrictions and restrictions imposed by shareholders agreement, if any. Shareholders may also agree not to make transfers that would terminate S election.	Securities law restrictions and restrictions imposed by shareholders agreement, if any.	Securities law restrictions and restrictions imposed under Partnership Agreement. A partner may assign his right to distributions, but the assignee becomes a partner only if the other partners consent.
Term	Determined by Operating Agreement.	Perpetual.	Perpetual.	Determined by Partnership Agreement.
Securities Issues	Membership interests are generally securities.	Shares of stock are securities.	Shares of stock are securities.	Limited partnership interests are securities.
Entity Level Federal Income Taxes	No federal tax at LLC level unless LLC elects to be taxed as corporation	Generally no tax at S corporation level; some excise taxes, and built in gains taxes may apply	Income tax on earnings at corporate level.	No federal tax at partnership level.

ENTITY	LLC	S Corporation	C Corporation	Partnership
Number of Required Owners	Any number.	No more than 100.	Any number.	At least two.
Eligibility Requirements of Owners	No restrictions.	US citizens or resident individuals, certain trusts, and certain tax exempt entities.	No restrictions.	No restrictions.
Entity Level California Taxes	$800 minimum franchise tax plus gross receipts fee.	Minimum franchise tax of $800 or 1.5% taxable income.	State income taxes on California apportioned income ($800 minimum).	$800 minimum franchise tax on limited partnerships, no California income tax on general partnerships
Tax on Distributions of Appreciated Property	Generally, no tax to either LLC or member (certain exceptions apply).	Taxable gain on distribution passed through to shareholders.	Taxable gain to corporation and dividend to shareholders.	Generally, no tax (certain exceptions apply).
Special Allocations of Income or Deduction	Allowed, subject to substantial economic effect rules.	Not allowed - all allocations are pro rata.	Not allowed.	Allowed, subject to substantial economic effect rules.
Distribution Preferences	Allowed.	Not allowed - one class of stock requirement.	Preferred stock allowed.	Allowed.
Deductibility of losses by Owners	Members may deduct their shares of losses to extent of basis, which includes LLC level debt.	Shareholders may deduct their shares of losses to extent of basis.	No deduction at shareholder level.	Partners may deduct their shares of losses to extent of basis, which includes partnership level debt.
Self Employment and Social Security Taxes	Earnings generally subject to self employment taxes, except for earnings of limited partnership type interests.	Social security taxes imposed on wages of employee-owners/ no self employment tax on distributions.	Social security taxes imposed on wages of employee-owners/ no self employment tax on distributions.	Earnings generally subject to self employment taxes, except for earnings attributable to limited partnership interests.

ENTITY	LLC	S Corporation	C Corporation	Partnership
Non-Taxable Fringe Benefits (group health insurance, accident or health benefits, meals or lodging, cafeteria plan benefits)	Cash value of fringe benefits generally not excludable from member's income.	Cash value of fringe benefits generally not excludable from owner-employee's income.	Deductible by corporation - not included in income of employee.	Cash value of fringe benefits generally not excludable from partner's income.
Option Plans, NSO's, ISO's	Employees & consultants can be given options to acquire LLC interests, but such options are generally more complex. ISO's not available.	ISO's commonly granted to employees. NSO's may be granted to consultants and advisors.	ISO's commonly granted to employees. NSO's may be granted to consultants and advisors.	Employees & consultants can be given options to acquire partnership interests, but such options are generally more complex. ISO's not available.
Adjustments to Basis on Death of Owner	Inside basis may be adjusted on death or transfer under Code section 754.	No Section 754 adjustments to basis.	No Section 754 adjustments to basis.	Inside basis may be adjusted on death or transfer under Code section 754.
Increase in Basis for Debt	Members increase outside basis by share of LLC debt.	No increase in basis in stock for corporate level debt.	No increase in basis in stock for corporate level debt.	Partners increase outside basis by share of partnership debt.
Treatment of Foreign Owners	Foreign members subject to US tax on their share of effectively connected income of LLC; branch profits tax may apply.	Foreigners cannot be shareholders of S corporation.	Foreigners are subject to withholding tax on dividends from US corporation, subject to treaty rate or exemption.	Foreign partners subject to US tax on their share of partnership's effectively connected income; branch profits tax may apply.
Foreign Individual Owners - Transfer Taxes	Membership interest may be subject to US estate and gift taxes.	N/A. Foreigners cannot be shareholders of S corporation.	Corporate stock is not US situs asset for gift tax purposes.	Partnership interest may be subject to US estate and gift taxes.

ENTITY	LLC	S Corporation	C Corporation	Partnership
Conversion to Another Entity	May be incorporated tax free.	Can convert to C corporation by revoking election; may be tax on converting to LLC.	Can convert to S corporation by making election (built in gains tax may apply to later dispositions of appreciated property). Conversion to LLC may be taxable.	Easily converted to LLC or incorporated tax free.
Taxes on Sale or Liquidation	One level of tax, generally capital gain except for amount allocable to certain assets.	One level of tax on sale of stock or assets, generally capital gain on stock sale.	Potential double tax. Corporate tax on sale of assets. Shareholder level tax on sale of stock or liquidation	One level of tax, generally capital gain except for amount allocable to certain assets
Self Employment and Social Security Taxes	Earnings generally subject to self employment taxes, except for earnings of limited partnership type interests.	Social security taxes imposed on wages of employee-owners/ no self employment tax on distributions.	Social security taxes imposed on wages of employee-owners/ no self employment tax on distributions.	Earnings generally subject to self employment taxes, except for earnings attributable to limited partnership interests.
Non-Taxable Fringe Benefits (group health insurance, accident or health benefits, meals or lodging, cafeteria plan benefits)	Cash value of fringe benefits generally not excludable from member's income or deductible by LLC.	Cash value of fringe benefits generally not excludable from owner-employee's income or deductible by S corporation.	Deductible by corporation - not included in income of employee.	Cash value of fringe benefits generally not excludable from partner's income or deductible by partnership.
Option Plans, NSO's, ISO's	Employees & consultants can be given options to acquire LLC interests, but such options are generally more complex. ISO's not available.	ISO's commonly granted to employees. NSO's may be granted to consultants and advisors.	ISO's commonly granted to employees. NSO's may be granted to consultants and advisors.	Employees & consultants can be given options to acquire partnership interests, but such options are generally more complex. ISO's not available.

ENTITY	LLC	S Corporation	C Corporation	Partnership
Adjustments to Basis on Death of Owner	Inside basis may be adjusted on death or transfer under Code section 754.	No Section 754 adjustments to basis.	No Section 754 adjustments to basis.	Inside basis may be adjusted on death or transfer under Code section 754.
Termination on Transfer of Interests	LLC terminates for tax purposes on transfer of 50% or more of capital and profits in 12 mos.	No termination of entity on transfer of interests.	No termination of entity on transfer of interests.	LLC terminates for tax purposes on transfer of 50% or more of capital and profits in 12 mos.
Increase in Basis for Debt	Members increase outside basis by share of LLC debt.	No increase in basis in stock for corporate level debt. Exception for shareholder debt.	No increase in basis in stock for corporate level debt.	Partners increase outside basis by share of partnership debt.
Treatment of Foreign Owners	Foreign members subject to US tax on their share of effectively connected income of LLC; branch profits tax may apply.	Foreigners cannot be shareholders of S corporation. Exception for ESBT.	Foreigners are subject to withholding tax on dividends from US corporation, subject to treaty rate or exemption.	Foreign partners subject to US tax on their share of partnership's effectively connected income; branch profits tax may apply.
Foreign Individual Owners - Transfer Taxes	Membership interest may be subject to US estate and gift taxes.	N/A. Foreigners cannot be shareholders of S corporation.	Corporate stock is not US situs asset for gift tax purposes.	Partnership interest may be subject to US estate and gift taxes.
Conversion to Another Entity	May be incorporated tax free.	Can convert to C corporation by revoking election; may be tax on converting to LLC.	Can convert to S corporation by making election (built in gains tax may apply to later dispositions of appreciated property). Conversion to LLC may be taxable.	Easily converted to LLC or incorporated tax free.

Appendix B

QSBS

This appendix provides an overview of the federal capital gain exclusion available on the sale of certain qualified small business stock ("QSBS") under Section 1202 of the Internal Revenue Code of 1986, as amended. In general, a non-corporate taxpayer can exclude 50%, 75% or 100% of the gain (depending on when the QSBS was issued) arising on the sale of QSBS held for at least five (5) years under U.S. federal income tax rules.

Criteria for Gain Exclusion on the Sale of QSBS

The four main requirements to qualify for QSBS relief on the sale of stock are: (1) the stock sold is stock of a C corporation acquired at original issuance; (2) the issuing corporation is a qualified small business; (3) the issuing corporation had an active trade or business during substantially all of the taxpayer's holding period; and (4) the QSBS was held for at least five years prior to the sale.

A. Stock of a C Corporation Acquired at Original Issuance

The issuing corporation must be an "eligible corporation" which is any domestic C corporation except:

(1) a current or former "domestic international sales corporation"; (2) a regulated investment company , real estate investment trust , or real estate mortgage investment conduit ; (3) a cooperative.

QSBS must be acquired at the original issuance in exchange for money, property, or as compensation for services. The term "property" generally encompasses anything of value; however the IRS takes a narrower view where the property transferred is intellectual property. In this case, the transfer must be one of substantially all the rights to the intellectual property.

There are exceptions to the original issuance requirement for stock received by way of gift or upon the death of the holder, or for stock received in a Section 368 reorganization.

B.   Qualified Small Business

The "qualified small business" test is met where the corporation has "aggregate gross assets" of not more than $50 million at all times from September 1993 (the enactment of the QSBS exclusion) to the date immediately after the issuance of the stock in question. "Aggregate gross assets" means the cash and the aggregate adjusted bases of all other property held by the corporation. Generally, the assets of subsidiary corporations are included when calculating the aggregate gross assets of a parent company.

C.   Active Business Requirement

The corporation must meet the active business requirement for substantially all of the taxpayer's holding period. To meet the active business requirement, at least 80% of the corporation's assets must be used in a "qualified trade or business." A "qualified trade or business" is any business except:

(1) businesses providing services such as healthcare, law, engineering, architecture, accounting, athletics, financial services, etc.; (2) banking, insurance, or similar businesses; (3) farming businesses; (4) certain oil and gas businesses; and (5) hotel, restaurant, or similar businesses.

D.   Five Year Holding Period

For gain exclusion on the sale of QSBS, the taxpayer must hold the qualifying stock for five years from the date of issuance. In circumstances such as the transfer of stock via a gift there may be tacking of the holding period such that the new stock is considered held for the length of time attributable to the previous owner. Similarly, in the case of stock received in a Section 368 reorganization, the holding period of the new stock may include the holding period of the stock exchanged.

E.   Gain Exclusion on the Sale of QSBS

On the sale of QSBS, a taxpayer's income shall not include 50% of the gain on the sale of the stock. The 50% exclusion has been increased in recent years, such that a gain on stock issued after September 28, 2010 will qualify for a 100% exclusion. Stock issued in 2009 but before September 28, 2010 qualifies for a gain exclusion of 75%.[20]

The amount of gain that a taxpayer can take into account for QSBS relief in any one tax year is the greater of $10 million or ten (10) times the aggregate adjusted bases of the stock disposed of in the year. The cap on the gain likely applies to the total gain before the application of the exclusion. Therefore, if the exclusion rate is 50% and the $10 million cap applies, the maximum gain that can likely be excluded is $5 million per taxpayer per tax year.

Appendix C
Delaware Tax Memo

All domestic corporations formed or doing business in Delaware are required to file an Annual Franchise Tax Report ("Report") and pay a Franchise Tax ("Tax") in order to avoid paying a $125 late fee and interest at 1.5% per month is applied to any unpaid tax balance. Domestic corporations must file the Report and pay both a $50 filing fee and the Tax owed by March 1 of each year. The Delaware Division of Corporations now requires filing and payment to be completed on-line at http://corp.delaware.gov/paytaxes.shtml. Failure by the corporation to the file the Report and pay the Tax by March 1 of each year, the Delaware Secretary of State shall place the corporation out of good standing. Should the Report not be filed for three consecutive years, the Delaware Secretary of State can void the corporation.

One of two methods can be used to determining the Tax: 1) Authorized Shares Method and 2) Assumed Par Value Method. Two factors are used to determine the Tax liability within the Assumed Par Value Method – the number of outstanding shares issued and the total gross assets of the corporation as of December 31st of each year. For start-up corporations and emerging growth corporations, using the Assumed Par Value Method should greatly reduce the Tax.

For corporations in which 5,000 shares or less are authorized, the Authorized Shares Method should be used and the Tax shall be $175, plus $50 for filing the Report for a total of $225 being owned. For corporations in which more than 5,000 shares are authorized, in most cases, the Assumed Par Value Method should be used to determine the Tax and the minimum amount owed will be $350, plus $50 for filing the Report for a total of $400 being owed.

Please note that when the Report is viewed online, the Delaware Division of Corporations uses the Authorized Shares Method as the default method to determine the Tax since the total number of shares issued and the gross assets are not known at the time of filing.　This results in a huge tax liability being shown as owed.　Using the Assumed Par Value Method should result in a much lower and reasonably Tax liability.

To use the Assumed Par Value Method, please follow the steps below:

1. Access the Delaware Division of Corporations at http://corp. delaware.gov/paytaxes.shtml

2. Click on "Click Here to Pay Taxes/ File Annual Report"

3. Enter the seven digit DE file number.　This number is contained on the filed Certificate of Incorporation.　Should you not know the number, you can conduct a search using the name of the Corporation to determine its file number.

4. Click on "Continue"

5. Enter the number of issued shares as of December 31 of the previous tax year for each type of authorized stock

6. Enter the total issued shares for each type of authorized stock

7. Enter the total gross assets of the Corporation as of December 31

8. Enter 12/31 and the last two numbers of the end of the last tax year

9. Click on "recalculate tax" and the tax owed shall be updated

10. Disclose the principal place of business and the officers and directors as of the date in which the Report is filed

11. Complete the authorization field

12. Click on "Continue Filing" then process payment with a credit/ debit card

13. Once the Report has been filed and taxes paid, you should print out a copy of the filed Report and retain with your records.

Corporations that owe $5,000.00 or more must also pay estimated Tax in quarterly installments with 40% due on June 1, 20% due by September 1, 20% due by December 1, and the remained due on March 1.

Appendix D
Flip Transaction

The Inbound Flip Transaction

Description: The shareholders create a new US entity ("Domco"), and exchange their Forco stock for Domco stock. After the exchange, the shareholders will own Domco, and Domco will own Forco. Angel investors and venture capital funds would invest at the Domco level.

Appendix E
Stock Option Plans

This explanation provides a brief summary of the tax consequences of exercising an option. This explanation is no substitute for personal tax advice:

Limit on ISO Treatment

The Notice of Stock Option Grant indicates whether an option is a nonstatutory stock option (NSO) or an incentive stock option (ISO). The favorable tax treatment for ISOs is limited, regardless of what the Notice of Stock Option Grant indicates. Of the options that become exercisable in any calendar year, only options covering the first $100,000 of stock are eligible for ISO treatment. The excess over $100,000 automatically receives NSO treatment. For this purpose, stock is valued at the time of grant. This means that the value is generally equal to the exercise price.

For example, assume that you hold an option to buy 50,000 shares for $4 per share. Assume further that the entire option is exercisable immediately after the date of grant. (It is irrelevant when the underlying stock vests.) Only the first 25,000 shares qualify for ISO treatment. (25,000 times $4 equals $100,000.) The remaining 25,000 shares will be treated as if they had been acquired by exercising an NSO. This is true regardless of when the option is *actually* exercised; what matters is when it first *could* have been exercised.

Exercise of Nonstatutory Stock Option to Purchase Vested Shares

The Notice of Stock Option Grant indicates whether your Purchased Shares are already vested. Vested shares are no longer subject to the Company's right to repurchase them at the exercise price, although they are still subject to the Company's right of first refusal. If you know that your Purchased Shares are already vested, there is no need to file a section 83(b) election.

If you are exercising an NSO to purchase vested shares, you will be taxed now. You will recognize ordinary income in an amount equal to the difference between (a) the fair market value of the Purchased Shares on the date of exercise and (b) the exercise price you are paying. If you are an employee or former employee of the Company, this amount is subject to withholding for income and payroll taxes. Your tax basis in the Purchased Shares (to calculate capital gain when you sell the shares) is equal to their fair market value on the date of exercise.

Exercise of NSO to Purchase Non-Vested Shares

If you are exercising an NSO to purchase non-vested shares, and if you do not file a timely election under section 83(b) of the Internal Revenue Code, then you will not be taxed now. Instead, you will be taxed whenever an increment of Purchased Shares vests—in other words, when the Company no longer has the right to repurchase those shares at the exercise price. The Notice of Stock Option Grant indicates when this occurs, generally over a period of several years. Whenever an increment of Purchased Shares vests, you will recognize ordinary income in an amount equal to the difference between (a) the fair market value of those Purchased Shares on the date of vesting and (b) the exercise price you are paying for those Purchased Shares. If you are an employee or former employee of the Company, this amount will be subject to withholding for income and payroll taxes. Your tax basis in the Purchased Shares (to calculate capital gain when you sell the shares) will be equal to their fair market value on the date of vesting.

If you are exercising an NSO to purchase non-vested shares, and if you file a timely election under section 83(b) of the Internal Revenue Code, then you will be taxed now. You will recognize ordinary income in an amount equal to the difference between (a) the fair market value of the Purchased Shares on the date of exercise and (b) the exercise price you are paying. If you are an employee or former employee of the Company, this amount is subject to withholding for income and payroll taxes. Your tax basis in the Purchased Shares (to calculate capital gain when you sell the shares) is equal to their fair market value on the date of exercise. Even if the fair market value of the Purchased Shares on the date of exercise equals the exercise price (and thus no tax is payable), the section 83(b) election must be made in order to avoid having any subsequent appreciation taxed as ordinary income at the time of vesting.

YOU MUST FILE A SECTION 83(B) ELECTION WITH THE INTERNAL REVENUE SERVICE WITHIN 30 DAYS AFTER THE NOTICE OF STOCK OPTION EXERCISE IS SIGNED. The 30-day filing period cannot be extended. If you miss the deadline, you will be taxed as the Purchased Shares vest, based on the value of the shares at that time. (See above.) The form for making the 83(b) election is attached. Additional copies of the form must be filed with the Company and with your tax return for the year in which you make the election.

EXERCISE OF ISO AND ISO HOLDING PERIODS

If you are exercising an ISO, you will not be taxed under the *regular* tax rules until you dispose of the Purchased Shares.[1] (The alternative minimum tax rules are described below.) The tax treatment at the time of disposition depends on how long you hold the shares. You will satisfy the ISO holding periods if you hold the Purchased Shares until the *later* of the following dates:

- The date two years after the ISO was granted, and
- The date one year after the ISO is exercised.

DISPOSITION OF ISO SHARES

If you dispose of the Purchased Shares after satisfying *both* of the ISO holding periods, then you will recognize only a long-term capital gain at the time of

---

1   Generally, a "disposition" of shares purchased under an ISO encompasses any transfer of legal title, such as a transfer by sale, exchange or gift. It generally does not include a transfer to your spouse, a transfer into joint ownership with right of survivorship (if you remain one of the joint owners), a pledge, a transfer by bequest or inheritance, or certain tax-free exchanges permitted under the Internal Revenue Code. A transfer to a trust is a "disposition" unless the trust is an eligible revocable trust, as described in the attached explanation.

disposition. The amount of the capital gain is equal to the difference between (a) the sales proceeds and (b) the exercise price. In general, the maximum marginal federal income tax rate on long-term capital gains is 20%.

If you dispose of the Purchased Shares before either or both of the ISO holding periods are met, then you will recognize ordinary income at the time of disposition. The calculation of the ordinary income amount depends on whether the shares are vested at the time of exercise.

- **Shares Vested**. If the shares are vested at the time of exercise, the amount of ordinary income will be equal to the difference between (a) the fair market value of the Purchased Shares on the date of exercise and (b) the exercise price. But if the disposition is an arm's length sale to an unrelated party, the amount of ordinary income will not exceed the total gain from the sale. Under current IRS rules, the ordinary income amount will not be subject to withholding for income or payroll taxes. Your tax basis in the Purchased Shares will be equal to their fair market value on the date of exercise. Any gain in excess of your basis will be taxed as a capital gain—either long-term or short-term, depending on how long you hold the Purchased Shares after the date of exercise.

- **Shares Not Vested—No 83(b) Election Filed**. If the Purchased Shares are not vested at the time of exercise, and if you do not file a timely election under section 83(b) of the Internal Revenue Code, then the amount of ordinary income will be equal to the difference between (a) the fair market value of the Purchased Shares on the date of vesting and (b) the exercise price. But if the disposition is an arm's length sale to an unrelated party, the amount of ordinary income will not exceed the total gain from the sale. Under current IRS rules, the ordinary income amount will not be subject to withholding for income or payroll taxes. Your tax basis in the Purchased Shares will be equal to their fair market value on the date of vesting. Any gain in excess of your basis will be taxed as a capital gain—either long-term or short-term, depending on how long you hold the Purchased Shares after the date of vesting.

- **Shares Not Vested—Timely 83(b) Election Filed.** If the shares are not vested at the time of exercise, and if you file a timely election under section 83(b) of the Internal Revenue Code, then the amount of ordinary income should be equal to the difference between (a) the fair market value of the Purchased Shares on the date of exercise and (b) the exercise price. In other words, the 83(b) election should cause the ordinary income to be calculated as if the shares were vested at the time of exercise. All other rules described above for the purchase of vested shares by exercising an ISO apply here as well. **You must file an 83(b) election with the Internal Revenue Service within 30 days after the Notice of Stock Option Exercise is signed.** The 30-day filing period cannot be extended. Note that, in the case of an ISO, the 83(b) election does not trigger an immediate tax; it merely affects how the ordinary income should be calculated when you dispose of the Purchased Shares. If you miss the filing deadline, the amount of your ordinary income will be based on the value of the Purchased Shares at the time they vest. (See above.) The form for making the 83(b) election is attached. Additional copies of the form must be filed with the Company and with your tax return for the year in which you make the election.

You may not know at this time whether you will dispose of your Purchased Shares before meeting the two holding periods. You should nevertheless consider filing an 83(b) election. If you meet the holding periods, the election will be moot for purposes of the *regular* tax system, since you will have no ordinary income. (The effect of the election under the alternative minimum tax system is discussed below.) If you do not satisfy the holding periods, then the election should take effect and should limit your ordinary income to the gain that existed at the time of exercise.

It is not certain that an 83(b) election is effective in conjunction with an ISO. The Internal Revenue Service may take the position that the 83(b) election—even if filed on time—must be disregarded for purposes of the regular tax system. The Company strongly encourages you to consult your own tax adviser before exercising an ISO and before making a decision about filing or not filing a section 83(b) election in conjunction with an ISO.

Summary of Alternative Minimum Tax

The alternative minimum tax (AMT) must be paid if it exceeds your regular income tax. The AMT is equal to 26% of your alternative minimum tax base up to \$_____ and 28% of the excess over \$_____. (In the case of married individuals filing separately, the breakpoint is \$_____ rather than \$_____.) Your alternative minimum tax base is equal to your alternative minimum taxable income (AMTI) minus your exemption amount.

- **Alternative Minimum Taxable Income**. Your AMTI is equal to your regular taxable income, subject to certain adjustments and increased by items of tax preference. Among the many adjustments made in computing AMTI are the following:
    - State and local income and property taxes are not allowed as a deduction.
    - Miscellaneous itemized deductions are not allowed.
    - Medical expenses are not allowed as a deduction until they exceed 10% of adjusted gross income (as opposed to the 7.5% floor that applies to regular income taxes).
    - Certain interest deductions are not allowed.
    - The standard deduction and personal exemptions are not allowed.
    - When an ISO is exercised, the spread is treated as if the option were an NSO. (See discussion below.)
- **Exemption Amount**. Before AMT is calculated, AMTI is reduced by the exemption amount. The exemption amount is as follows:

Joint Returns: \$_____	Single Returns: \$_____	Separate Returns: \$_____

The exemption amount is phased out by 25 cents for each \$1 by which AMTI exceeds the following levels:

| Joint Returns: $_____ | Single Returns: $_____ | Separate Returns: $_____ |

This means, for example, that the entire $45,000 exemption amount disappears for married individuals filing joint returns when AMTI reaches $330,000.

Application of AMT When ISO Is Exercised

As noted above, when an ISO is exercised, the spread is treated for AMT purposes as if the option were an NSO. In other words, the spread is included in AMTI at the time of exercise, unless the Purchased Shares are not yet vested at the time of exercise. If the Purchased Shares are not yet vested, the value of the shares minus the exercise price is included in AMTI when the shares vest. If you make an election under section 83(b) within 30 days after exercise, then the spread is included in AMTI at the time of exercise. **You MUST FILE AN 83(b) ELECTION WITH THE INTERNAL REVENUE SERVICE WITHIN 30 DAYS AFTER THE NOTICE OF STOCK OPTION EXERCISE IS SIGNED**. The 30-day filing period cannot be extended.

A special rule applies if you dispose of the Purchased Shares in the same year in which you exercised the ISO. If the amount you realize on the sale is less than the value of the stock at the time of exercise, then the amount includible in AMTI on account of the ISO exercise is limited to the gain realized on the sale.[2]

To the extent that your AMT is attributable to the spread on exercising an ISO (and certain other items), the AMT paid may be applied as a credit against your *regular* income tax liability in future years. But this tax credit cannot reduce your regular income tax liability in any future tax year below your AMT for that year. The AMT credit may be carried forward indefinitely, but it may not be carried back. (In practice, many optionees who paid AMT

---

[2]   This is similar to the rule that applies under the regular tax system in the event of a disqualifying disposition of ISO stock. The amount of ordinary income that must be recognized in that case generally does not exceed the amount of the gain realized in the disposition.

upon exercising an ISO find that they cannot fully use this tax credit for many years, if at all.)

When Purchased Shares are sold, your basis for purposes of computing the capital gain or loss under the AMT system is increased by the option spread that exists at the time of exercise. Again, an ISO is treated under the AMT system much like an NSO is treated under the regular tax system. But your basis in the ISO shares for purposes of computing gain or loss under the regular tax system is equal to the exercise price; it does *not* reflect any AMT that you pay on the spread at exercise. Therefore, if you pay AMT in the year of the ISO exercise and regular income tax in the year of selling the Purchased Shares, you could pay tax twice on the same gain (except to the extent that you can use the AMT credit described above).

Section 83(b) Election

This statement is made under Sections 55 and 83(b) of the Internal Revenue Code of 1986, as amended, pursuant to Treasury Regulations Section 1.83-2.

A.   The taxpayer who performed the services is:

Name: _____

Address: _____

Social Security No.:   _____

B.   The property with respect to which the election is made is _____ shares of the common stock of _____ .

C.   The property was transferred on _____ _____ , _____ .

D.   The taxable year for which the election is made is the calendar year _____ .

E.   The property is subject to a repurchase right pursuant to which the issuer has the right to acquire the property at the original purchase price if for any reason taxpayer's service with the issuer terminates. The issuer's repurchase right lapses in a series of installments over a _____-year period ending on _____ _____ ,

_____ .

F.   The fair market value of such property at the time of transfer (determined without regard to any restriction other than a restriction which by its terms will never lapse) is _____ per share.

G.   The amount paid for such property is _____ per share.

H.   A copy of this statement was furnished to _____ , for whom taxpayer rendered the services underlying the transfer of such property.

_____   _____

Signature of Spouse (if any)   Signature of Taxpayer

Within 30 days after the date of exercise, this election must be filed with the Internal Revenue Service Center where the Optionee files his or her federal income tax returns. The filing should be made by registered or certified mail, return receipt requested. The Optionee must (a) file a copy of the completed form with his or her federal tax return for the current tax year and (b) deliver an additional copy to the Company.

Appendix F
351

IRC section 351. General rule. No gain or loss shall be recognized if property is transferred to a corporation by one or more persons solely in exchange for stock in such corporation, and immediately after the exchange such person or persons are in control—as defined in IRC section 368(c)—of the corporation.

Control. The term control means the ownership of stock possessing at least 80% of the total combined voting power of all classes of stock entitled to vote and at least 80% of the total number of shares of all other classes of stock of the corporation. IRC §368(c). A group of investors can combine to meet the 80% control requirement.

Property. Stock must be issued for property. Services do not qualify as property but the property created by services does. Know-how, trade secrets and processes may be considered property for purposes of IRC section 351. (Rev. Rul. 64-56)

Immediately after the exchange. Control of the corporation immediately after the exchange includes agreements where the rights of the parties have been previously defined, and execution of the agreement proceeds in a timely manner consistent with the agreement. Treas. Reg. §1.351-1(a)(1). However, a transferor may fail this prong if the transferor is obligated or transfers control after the exchange.

Solely in exchange for stock. If the transferor receives property other than stock in the exchange ("boot"), gain is realized to the extent of the money or other property received. IRC §351(b).

Nonqualified transactions. Section 351 does not apply to transfers to investment companies, transfers in a bankruptcy or similar proceeding in exchange for stock used to pay creditors or if stock is received in exchange for the corporation's debt.

Nonqualified preferred stock. Nonqualified preferred stock is treated as boot and does not count for purposes of the 80% control test. Nonqualified preferred stock means preferred stock if:

The holder of the stock has the right to require the issuer or a related person to redeem or purchase the stock,

The issuer or a related person is required to redeem or purchase the stock,

The issuer or a related person has the right to redeem or purchase the stock and, as of the issue date, it is more likely than not that such right will be exercised, or

The dividend rate on such stock varies in whole or in part (directly or indirectly) with reference to interest rates, commodity prices, or other similar indices. IRC §351(g).

Liabilities. A corporation can assume liability without triggering gain except for debt in excess of basis. IRC §357(a)]. The shareholder's basis in stock is reduced by the amount of liability transferred. If the liability assumed by the corporation is more than the contributing shareholder's adjusted basis, the excess is treated as gain. Even if the shareholder remains liable on the debt, gain maybe recognized. *Seggerman Farms Inc. v. Comr.*, 308 F.3d 803 (7th Cir. 2002).

Shareholder's Basis. A shareholder's basis in stock is the adjusted basis of the contributed property plus gain recognized and cash paid, less cash and property received and liabilities assumed. If the basis of the property transferred exceeds its fair market value, the parties may elect to treat the basis of the stock received as having a basis equal to the fair market value of the property transferred.

Corporation's Basis. The corporation's basis in contributed property is the shareholder's basis plus gain recognized by the shareholder on the transfer.

<u>Holding period</u>. The holding period for stock received includes the time the shareholder held the property before the exchange. The corporation's holding period for the contributed property includes the time the property was held by the shareholder.

<u>Reporting</u>. The corporation and significant transferors (1% or more of a privately held company) must attach a statement to their income tax returns.

Appendix G

Independent Contractor Guidelines

In determining whether a service provider is an employee or an independent contractor, the IRS will consider the degree of control and independence.

<u>Common Law Rules (IRS Publication 15-A)</u>

Facts that provide evidence of the degree of control and independence fall into three categories:

1 <u>Behavioral control</u>: Does the company control or have the right to control what the worker does and how the worker does his or her job? Facts that show whether the business has a right to direct and control how the worker does the task for which the worker is hired include the type and degree of:

<u>Instructions that the business gives to the worker</u>. An employee is generally subject to the business' instructions about when, where, and how to work. All of the following are examples of types of instructions about how to do work.

- When and where to do the work.
- What tools or equipment to use.
- What workers to hire or to assist with the work.
- Where to purchase supplies and services.
- What work must be performed by a specified individual.
- What order or sequence to follow.

The amount of instruction needed varies among different jobs. Even if no instructions are given, sufficient behavioral control may exist if the employer has the right to control how the work results are achieved. A business may lack the knowledge to instruct some highly specialized professionals; in other cases, the task may require little or no instruction. The key consideration is whether the business has retained the right to control the details of a worker's performance or instead has given up that right.

Training that the business gives to the worker. An employee may be trained to perform services in a particular manner. Independent contractors ordinarily use their own methods.

2. Financial control: Are the business aspects of the worker's job controlled by the payer? Facts that show whether the business has a right to control the business aspects of the worker's job include:

The extent to which the worker has unreimbursed business expenses. Independent contractors are more likely to have unreimbursed expenses than are employees. Fixed ongoing costs that are incurred regardless of whether work is currently being performed are especially important. However, employees may also incur unreimbursed expenses in connection with the services that they perform for their employer.

The extent of the worker's investment. An independent contractor often has a significant investment in the facilities or tools he or she uses in performing services for someone else. However, a significant investment isn't necessary for independent contractor status.

The extent to which the worker makes his or her services available to the relevant market. An independent contractor is generally free to seek out business opportunities. Independent contractors often advertise, maintain a visible business location, and are available to work in the relevant market.

How the business pays the worker. An employee is generally guaranteed a regular wage amount for an hourly, weekly, or other period of time. This usually indicates that a worker is an employee, even when the wage or salary is supplemented by a commission. An independent contractor is often paid a flat fee or on a time and materials basis for the job. However, it is common in some professions, such as law, to pay independent contractors hourly.

The extent to which the worker can realize a profit or loss. An independent contractor can make a profit or loss.

3. Type of Relationship: Are there written contracts or employee type benefits (i.e. pension plan, insurance, vacation pay, etc.)? Will the relationship continue and is the work performed a key aspect of the business? Facts that show the parties' type of relationship include:

- Written contracts describing the relationship the parties intended to create.

- Whether or not the business provides the worker with employee-type benefits, such as insurance, a pension plan, vacation pay, or sick pay.

- The permanency of the relationship. If you engage a worker with the expectation that the relationship will continue indefinitely, rather than for a specific project or period, this is generally considered evidence that your intent was to create an employer-employee relationship.

- The extent to which services performed by the worker are a key aspect of the regular business of the company. If a worker provides services that are a key aspect of your regular business activity, it is more likely that you'll have the right to direct and control his or her activities. For example, if a law firm hires an attorney, it is likely that it will present the attorney's work as its own and would have the right to control or direct that work. This would indicate an employer-employee relationship.

https://www.irs.gov/businesses/small-businesses-self-employed/independent-contractor-self-employed-or-employee

California AB-5 (the *ABC Test*).

A worker is presumed to be an employee unless all of the following tests are satisfied:

A. Worker is free from control and direction of hiring authority,
B. Worker performs work outside the usual course of the hiring entity's business, and
C. Worker is engaged in an independently established trade, occupation of business of the same nature.

AB-2257 contains numerous carveouts and exceptions.

Appendix H

Buy Sell Questionnaire

Date: _____   File No.: _____

Corporation: _____

Telephone #: _____   Fax #: _____

Shareholders:

Name	Address	Number of Shares

Total Number of Shares outstanding: _____

RIGHT OF FIRST REFUSAL.

Will the company have a right of first refusal for each shareholder's shares?
_____

Will the Company's right of first refusal be assignable to the other Shareholders?
_____ If so, is the right of first refusal assignable to shareholders in proportion to share ownership or as the directors determine? _____

Is the Company's purchase price

    (i)   the third party offer price? _____ or

    (ii)   fair market value as determined by the Board of Directors? _____

Must the Company close the purchase in cash? Or can in make payments in installments? If so, over how long a period?

How is the purchase price determined in the case of an involuntary transfer (e.g. by death of a shareholder)? _____ (e.g. appraisal, financial consultants, arbitration)

Is a transfer to a family member (or family trust) subject to the Company's right of first refusal?

SHAREHOLDER TERMINATION PURCHASE RIGHTS.

Upon what events must a shareholder offer his shares to the company?

    _____ Death

    _____ Disability

    _____ Termination of employment with the Company

    _____ Bankruptcy

    _____ Insolvency

At what price?

    Formula (please specify)

    Appraised Value

    Value determined by arbitrators or appraisers

    Previously Agreed Value (please specify)

Is the Company required to purchase part, all or none of those shares? _____

SPOUSAL RIGHTS

On divorce of a shareholder:

    The shareholder's spouse (Spouse) must offer the shares to the Company;

    The Spouse must offer the shares to the shareholder;

    The Spouse's shares convert to nonvoting shares;

LIFE INSURANCE

    Will the repurchase of shares on death be funded by insurance? _____

    Who owns the policy?

_____ The Company pays the premiums and is the beneficiary of the policy proceeds.

_____ The Company pays the premiums and the shareholders are the beneficiaries of the policy proceeds, and must _____ / may _____ use the proceeds to by the decedent's shares.

_____ The shareholders pay the premiums and are the beneficiaries of the policy proceeds, and must _____ / may _____ use the proceeds to by the decedent's shares.

INTERNAL DISSENSION

Should the agreement contain provisions regarding procedures in the case of a deadlock? _____

Blind Option _____

Company Repurchase Option _____

SHAREHOLDER WILLS

Are the shareholders obligated to amend their wills to direct their executor to comply with this agreement?

Appendix I

Patent Process*

Step 1

Determine the type of Intellectual Property protection that you need. To protect your invention, you may need a patent, trademark, copyright, marketing plan, trade secrets, or some combination of these. Before you begin preparing a patent application, find out if you really need a patent or some other form of Intellectual Property protection.

Step 2

Determine if your invention is patentable. To determine if you can patent your invention, you will need to know the answers to a few simple questions.

> Who can apply for a patent?
> What can and cannot be patented?
> How do I know if my invention is patentable?
> How long does patent protection last?
> How much does it cost to get a patent?

You cannot get a patent if your invention has already been publicly disclosed. Therefore, a search of all previous public disclosures should be conducted. A search of foreign patents and printed publications should also be conducted. If you are not experienced at performing patent searches, a registered attorney or agent is recommended.

Step 3

What kind of patent do you need?

There are three types of patents - Utility, Design, and Plant.

Utility Patent. Utility patents may be granted to anyone who invents or discovers any new and useful process, machine, article of manufacture, or compositions of matters, or any new useful improvement thereof. By far, most patent applications filed at the USPTO are utility applications.

Design Patent. Design patents may be granted to anyone who invents a new, original, and ornamental design for an article of manufacture.

Plant Patent. Plant patents may be granted to anyone who invents or discovers and asexually reproduces any distinct and new variety of plant.

Step 4

Get ready to apply. Once you have determined the type of Patent that you need, you can consider your application strategy and whether to use professional legal services. A patent application is subject to the payment of a basic fee and additional fees that include a search fee, an examination fee, and issue fee. Depending on your application, there may also be excess claims fees. Fees vary depending on the type of patent application that you submit. See the Patents Data Visualization Center for an overall average First Office Action estimate and Total Pendency.

Consider expedited examination options. The USPTO Patent Application Initiatives Timeline displays various programs and initiatives that are available to applicants during each phase of the application process. Each program is designed to advance the progress of a patent application and to provide applicant assistance. View a detailed Matrix of programs available Prior to Examination.

Do you need International protection?

Do you want to file a Provisional or Nonprovisional application?

Utility and Plant patent applications can be filled using either a provisional or nonprovisional application. A provisional application is a quick and inexpensive way for inventors to establish a U.S. filing date for their invention which can be claimed in a later filed nonprovisional application.

Should you hire a Patent Attorney or Agent?

The preparation of an application for patent and the conducting of the proceedings in the United States Patent and Trademark Office (USPTO or Office) to obtain the patent is an undertaking requiring the knowledge of patent law and rules and Office practice and procedures, as well as knowledge of the scientific or technical matters involved in the particular invention.

Inventors may prepare their own applications and file them in the USPTO and conduct the proceedings themselves, but unless they are familiar with these matters or study them in detail, they may get into considerable difficulty. While a patent may be obtained in many cases by persons not skilled in this work, there would be no assurance that the patent obtained would adequately protect the particular invention.

Most inventors employ the services of registered patent attorneys or patent agents

Step 5

Prepare and submit your initial application. See the Patent Application Guides for the detailed legal requirements for filing the type of Patent Application you have determined is right for you. Submit your initial application with all the required parts needed for obtaining a filing date and include the correct fee.

Submit your application online: Use EFS-Web, the USPTO's electronic filing system for patent applications, to submit Utility patent applications, Provisional applications and many other types of Office correspondence to the USPTO via the Internet.

Before you sign your application, make sure that you read the written specification and claims. You will not be able to add anything new to your application once it has been filed with the USPTO.

Step 6

Work with your examiner. If your application is incomplete, you will be notified of the deficiencies by an official letter from the USPTO, known as an Office Action. You will be given a time period to complete the application filing (a surcharge may be required). If the omission is not corrected within a specified time period, the application will be returned or otherwise disposed of; the filing fee if submitted will be refunded less a handling fee as set forth in the fee schedule. Learn more about responding to Office Actions.

Estimate how long it will be until you receive your first official correspondence from the USPTO in response to your application. Once your application has been accepted as complete, it will be assigned for examination. Your examiner will review the contents of the application to determine if the application meets the requirements of 35 U.S.C. 111(a). If the examiner does not think your application meets the requirements, the examiner will explain the reason(s). You will have opportunities to make amendments or argue against the examiner's objections. If you fail to respond to the examiner's requisition, within the required time, your application will be abandoned. If your application is twice rejected, you may appeal the examiner's decision to the Patent Trial and Appeal Board (PTAB) If your response to a Final Action does not overcome all of the examiner's objections or if any of the claims have been twice rejected. You can consider filing an appeal with the Patent Trial and Appeal Board (PTAB)

If you have chosen legal representation, remember that once an application is filed by a patent attorney or agent, the USPTO will only communicate with the attorney or agent. Inventors often call the USPTO for updates, but they have a designated attorney or agent representing them. The USPTO does not engage in double correspondence with an applicant and a patent practitioner (37 CFR 1.33).

Sign up to view your pending application and documents in Private PAIR. You can also sign up for the PAIR e-Office Action Program to receive an email notification when a new Office communication is available for viewing and download in PAIR.

Consider an Interview with your examiner - The USPTO encourages examiners to take a proactive approach to examination by reaching out and engaging our stakeholders in an effort to resolve issues and shorten prosecution.

Step 7

Receive your approval. If the examiner determines that your application is in satisfactory condition and meets the requirements, you will receive a Notice of Allowance. The notice of allowance will list the issue fee and may also include the publication fee that must be paid prior to the Patent being issued. Utility and reissue patents are issued within about four weeks after the issue fee and any required publication fee are received in the Office. A patent number and issue date will be assigned to an application and an Issue Notification will be mailed after the issue fee has been paid and processed by the USPTO. The patent grant is mailed on the issue date of the patent. It includes any references to prior patents, the inventor(s)') names, specification, and claims (to name a few). It is bound in an attractive cover and includes a gold seal and red ribbon on the cover.

Order certified documents - Order certified documents with the USPTO ribbon and seal as well as the signature of an authorized certifying officer.

Step 8

Maintain your patent.

Pay Maintenance Fees and Check the Status

Maintenance fees are required to maintain a patent in force beyond 4, 8, and 12 years after the issue date for utility and reissue utility patents. If the maintenance fee and any applicable surcharge are not paid in a timely manner, the patent will expire.

After your Patent is issued and published, change the ownership of a Patent (Assignments).

Patent Process Overview, https://www.uspto.gov/patents/basics/patent-process-overview#step6

Appendix J

Scoggins Partnership

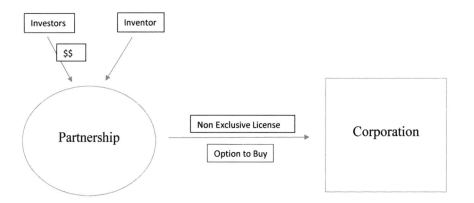

Dynamic Split Models

Inputs:
The dynamic model assigns a relative FMV weight to various contributions from each participant and contributions put into model:

- Time spent working
- Intellectual property
- Commissions
- Cash
- Facilities
- Equipment and Supplies

Outputs:
Depending on the relative weighted contributions of each team member, that member is allocated a corresponding percentage of outstanding equity.
On "split," members could return old equity, or be given new equity, to ensure each member gets appropriate percentage of company.

Appendix L

Founders Pie

Created by Frank Demmler, professor, Tepper School of Business at Carnegie Mellon University

1. A founder's value add is divided into 5 categories: Idea, Business Plan Preparation, Domain Expertise, Commitment and Risk, and Responsibilities
2. Each category is given a value
3. The value is multiplied by the founder's score to come up with a weighted score

	Founder 1	Founder 2
Idea	70	21
Business Plan	10	2
Domain Expertise	15	30
Commitment & Risk	28	42
Responsibilities	12	18
Total Points	135	113
% of Total Founder Equity Pool	54.43%	45.57%

Securities Exemptions

Type of Offering	Offering Limit within 12-month Period	General Solicitation	Issuer Requirements	Investor Requirements	SEC Filing or Disclosure Requirements	Restrictions on Resale	Preemption of State Registration and Qualification
Section 4(a)(2)	None	No	None	Transactions by an issuer not involving any public offering. *See SEC v. Ralston Purina Co.*	None	Yes. Restricted securities	No
Rule 506(b) of Regulation D	None	No	"Bad actor" disqualifications apply	Unlimited accredited investors Up to 35 sophisticated but non-accredited investors in a 90 day period	Form D Financial statement requirements for non-accredited investors consistent with Regulation A	Yes. Restricted securities	Yes
Rule 506(c) of Regulation D	None	Yes	"Bad actor" disqualifications apply	Unlimited accredited investors Issuer must take reasonable steps to verify that all purchasers are accredited investors	Form D	Yes. Restricted securities	Yes
Regulation A: Tier 1	$20 million	Permitted; before qualification, testing-the-waters permitted before and after the offering statement is filed	U.S. or Canadian issuers Excludes blank check companies, registered investment companies, business development companies, issuers of certain securities, certain issuers subject to a Section 12(j) order, and Regulation A and reporting issuers that have not filed certain required	None	Form 1 A, including two years of financial statements Exit report	No	No
Regulation A: Tier 2	$75 million			Non-accredited investors are subject to investment limits based on the greater of annual income and net worth, unless securities will be listed on a national securities exchange	Form 1 A, including two years of audited financial statements Annual, semi-annual, current, and exit reports	No	Yes
Rule 504 of Regulation D	$10 million	Permitted in limited circumstances	Excludes blank check companies, Exchange Act reporting companies, and investment companies "Bad actor" disqualifications apply	None	Form D	Yes. Restricted securities except in limited circumstances	No

SEC.gov | Overview of Capital-Raising Exemptions
https://www.sec.gov/smallbusiness/exemptofferings/exemptofferingschart

Appendix N

SAFE

An angel investment can be convertible debt, convertible equity (e.g. SAFE) or stock (a priced round). A convertible instrument means that the investor is not receiving any ownership upon investing, they are instead getting a right to convert their investment into equity in the first (or next) sale of stock by the company that establishes a valuation of the company. Because a sale of stock will require a price per share of the stock, and therefore a valuation of the company, they are often called priced rounds.

For a variety of reason, most angel financings are structured as convertible debt, SAFEs or similar instruments. There are subtle differences in each instrument that can have significant impact on the company and the investors, as discussed below.

Below are major features of SAFEs and convertible notes.

1. Pre money vs post money. The valuation cap at which a pre money SAFE converts into stock is based on the capitalization immediately before the financing. A post-money SAFE converts at a valuation cap immediately after the financing. In the post money scenario, the investor always knows what their percent of the company will be after the financing.

    There are significant differences between pre and post money SAFE. In the pre-money scenario, if the Company sells additional SAFEs, the investor and founder both share that dilution. In the post money scenario, only the founder is diluted. Generally, the pre money SAFE favors the company and its existing stakeholders while the post money SAFE favors the investor.

2. Discounts. Because the investor is the early money in, they usually receive a discount to the preferred stock price in the equity financing. That discount would range from 10% to 30% and is usually 20%. This means that every $80 of note investment would buy $100 of stock in the priced round.

3. Valuation Caps. Notes and SAFEs convert at a future value that could be much higher than the value at the time of the investment. There, the SAFE or note holder would receive proportionately less stock than they would have had they purchased stock instead of convertible debt. To deal with that problem, SAFEs and convertible notes usually contain a valuation cap, meaning that the note converts at no more than a maximum valuation. For example, if a note had a valuation cap of $10 million, and the company did not do a financing until the company was worth $20 million, the note investor would receive stock at a price per share based on a $10 million valuation, not the $20 million. Most convertibles today contain a valuation cap.

4. Convertible Note Interest and Maturity Date. Convertible note is technically debt and would carry interest since the US Internal Revenue Code would impute interest income to the noteholder if it did not. More significantly, a feature of debt is that it has a maturity date. Due to state banking and finance laws, most of these notes have a relatively short term (1 to 2 years) and if the company does not conclude its financing in that amount of time, the note would be due and in default. A SFE has another an interest component nor a maturity date.

5. Shadow preferred. Early convertibles had the investment amount convert into the same preferred stock being issued in the financing. That preferred stock would have a liquidation preference equal to the issue price. This, even though convertible might have had a discount, it would have received stock with a liquidation price over the amount paid by the investor. For example, if the preferred stock price is $1, and a SAFE or convertible debt converted at $.80, then the investor would receive $1 in liquidation proceeds for every $.80 invested. To address this windfall, well drafted convertibles will have the note or SAFE convert into a shadow stock that has the same rights and preferences as the preferred stock being issued to equity investors, except that the per share liquidation preference will equal the SAFE Price.

Price-based antidilution protection and dividend rights would also be based on the SAFE Price.

6. Pro rata rights. A pro rata right is a right of the investor to purchase more stock if the company raises another round. The pro rata is usually expressed in a side letter and typically refers to a financing round after the round in which the SAFE converts. For example, if the SAFE converts in the Series A round, the pro rata rights would apply at the next financing round.

7. Most Favored Nation (MFN). An MFN clause protects the investor from a later more favorable sale of SAFEs. Under an MFN clause, if the company subsequently issues SAFEs with provisions that are advantageous to the investors (such as valuation cap or discount), this SAFE is amended to reflect the more favorable terms.

8. Conversion. SAFEs and notes will convert to stock in the next financing that meets certain conditions, such as an equity financing of a certain size (a "qualified financing"). With a note, that qualified financing must occur before the maturity date of the note to effect an automatic conversion. The investor may also convert (an optional conversion) in the event of a financing that does not meet the criteria for a qualified financing. The note of SAFE may also convert if there is a sale of the company before a financing (a liquidation event).

With a conversion on a liquidation event, a note may provide that it converts to common at some price (the valuation cap for example) or is repaid at a multiple of the amount of the note. A SAFE investor will typically have the option on a liquidation event to a repayment of the purchase price of the SAFE (or some multiple) or to convert to common immediately before the liquidation event.

9. Dissolution. The SAFE or note will typically become payable if the company ceases business operations or enters into a liquidation or insolvency proceeding.

10. Representations. Investors do far less diligence in a SFAE or note investment than in a priced round. But there will some basic representations by both the company and the investor. The company will represent as to the absence its corporate status, power and authority, no violation, no consents and ownership of its IP. The investor will make representations as to its power and authority to enter into the agreement and securities related representations. The investors will almost always be required to represent that they are accredited under US securities laws.

11. Other Rights. Sometimes investors ask for additional rights to be contained in side letters. An investor may ask for a board seat (rare at this stage) or a board observer right, so the investor could attend board meetings but would not have a vote. They might also ask for information and reporting rights.

12. Securities Laws. Both the SAFE and the convertible note are securities, the sale of which must comply with US federal and state securities laws. The usual exemption from federal registration that companies rely on is Reg D, which is a safe harbor that generally requires the investors to represent that they are accredited. A federal Form D filing is required under this exemption. The states of residence of the investors may also have notice filing requirements.

13. Tax. For tax, a SAFE is probably treated as a prepaid forward contract, meaning that it is a right to buy stock in the company at a later date. Some SAFEs attempt to treat SAFEs as stock for qualified small business stock purposes (QSBS), but the IRS has not ruled on this issue. Convertible notes are treated as debt, so the company can deduct the interest paid or accrued to the investor. A taxpayer's holding period for capital gains and QSBS should start when the SAFE is converted to stock. In the case of a convertible note, the holding period of the note should tack to the holding period of the stock for capital gains purposes but not for QSBS.

Appendix O

Forward-Looking Statements

Certain information set forth in this presentation contains "forward-looking information", including "future-oriented financial information" and "financial outlook", under applicable securities laws (collectively referred to herein as forward-looking statements). Except for statements of historical fact, the information contained herein constitutes forward-looking statements and includes, but is not limited to, the (i) projected financial performance of the Company; (ii) completion of, and the use of proceeds from, the sale of the shares being offered hereunder; (iii) the expected development of the Company's business, projects, and joint ventures; (iv) execution of the Company's vision and growth strategy, including with respect to future M&A activity and global growth; (v) sources and availability of third-party financing for the Company's projects; (vi) completion of the Company's projects that are currently underway, in development or otherwise under consideration; (vi) renewal of the Company's current customer, supplier and other material agreements; and (vii) future liquidity, working capital, and capital requirements.

These statements are not guarantees of future performance and should not be relied on. Such forward-looking statements necessarily involve known and unknown risks and uncertainties, which may cause actual performance and financial results in future periods to differ materially from any projections of future performance or result expressed or implied by such forward-looking statements.

There can be no assurance that forward-looking statements will prove to be accurate, as actual results and future events could differ materially from those anticipated in such statements. The Company undertakes no obligation to update forward-looking statements if circumstances or management's estimates or opinions should change except as required by applicable securities laws.

Appendix P
Risk Factors

An investment in Shares is speculative in nature and involves a high degree of risk. In addition to the other information in this Statement, you should consider carefully the following risk factors before you decide whether or not to accept or reject a rescission or conversion offer. This Statement contains forward-looking statements that involve risks and uncertainties. Our actual results may differ materially from the results discussed in those forward-looking statements. We discuss below some of the factors that may cause such a difference. Moreover, the risks and uncertainties described below may not be the only ones we face. If any of the risks actually occur, our business, financial condition, operating results and prospects could be materially and adversely affected. In that event, the value of our Shares could decline, and you could lose part or all of your investment. "We" as used in this Risk Factors section refers to the Company and its affiliates.

THE INCLUSION OF RISK FACTORS IN THIS STATEMENT SHOULD NOT BE CONSTRUED TO IMPLY THAT THEY ARE DESCRIBED IN COMPLETE DETAIL OR THAT THERE ARE NO OTHER RISK FACTORS THAT APPLY TO AN INVESTMENT IN THE COMPANY.

General Risks

General Economic and Market Conditions. Changes or material developments or occurrences in U.S. market conditions, especially such as the economic downturn currently due to the COVID-19 pandemic, will affect the activities of the Company. The short-term and longer-term impacts of these events are uncertain, but they could continue to have a material effect on general economic conditions, consumer and business confidence.

Epidemics, Pandemics, Outbreaks of Disease and Public Health Issues. The operations and business activities of the hospitality industry has been materially adversely impacted by the outbreak of COVID-19 and could be further impacted in the future by the continuation or worsening of the COVID-19 global pandemic and/or any other outbreaks of disease, epidemics, pandemics and public health issues, such as those caused by other novel coronaviruses (including as a result of the emergence of new coronaviruses), Ebola virus disease, H1N1 flu, H7N9 flu, H5N1 flu (and other types or subtypes of influenza viruses), or Severe Acute Respiratory Syndrome (SARS), whether globally or in any particular regions of the world.

Force Majeure Risks. Force majeure is the term generally used to refer to an event beyond the control of the party subject to the obligation to perform claiming that such event has occurred, including, but not limit to, acts of God, fire, flood, weather, earthquakes, war, terrorism, labor strikes, outbreaks of disease and potentially other unpredictable events or occurrences. Force majeure events in the United States and elsewhere in the world may adversely affect the ability of the Company or the parties with whom they do business to perform their respective obligations under a contract or other arrangements. In addition, dealing with any force majeure event will divert the time and effort of the Company management and the cost of repairing or replacing damaged assets could be considerable. Repeated or prolonged service interruptions caused by force majeure events may result in permanent loss of customers, substantial litigation, or penalties due to regulatory or contractual non-compliance. In some cases, agreements may be terminated if the force majeure event is so catastrophic as to render it incapable of remedy within a reasonable, pre-agreed time period. All such force majeure events may have a permanent adverse effect on the Company and the potential returns will be diminished as a result.

No Assurance of Returns. A private company typically distributes money when it is sold to another company or a new set of investors, when it pays a dividend, or when it is listed on a stock exchange or other public trading platform. The Company may take a long time to, or may never, achieve one of these events. As such, there can be no assurance that investors will receive any returns. The timing of profit realization, if any, is highly uncertain.

Reliance on Management. The CEO and Directors ("Management") will have sole discretion over the investment of the capital committed to the Company. The investors will not receive detailed financial information and will be relying on Management to operate the businesses of the Company. The loss of one or more of the principals of Management would likely have a significant adverse impact on the business of the Company. No assurances can be given that the principals of Management will continue to be affiliated with the Company throughout its term. There can be no assurance that the principals of Management will be able to duplicate any previous levels of success.

No Assurance of Additional Capital. The Company may have additional capital needs. No assurance can be made that such additional financing will be available and no assurance can be made as to the terms upon which such financing may be obtained.

Indemnification. The Company will be required to indemnify Management for liabilities incurred in connection with the affairs of the Company. Such liabilities may be material and have an adverse effect on the returns to the investors.

Future and Past Performance. The performance of any prior investments affiliated with any of the principals of Management is not necessarily indicative of the future results that will be realized by the Company. There can be no assurance that targeted results will be achieved. Loss of principal is possible.

No Market; Illiquidity of Company Interest. An investment in the Company will be illiquid and involves a high degree of risk. Because Company interests will not be registered under the Securities Act there will be no public market for Company interests, and it is not expected that a public market will develop. The investors may not be able to avail itself of the provisions of Rule 144 of the Securities Act with respect to a proposed transfer of its shares, and the Investors will not be permitted to sell its shares unless such interests are subsequently registered under the Securities Act or an exemption from registration is available. Consequently, the investors will bear the economic risks of its investment for the term of the Company.

Certain Limitations on the Ability of the Investors to Transfer Company Interest. The transferability of Company interests will be restricted by agreement and by United States federal and state securities laws. In general, the investors will not be able to sell or transfer shares to third parties without the consent of Management.

Risks Related to the Company, Business and Industry

In making an investment decision, you must rely on your own examination of the Company and the terms provided for in the Offering Materials, including the merits and risks involved. These securities have not been recommended or approved by any federal or state securities commission or regulatory authority. Furthermore, these authorities have not passed upon the accuracy or adequacy of this document.

The risks related to making an investment in the Shares, as of this date, include the following:

If there is a Dissolution Event, the Company will make commercially reasonable efforts to reimburse Investments received from Investors, but the Company cannot guarantee that sufficient funds will be available for any such reimbursement.

The Shares are being offered in reliance upon exemptions from the registration requirements of the Securities Act and, as a result, will fall within the definition of "restricted securities," as set forth in Securities Act Rule 144. As a result, the Shares may not be transferred except in compliance with applicable securities law. Any transfer of the Shares made in violation of Securities Act restrictions will be treated by the Company as void.

There can be no assurance that any Investor will achieve his or her investment objective or avoid substantial losses by investing in Shares. Instruments like the purchase documents for the Shares entail a high degree of risk, and Investors may lose some or all of their Investment. A potential Investor should execute the purchase documents for the Shares and invest in Shares only if able to withstand a total loss of the Investment. Potential Investors are urged to consult with their personal investment, legal and tax advisors before executing the purchase documents for the Shares.

The Shares have numerous transfer restrictions and will likely be highly illiquid, with no secondary market on which to sell them. The Shares are equity interests, have ownership rights, have no rights to the Company's assets or profits and have no voting rights or ability to direct the Company or its actions. The Company intends on allowing holders of Shares to either resell their Shares to the Company or to sell their Shares to existing shareholders or new shareholders, subject to the approval of the Company.

The Company is offering the Shares under an exemption from registration under the Securities Act, and neither the Company nor any affiliate will be registered under any U.S. securities or commodities laws. It is possible that a regulator could disagree with the Company's position that it is not required to register under those laws. This could lead to significant changes with respect to how the Shares are issued, how they are purchased and sold, and other issues that would greatly increase the Company's costs in creating and facilitating business. It could even lead to the termination of the Shares. Further, a regulator could take action against the Company if it views the Shares and the Company's offering as a violation of existing law. Any of these outcomes would negatively affect the value of the Shares.

The terms described in this Statement are subject to change prior to the completion of this Offering, possibly substantially. The Company cannot guarantee that the Shares will have the same characteristics as described herein following this restructuring and close of this Offering.

Executive Summary

[company logo] [website] **Management:** [name] [name]	**Mission:** [short description of company's mission]
	Business Description: [further explication of company's mission and how it will be achieved, brief description of target market and/or progress/success so far]
Industry: [name] **Number of Employees:** [#] **Financing Sought:** [$]	**Company Background:** [background, relevant previous experience of management and team in start-ups/the industry; advisors; other relevant qualifications]
Current Investors: [name] [name] **Use of Funds:** [use 1] [use 2] [use 3]	**Products/Services:** [brief description of competing products/services already on the market and comparison to company's products/services; explanation of how company's products/services fill a niche or are innovative/offer something different]

Technologies: [specialized technologies involved in the products/services; barriers to market entry, patents, trademarks, need for IP protection]

Markets: [current and projected market and growth of the industry; target market/ audience and company's projected market value in 5 years; whether different versions of the products/services are tailored to specific subgroups/segments of the market]

Distribution Channels: [strategy and timeline for entering the market and expanding market share; description of sales/advertisement strategy and media, how they are effective in reaching the target market; how/where products/services will be made available to customers]

Competition: [description of competitors and their products/services, how company's products/services are unique and offer something different]

Financial Projections:

Appendix R

Valuation Methods

I. **Scorecard Valuation Methodology**
a. **Two-Step Process:**
    i. **First step** is to determine the average pre-money valuation of pre-revenue companies in the region and business sector of the target company.
        1. Pre-money valuation varies with the economy and competitive environment for startup ventures within a region. For most regions, the pre-money valuation does not vary significantly from one business sector to another.
        2. In 2011, pre-money valuation of pre-revenue companies typically varies in the range of $1.5-2.5 million with an average of $2 million.
    ii. **Second step** is to compare the target company to your perception of similar deals done in your region. Use the following factors:
        1. **Strength of Management Team**   0-30%
        2. **Size of the Opportunity**   0-25%
        3. **Product/Technology**   0-15%
        4. **Competitive Environment**   0-10%
        5. **Marketing/Sales Channels/Partnerships**   0-10%
        6. **Need for Additional Investment**   0-5%
        7. **Other**   0-5%

        The subjective ranking of factors above is typical for investor appraisal of startup ventures. Some people are surprised that product/technology is below management team and size of opportunity. However, in building a business, the *quality of the team* is paramount to success. A great management team will fix early product flaws, but the reverse is not true.

b. **Example:** A company has an average product and technology (100% of norm), a strong management team (125% of norm) and a large market opportunity (150% of norm). The company can get to positive cash flow with just a single round of angel investment (100% of norm). Looking at the strength of competition in the market, the target is weaker (75%) but early customer feedback on the product is excellent (Other = 100%). The company needs some additional work on building sales channels and partnerships (80%). Using this data, we complete the following calculation using the above factors:

COMPARISON FACTOR	RANGE	TARGETCOMPANY	FACTOR
Strength of Management Team	30%	125%	0.3750
Size of Opportunity	25%	150%	0.3750
Product/Technology	15%	100%	0.1500
Competitive Environment	10%	75%	0.0750
Marketing/Sales/Partnerships	10%	80%	0.0800
Need for Additional Investment	5%	100%	0.0500
Other factors	5%	100%	0.0500
		Sum	**1.0750**

Assuming the average pre-money valuation is $2 million, we multiply that figure with the Sum of Factors (1.075 x $2.0 million). Therefore, we arrive at a pre-money valuation of $2.15 million.

NOTE: $2 million was the average valuation in 2012. **In 2014 the average valuation rose to around $2.7 million.**

II. **The Venture Capital Method**

    a. One of the useful methods for establishing the pre-money valuation of startup ventures.

    b. Formulas for post-money and pre-money valuation

        i. **Post-money Valuation** = Terminal (or Harvest) Value ÷ Anticipated ROI

1. **Terminal value** is the anticipated selling price for the company at some point down the road (5-8 years).
   a. The selling price can be estimated by establishing a reasonable expectation for revenues in the year of the sale, and based on those revenues, estimating earnings in the year of the sale from industry-specific statistics.
   b. **Calculating TV:** For example, a software company with revenues of $20 million in the harvest year might be expected to have after-tax earnings of 15%, or $3 million. Using industry specific Price/Earnings ratios, we can then determine the Terminal Value (a 15X P/E ratio for the software company would give an estimated Terminal Value of $45). It is also known that software companies often sell for two times their revenue (2 x $20M = $40M). So the TV can be set at around $40-50 million. We'll assume it's **$42.5 million** here.
2. **Anticipated ROI**: Most angels understand that half of new ventures fail and the best an investor can expect from 9/10 investments is return of capital for a portfolio of ten. Consequently, the tenth investment must be a home run of 20X or more. Since investors do not know which of the ten will be the homerun, all investments must demonstrate the possibility of a 10X-30X return. In this scenario, we'll assume a **20X** ROI.
3. **Therefore**, the Post-Money Valuation = $42.5 million ÷ 20 = **$2.125M**

ii. **Pre-money Valuation:** To calculate this, you need to know how much the initial investment is. **Pre-money Valuation = Post-money Valuation - Investment**
   1. Assume the software company needs $500,000 to achieve positive cash flow and will grow organically thereafter.

    2. **Therefore**, Pre-money Valuation = $2.125M - $0.5M = **$1.625M**

III. Berkus Method

    a. Dave Berkus is a founding member of the Tech Coast Angels in Southern CA. His valuation method first appeared in a book in the mid-90s. It has been used by angels since.

Characteristic	Add to Pre-money Valuation
Quality Management Team	0 - $500,000
Sound Idea	0 - $500,000
Working Prototype	0 - $500,000
Quality Board of Directors	0 - $500,000
Product Rollout or Sales	0 - $500,000

    b. Comments:

        i. This can be a very useful method.

        ii. However, some issues are missing from this methodology.

            1. Is the competitive environment important in the business sector of the target venture? If so, it must be considered.

            2. Is the depth of intellectual property and competitive differentiation important to the target venture? If so, it must be considered.

            3. Is the size of the opportunity to investors considering funding this target company? If so, it must be considered.

        iii. Therefore, while this method is useful in valuing a company, however, it should not be the only method used.

IV. Cayenne Calculator

    a. This is pretty straightforward. You fill out a 25 question survey about your company. After answering the questions, the website calculates an estimate of what the Pre-money value is.

    b. http://www.caycon.com/valuation.php

V. Risk Factor Summation

    a. This method assesses various risk factors.

      i.   Management

      ii.   State of the business

      iii. Legislation/Political risk

      iv. Manufacturing risk

      v.   Sales and marketing risk

      vi.   Funding/capital risk

      vii. Competition risk

      viii. Technology risk

      ix.   Litigation risk

      x.   International risk

      xi.   Reputation risk

      xii. Potential lucrative exit

b. Each risk is assessed as followed:

      i.   +2   very positive for growing the company and executing a wonderful exit

      ii.   +1   positive

      iii. 0   neutral

      iv. -1   negative for growing the company and executing a wonderful exit

      v.   -2   very negative

c. For every +1 you add \$250,000 (+\$500k for +2) and subtract \$250,000 for every -1 (-\$500k for a -2).

d. Once you've tallied up the points and multiplied the sum by \$250k, you then add that number to the **Average Pre-money Valuation** in the area

      i.   Example: Assume the average pre-money valuation is \$1.5 million, and after tallying the points, the sum is +2. Therefore, you would add \$500,000 to the \$1.5M average, bringing the company's pre-money value to \$2 million.

VI. **Negotiation**

  a. Pretty straightforward, VCs and the startup can enter into negotiations and come to a mutually agreeable valuation number.

VII.   **(Patents + People) x \$1 million**

  a. A (rough) rule of thumb often used by investors is that each patent filed might justify $1 million increase in valuation.

    b. Valuations may rise $1 million for every paid full-time programmer, engineer, or designer.

VIII. **Comparable**

    a. Basic premise of the comparables approach is that an equity's value should bear some resemblance to other equities in a similar class.

        i. Look at competitors, what are they getting?

    b. Two primary comparable approaches:

        i. The first looks at market comparables for a firm and its peers.

            1. Common market multiples include the following:

                a. Enterprise value to sales (EV/S)

                b. Enterprise multiple

                c. Price to earnings (P/E)

                d. Price to book (P/B)

                e. Price to free cash flow (P/FCF)

            2. To get a better indication of how a firm compares to competitors, analysts can look at how its margin levels compare.

        ii. The second approach looks at market transactions where similar firms, or at least similar divisions, have been bout out or acquired.

            1. Using this approach, an investor can get a feel for the value of the equity being valued.

IX. **Discounted Cash Flow**

    a. DCF analysis is a method of valuing the intrinsic value of a company. DCF tries to work out the value today, based on projections of all of the cash that it could make available to investors in the future.

        i. It is described as "discounted" cash flow because of the principle of "time value of money" (i.e. cash in the future is worth less than cash today).

    b. **Advantage:** DCF analysis produces the closest thing to an intrinsic stock value.

i.   In addition, the DCF method is forward-looking and depends more on future expectations than historical results. The method is also based on free cash flow, which is less subject to manipulation than some other figures and ratios calculated out of the income statement or balance sheet.

c. **Disadvantage:** It is a mechanical valuation tool, so it is subject to the principle of "garbage in, garbage out." In particular, small changes in inputs can result in large changes in the value of a company, given the need to project cash-flow to infinity.

i.   James Montier argues that, "while the algebra of DCF is simple, neat and compelling, the implementation becomes a minefield of problems." Citing problems such as estimating cash flows and discount rates.

d. Despite the issues, DCF analysis is very widely used and is perhaps the primary valuation tool amongst the financial analyst community.

X. **Market Multipliers**

a. This method uses an income figure, such as gross sales and inventory, or net profit, and multiplies it by an appropriate coefficient to arrive at a value for the business.

i.   The coefficient used will be varied based on the industry, market conditions, and any special concerns within the business. This number is somewhat arbitrary in nature.

XI. **Discount to Public Company Values**

a. When comparing the value of a **private** company to a similar **public** company, you must discount the value of the publicly traded company to equal that of a similar private company.

i.   Discount for lack of marketability: Marketability is defined as the ability to convert the business interest into cash quickly. There is usually a cost and a time lag associated with locating interested and capable buyers of interests in privately held companies, because there is no established market of readily available buyers and sellers.

Appendix S

Pitch Decks

1. Getting to Wow! Silicon Valley Pitch Secrets for Entrepreneurs by Bill Reichert and Angelika Blendstrup
2. Get Your Venture Backed with Persuasive Data Viz: An HBR Collection for Building the Perfect Pitch Deck by Scott Berinato, Evan Baehr, et al
3. Pitch Decks: 31 Investor Marketing & Pitch Assets for Raising Capital by Andres Ospina
4. Presentation Zen: Simple Ideas on Presentation Design and Delivery (Voices That Matter) 3rd Edition, by Garr Reynolds

Appendix T

Rule 506*

Rule 506 provides two distinct exemptions from registration for companies when they offer and sell securities. Companies relying on the Rule 506 exemptions can raise an unlimited amount of money.

Under Rule 506(b), a "safe harbor" under Section 4(a)(2) of the Securities Act, a company can be assured it is within the Section 4(a)(2) exemption by satisfying certain requirements, including the following:

The company cannot use general solicitation or advertising to market the securities.

The company may sell its securities to an unlimited number of "accredited investors (/additional-resources/news-alerts/alerts-bulletins/investor-bulle-tin- accredited-investors) " and up to 35 other purchasers. All non-accredited investors, either alone or with a purchaser representative, must be sophisti-cated—that is, they must have sufficient knowledge and experience in finan-cial and business matters to make them capable of evaluating the merits and risks of the prospective investment.

Companies must decide what information to give to accredited investors, so long as it does not violate the antifraud prohibitions of the federal securities laws. This means that any information a company provides to investors must be free from false or misleading statements. Similarly, a company should not exclude any information if the omission makes what is provided to investors false or misleading. Companies must give non-accredited investors disclo-sure documents that are generally the same as those used in Regulation A (/additional- resources/general-resources/glossary/regulation) or registered offerings, including financial statements, which in some cases may need to be certified or audited by an accountant. If a company provides information to accredited investors, it must make this information available to non-accredited investors as well.

The company must be available to answer questions by prospective purchasers.

Under Rule 506(c), a company can broadly solicit and generally advertise the offering and still be deemed to be in compliance with the exemption's requirements if:

The investors in the offering are all accredited investors; and

The company takes reasonable steps to verify that the investors are accredited investors, which could include reviewing documentation, such as W-2s, tax returns, bank and brokerage statements, credit reports and the like.

Purchasers of securities offered pursuant to Rule 506 receive "restricted" securities (/additional-resources/general-resources/glossary/restricted-securities), meaning that the securities cannot be sold for at least six months or a year without registering them.

Companies that comply with the requirements of Rule 506(b) or (c) do not have to register their offering of securities with the SEC, but they must file what is known as a "Form D (http://www.sec.gov/about/forms/formd.pdf) " electronically with the SEC after they first sell their securities. Form D is a brief notice that includes the names and addresses of the company's promoters, executive officers and directors, and some details about the offering, but contains little other information about the company. You can access

the SEC's EDGAR database (http://www.sec.gov/edgar.shtml) to determine whether the company has filed a Form D.

Be sure to ask whether your state regulator has received notice of the offering for sale in your state. You can get the address and telephone number for your state securities regulator by calling the North American Securities Administrators Association at (202) 737- 0900 or by visiting its website (http://www.nasaa.org/about-us/contact-us/contact-your- regulator/).

Learn more (https://www.sec.gov/smallbusiness).

* https://www.investor.gov/introduction-investing/investing-basics/glossary/
rule-506-regulation-d

Appendix U

Donald Trump's Billion Dollar Loss: Good Tax Planning, or Dubious Trick?

Donald Trump's refusal to release his tax returns has led to intense interest in and speculation concerning his tax positions. His dealings relating to his charitable foundation have been perceived as dubious in some circles. [1] Moreover, a month ago, the New York Times[2] discovered he had nearly a billion dollars of net operating loss on his 1995 tax returns, reducing his taxable income for years to come.

Many tax commentators tried to figure out how Trump had received such a huge loss, as he should have had "cancellation of debt" income (discussed below) which would reduce the loss. Some commentators proposed that he used the "qualified real property business indebtedness" exclusion from cancellation of debt income, while others proposed an illegal tax shelter technique[3] and others yet proposed an S corporation technique that clearly worked,[4] but would have been unusual for a real property business to have used (because such businesses were typically organized as partnerships).

Finally, just yesterday, the New York Times[5] discovered the apparent method used, while implying the method was quite dubious. But was it? To answer this, we must first review the facts of the matter, and then we can provide a quick analysis based on the available facts.

Background of the Matter

In the early 1990s, Donald Trump lost considerable money on his real estate ventures, such as the Taj Mahal. He borrowed heavily to finance the projects. These enormous economic losses, by themselves, would have given Trump the losses we now see on his returns.

However, Donald Trump faced a challenge. In order to refinance his debt, Donald Trump demanded and apparently received modifications of his debt. Under normal tax rules, a dollar of cancelled debt is taxed just like any other dollar of income. Thus, it would appear Donald Trump would have received an enormous tax bill for income from the refinancing. This income should have offset any losses he otherwise had. From a policy perspective, this offset result makes sense; you should not be able to deduct losses economically belonging to your creditors. (This result does create some economic hardship, as people receiving cancellation of debt income are often insolvent, but there are rules to ease this pain.)[6]

But there appeared to be a potential way out of Trump's income offset problem. Once upon a time, if a corporation paid off its debt via issuing equity (i.e., stock), it would not receive any "cancellation of debt" income. By 1993, this technique had been banned specifically for corporations. However, it was (at the time) not clear what would happen if a partnership did the same technique. Perhaps the old corporation trick preventing cancellation of debt income would apply? Trump decided to take the position it would, and planned to issue equity from his real estate investment partnership to pay off the debt.

But there was another major hurdle not discussed in the New York Times article.[7] Specifically, in most circumstances, when entities issued equity to pay off debts and avoid cancellation of debt income, they paid off *their own* debts. But in this case, the debt being paid off was debt of Trump's related financing corporations (guaranteed by Trump's partnerships), which existed because of New Jersey casino regulations. Still, Trump was undeterred, and took the position that the corporations' debt was really the partnerships' debt, as the corporations were mere agents or nominees of the partnerships. This is often a difficult position to sustain in tax law, which is biased towards treating legal entities as separate and holding taxpayers to the form they select for a transaction.

Before taking this debt position, Trump made sure to reinforce his defenses: He requested a tax opinion from the law firm of Willkie Farr & Gallagher.

[8] Tax opinions are routinely requested by parties performing major transactions, particularly where there is tax uncertainty present. Such opinions provide various legal benefits, including (importantly here) mitigating potential tax penalties. That is, when someone underpays or misreports their taxes, they will always be liable for missed taxes and some level of interest (as the unpaid taxes are essentially "loans" from the government). The IRS may also apply penalties, intended to scare taxpayers into compliance. However, a tax opinion provides analysis and a confidence level which, if accurate, may help to reduce or eliminate many such penalties. A higher confidence level means more penalties will likely be mitigated. Further, the mere act of obtaining competent-seeming professional advice can help mitigate certain penalties.

The confidence levels expressed by tax opinions translate to the following probabilities:[9]

Confidence level	Probability of being upheld
Will	90-95%
Should	70%-75%
More likely than not	Greater than 50%
Substantial authority	33%-40%
Reasonable basis	20%-30%
Not frivolous	Some amount lower than reasonable basis, but not clear how low
Frivolous	Extremely unlikely, to the point special penalties are likely to apply for frivolousness

In the case of Trump's transaction, Willkie identified 8 key areas of tax uncertainty. It offered a more likely than not opinion on one issue, and a substantial authority level of confidence for the remainder of the issues. This meant that Trump was highly unlikely to face tax penalties for his position. But it also meant that, for many of Trump's positions, the law firm thought the most likely outcome was that Trump would lose against the IRS. Some tax experts speculate Trump had opinion shopped to get the most favorable opinion he could, as was common in the 1990s. Opinion practice has since been legally forced to become much more legitimate and thorough than it was in the

1990s. If the Willkie opinion, with its low confidence level, was the best he could do, perhaps his position was even less justifiable than it appears to be.

In 2004, Congress (including Sen. Hillary Clinton) explicitly removed from the Internal Revenue Code the ability to issue partnership equity for debt in order to avoid cancellation of debt income while recognizing a loss. Some see in this amendment an indication that Trump's position regarding the exchange of partnership equity for debt had some legitimacy, since Congress felt it had to step in to explicitly change the law.

Was Trump Wrong to Act this Way?

The New York Times is unambiguous in its verdict: Trump's technique was legally dubious and deserves our scorn.

But there is a different way of looking at it. Trump appears to have made a calculated decision: The tax benefits from his tax position would be enormous, and the Willkie opinion appeared to cover him from the downside of penalties. All he was likely risking was the additional interest he might owe. Trump apparently felt this was worth a shot. While the outcome doubtlessly violated good and fair tax policy, it appears Trump's position worked out for him in the end.

Even so, was the position too aggressive, and was Willkie wrong for issuing that position? It's unclear from the facts provided. The fact Congress needed to step in to amend the Code to eliminate the partnership-equity-for-debt rule does suggest this key ambiguity Trump exploited was a real, unforced reading of the law. But we cannot say for all the other ambiguities Trump exploited.

Thus, while we cannot know if Trump's actions were truly as dubious as the New York Times says, we do know that Trump's risks and the expiration of the applicable statute of limitations saved him from heavy income taxation and stiff sanctions. Trump's result, in short, shows what good tax lawyering and ambiguous tax law may allow.

[1] http://www.vox.com/policy-and-politics/2016/10/31/13474280/trump-foundation-criminal-charges

[2] http://www.nytimes.com/2016/10/02/us/politics/donald-trump-taxes.html

[3] http://brontecapital.blogspot.co.uk/2016/10/some-comments-on-new-york-times-story.html

[4] http://www.businessinsider.com/why-did-trump-pay-so-little-tax-2016-10

[5] http://www.nytimes.com/interactive/2016/us/politics/trump-taxes-loophole.html

[6] Insolvent or bankrupt taxpayers have an exception for reducing their cancellation of debt income, but it forces them to reduce their positive tax attributes, such as their net operating losses; Trump did not use this exception.

[7] http://www.taxanalysts.org/content/documents-reveal-dubious-tax-planning-behind-trumps-big-losses

[8] http://www.nytimes.com/interactive/2016/10/31/us/politics/trump-tax-letters.html?_r=0

[9] It should be noted that what these "probabilities" mean is somewhat opaque and uncertain. *See* http://danshaviro.blogspot.com/2016/11/latest-on-trumps-tax-scam.html?m=1.

https://rogerroyse.com/donald-trumps-billion-dollar-loss-good-tax-planning-or-dubious-trick/

INDEMNIFICATION AGREEMENT

This **Indemnification Agreement** ("**Agreement**") is made as of this _____ day of _____, 20___ by and between _____, a _____ corporation (the "**Company**"), and _____ ("**Indemnitee**").

Whereas, the Company and Indemnitee recognize the increasing difficulty in obtaining directors' and officers' liability insurance, the significant increases in the cost of such insurance and the general reductions in the coverage of such insurance;

Whereas, the Company and Indemnitee further recognize the substantial increase in corporate litigation in general, subjecting officers and directors to expensive litigation risks at the same time as the availability and coverage of liability insurance has been severely limited;

Whereas, Indemnitee does not regard the current protection available as adequate under the present circumstances, and Indemnitee and other officers and directors of the Company may not be willing to continue to serve as officers and directors without additional protection; and

Whereas, the Company desires to attract and retain the services of highly qualified individuals, such as Indemnitee, to serve as officers and directors of the Company and to indemnify its officers and directors so as to provide them with the maximum protection permitted by law.

Now, Therefore, the Company and Indemnitee hereby agree as follows:

1. **Indemnification.**

    (a) **Third Party Proceedings**. To the fullest extent allowed by law, the Company shall indemnify Indemnitee if Indemnitee is or was a party or is threatened to be made a party to any threatened, pending or completed action or proceeding, whether civil, criminal, administrative or investigative (other than an action by or in the right of the Company) by reason of the fact that Indemnitee is or was a director, officer, employee or agent of the Company, or any subsidiary of the Company, by reason of any action or inaction on the part of Indemnitee while an officer or director or by reason of the fact that Indemnitee is or was serving at the request of the Company as a director, officer, employee or agent of another corporation, partnership, joint venture, trust or other enterprise, against expenses (including attorneys' fees), judgments, fines and amounts paid in settlement (if such settlement is approved in advance by the Company, which approval shall not be unreasonable withheld) actually and reasonably incurred by Indemnitee in connection with such action or proceeding. The Company shall provide the Indemnitee all such indemnity benefits notwithstanding any allegations that the Indemnitee acted, in whole or in part, in anything other than good faith and in a manner Indemnitee believed to be in the best interests of the Company, and, with respect to any criminal action or proceeding, had no reasonable cause to believe Indemnitee's conduct was unlawful until and unless the Company proves these allegations by clear and convincing evidence and obtains a Final Judgment establishing the truth of such allegations. For purposes of this Agreement, the term "Final Judgment" shall mean a final judgment of a court of competent jurisdiction after all appellate rights have been exhausted or time barred. The termination of any action or proceeding by judgment, order, settlement, conviction, or upon a plea of nolo contendere or its equivalent, shall not, of itself, create a presumption that (i) Indemnitee did not act in good faith and in a manner which Indemnitee reasonably believed to be in the best interests of the Company, or (ii) with respect to any criminal action or proceeding, Indemnitee had reasonable cause to believe that Indemnitee's conduct was unlawful.

(b) **Proceedings by or in the Right of the Company**. The Company shall indemnify Indemnitee if Indemnitee was or is a party or is threatened to be made a party to any threatened, pending or completed action or proceeding by or in the right of the Company or any subsidiary of the Company to procure a judgment in its favor by reason of the fact that Indemnitee is or was a director, officer, employee or agent of the Company, or any subsidiary of the Company, by reason of any action or inaction on the part of Indemnitee while an officer or director or by reason of the fact that

Indemnitee is or was serving at the request of the Company as a director, officer, employee or agent of another corporation, partnership, joint venture, trust or other enterprise, against expenses (including attorneys' fees) and, to the fullest extent permitted by law, amounts paid in settlement, in each case to the extent actually and reasonably incurred by Indemnitee in connection with the defense or settlement of such action or proceeding if Indemnitee acted in good faith and in a manner Indemnitee believed to be in the best interests of the Company and its shareholders.

   2.   **Expenses; Indemnification Procedure.**

   (a)   **Advancement of Expenses.** The Company shall advance all expenses incurred by Indemnitee in connection with the investigation, defense, settlement or appeal of any civil or criminal action or proceeding referenced in Section 1(a) or (b) hereof (but not amounts actually paid in settlement of any such action or proceeding). Indemnitee hereby undertakes to repay such amounts advanced only if, and to the extent that, it shall ultimately be determined by Final Judgment that Indemnitee is not entitled to be indemnified by the Company as authorized hereby. The advances to be made hereunder shall be paid by the Company to Indemnitee within 20 days following delivery of a written request therefor by Indemnitee to the Company.

   (b)   **Notice/Cooperation by Indemnitee.** Indemnitee shall, as a condition precedent to his right to be indemnified under this Agreement, give the Company notice in writing as soon as practicable of any claim made against Indemnitee for which indemnification will or could be sought under this Agreement. Notice to the Company shall be directed to the President of the Company at the address shown on the signature page of this Agreement (or such other address as the Company shall designate in writing to Indemnitee). Notice shall be deemed received three business days after the date postmarked if sent by domestic certified or registered mail, properly addressed; otherwise notice shall be deemed received when such notice shall actually be received by the Company. In addition, Indemnitee shall give the Company such information and cooperation as it may reasonably require and as shall be within Indemnitee's power. Notwithstanding the foregoing, the Company may not reduce or refuse indemnity benefits except to the extent it obtains a Final Judgment that any late notice or refusal to cooperate caused the Company actual and substantial prejudice.

(c) **Procedure**. Any indemnification provided for in Section 1 shall be made no later than 45 days after receipt of the written request of Indemnitee. If a claim under this Agreement, under any statute, or under any provision of the Company's Articles of Incorporation or Bylaws providing for indemnification, is not paid in full by the Company within 45 days after a written request for payment thereof has first been received by the Company, Indemnitee may, but need not, at any time thereafter bring an action against the Company to recover the unpaid amount of the claim and, subject to Section 13 of this Agreement, Indemnitee shall also be entitled to be paid for the expenses (including attorneys' fees) of bringing such action. It shall be a defense to any such action (other than an action brought to enforce a claim for expenses incurred in connection with any action or proceeding in advance of its final disposition) that Indemnitee has not met the standards of conduct which make it permissible under applicable law for the Company to indemnify Indemnitee for the amount claimed, and Indemnitee shall be entitled to receive interim payments of expenses pursuant to Subsection 2(a) unless and until such defense may be finally adjudicated by court order or judgment from which no further right of appeal exists. It is the parties' intention that if the Company contests Indemnitee's right to indemnification, the question of Indemnitee's right to indemnification shall be for the court to decide, and neither the failure of the Company (including its Board of Directors, any committee or subgroup of the Board of Directors, independent legal counsel, or its shareholders) to have made a determination that indemnification of Indemnitee is proper in the circumstances because Indemnitee has met the applicable standard of conduct required by applicable law, nor an actual determination by the Company (including its Board of Directors, any committee or subgroup of the board of Directors, independent legal counsel, or its shareholders) that Indemnitee has not met such applicable standard of conduct, shall create a presumption that Indemnitee has or has not met the applicable standard of conduct.

(d) **Notice to Insurers**. If, at the time of the receipt of a notice of a claim pursuant to Section 2(b) hereof, the Company has director and officer liability insurance in effect, the Company shall give prompt notice of the commencement of such proceeding to the insurers in accordance with the procedures set forth in the respective policies. The Company shall thereafter take all necessary or desirable action to cause such insurers to pay, on behalf of the Indemnitee, all amounts payable as a result of such proceeding in accordance with the terms of such policies.

(e)   **Selection of Counsel.** In the event the Company shall be obligated under Section 2(a) hereof to pay the expenses of any proceeding against Indemnitee, the Company, if appropriate, shall be entitled to assume the defense of such proceeding, with counsel approved by Indemnitee, which approval shall not be unreasonably withheld, upon the delivery to Indemnitee of written notice of its election so to do. After delivery of such notice, approval of such counsel by Indemnitee and the retention of such counsel by the Company, the Company will not be liable to Indemnitee under this Agreement for any fees of counsel subsequently incurred by Indemnitee with respect to the same proceeding, provided that (i) Indemnitee shall have the right to employ his counsel in any such proceeding at Indemnitee's expense; and (ii) if (A) the employment of counsel by Indemnitee has been previously authorized by the Company, (B) Indemnitee shall have reasonably concluded that there may be a conflict of interest between the Company and Indemnitee in the conduct of any such defense or (C) the Company shall not, in fact, have employed counsel to assume the defense of such proceeding, then the fees and expenses of Indemnitee's counsel shall be at the expense of the Company. Notwithstanding the foregoing, in the event an actual or potential conflict of interest develops between the Company and the Indemnitee as to any issue related to the claim as to which indemnity is requested, then the Indemnitee shall be entitled to select his/her counsel without any reduction in indemnity benefits.

3.   **Additional Indemnification Rights; Nonexclusivity.**

(a)   **Scope.** Notwithstanding any other provision of this Agreement, the Company hereby agrees to indemnify the Indemnitee to the fullest extent permitted by law, notwithstanding that such indemnification is not specifically authorized by the other provisions of this Agreement, the Company's Articles of Incorporation, the Company's Bylaws or by statute.

In the event of any change, after the date of this Agreement, in any applicable law, statute or rule which expands the right of a California corporation to indemnify a member of its board of directors, an officer or other corporate agent, such changes shall be, _ipso facto_, within the purview of Indemnitee's rights and Company's obligations, under this Agreement. In the event of any change in any applicable law, statute or rule which narrows the right of a California corporation to indemnify a member of its Board of Directors, an officer or other corporate agent, such changes, to the extent required by such law, statute or rule to be applied to this Agreement, shall have the effect on this Agreement and the parties' rights and obligations hereunder as is required by such law, statute or rule.

(b) **Nonexclusivity**. The indemnification provided by this Agreement shall not be deemed exclusive of any rights to which Indemnitee may be entitled under the Company's Articles of Incorporation, its Bylaws, any agreement, any vote of shareholders or disinterested directors, the California General Corporation Law or otherwise, both as to action in Indemnitee's official capacity and as to action in another capacity while holding such office. The indemnification provided under this Agreement shall continue as to Indemnitee for any action taken or not taken while serving in an indemnified capacity even though he may have ceased to serve in such capacity at the time of any action or other covered proceeding.

4. **Partial Indemnification**. If Indemnitee is entitled under any provision of this Agreement to indemnification by the Company for some or a portion of the expenses, judgments, fines or penalties actually or reasonably incurred by him in the investigation, defense, appeal or settlement of any civil or criminal action or proceeding, but not, however, for the total amount thereof, the Company shall nevertheless indemnify Indemnitee for the portion of such expenses, judgments, fines or penalties to which Indemnitee is entitled. Unless an allocation between indemnifiable sums and unindemnifiable sums shall be proven by the Company by clear and convincing evidence resulting in a Final Judgment, all sums shall be presumed to be indemnifiable.

5. **Mutual Acknowledgement**. Both the Company and Indemnitee acknowledge that in certain instances, Federal law or applicable public policy

may prohibit the Company from indemnifying its directors and officers under this Agreement or otherwise. Indemnitee understands and acknowledges that the Company has undertaken or may be required in the future to undertake with the Securities and Exchange Commission to submit the question of indemnification to a court in certain circumstances for a determination of the Company's right under public policy to indemnify Indemnitee.

      6.   **Directors' and Officers' Liability Insurance.** The Company shall, from time to time, make the good faith determination whether or not it is practicable for the Company to obtain and maintain a policy or policies of insurance with reputable insurance companies providing the officers and directors of the Company with coverage for losses from wrongful acts, or to ensure the Company's performance of its indemnification obligations under this Agreement. Among other considerations, the Company will weigh the costs of obtaining such insurance coverage against the protection afforded by such coverage. In all policies of directors' and officers' liability insurance, Indemnitee shall be named as an insured in such a manner as to provide Indemnitee the same rights and benefits as are accorded to the most favorably insured of the Company's directors, if Indemnitee is a director; or of the Company's officers, if Indemnitee is not a director of the Company but is an officer; or of the Company's key employees, if Indemnitee is not an officer or director but is a key employee. Notwithstanding the foregoing, the Company shall have no obligation to obtain or maintain such insurance if the Company determines in good faith that such insurance is not reasonably available, if the premium costs for such insurance are disproportionate to the amount of coverage provided, if the coverage provided by such insurance is limited by exclusions so as to provide an insufficient benefit, or if Indemnitee is covered by similar insurance maintained by a subsidiary or parent of the Company.

      7.   **Severability.** Nothing in this Agreement is intended to require or shall be construed as requiring the Company to do or fail to do any act in violation of applicable law. The Company's inability, pursuant to court order, to perform its obligations under this Agreement shall not constitute a breach of this Agreement. The provisions of this Agreement shall be severable as provided in this Section 7. If this Agreement or any portion hereof shall be invalidated on any ground by any court of competent jurisdiction, then the Company shall nevertheless indemnify Indemnitee to the full extent permitted by any applicable portion of this Agreement that shall not have been invalidated, and the balance of this Agreement not so invalidated shall be enforceable in accordance with its terms.

    8. **Exceptions.** Any other provision herein to the contrary notwithstanding, the Company shall not be obligated pursuant to the terms of this Agreement:

    (a) **Excluded Acts.** To indemnify Indemnitee to the extent any acts or omissions or transactions from which a director may not be relieved of liability under the California General Corporation Law; or

    (b) **Claims Initiated by Indemnitee.** To indemnify or advance expenses to Indemnitee with respect to proceedings or claims initiated or brought voluntarily by Indemnitee and not by way of defense, except with respect to proceedings brought to establish or enforce a right to indemnification under this Agreement or any other statute or law or otherwise as required under Section 317 of the California General Corporation Law, but such indemnification or advancement of expenses may be provided by the Company in specific cases if the Board of Directors has approved the initiation or bringing of such suit; or

    (c) **Lack of Good Faith.** To indemnify Indemnitee for any expenses incurred by the Indemnitee with respect to any proceeding instituted by Indemnitee to enforce or interpret this Agreement, if a court of competent jurisdiction enters a Final Judgment based on the Company's proof by clear and convincing evidence that each of the material assertions made by the Indemnitee in such proceeding was not made in good faith or was frivolous; or

    (d) **Insured Claims.** To indemnify Indemnitee for expenses or liabilities of any type whatsoever (including, but not limited to, judgments, fines, ERISA excise taxes or penalties and amounts paid in settlement) which have been paid directly to Indemnitee by an insurance carrier under a policy of directors' and officers' liability insurance maintained by the Company; or

    (e) **Claims Under Section 16(b).** To indemnify Indemnitee for expenses and the payment of profits arising from the purchase and sale by Indemnitee of securities in violation of Section 16(b) of the Securities Exchange Act of 1934, as amended, or any similar successor statute.

9. **Effectiveness of Agreement.** To the extent that the indemnification permitted under the terms of certain provisions of this Agreement exceeds the scope of the indemnification expressly permitted by Section 317 of the California General Corporation Law, such provisions shall not be effective unless and until the Company's Articles of Incorporation authorize such additional rights of indemnification. In all other respects, the balance of this Agreement shall be effective as of the date set forth on the first page and may apply to acts or omissions of Indemnitee which occurred prior to such date if Indemnitee was an officer, director, employee or other agent of the Company, or was serving at the request of the Company as a director, officer, employee or agent of another corporation, partnership, joint venture, trust or other enterprise, at the time such act or omission occurred.

10. **Construction of Certain Phrases.**

(a)   For purposes of this Agreement, references to the "**Company**" shall also include, in addition to the resulting corporation, any constituent corporation (including any constituent of a constituent) absorbed in a consolidation or merger which, if its separate existence had continued, would have had power and authority to indemnify its directors, officers, employees or agents, so that if Indemnitee is or was a director, officer, employee or agent of such constituent corporation, or is or was serving at the request of such constituent corporation as a director, officer, employee or agent of another corporation, partnership, joint venture, trust or other enterprise Indemnitee shall stand in the same position under the provisions of this Agreement with respect to the resulting or surviving corporation as Indemnitee would have with respect to such constituent corporation if its separate existence had continued.

(b)   For purposes of this Agreement, references to "**other enterprises**" shall include employee benefit plans; references to "**fines**" shall include any excise taxes assessed on Indemnitee with respect to an employee benefit plan; and references to "serving at the request of the Company" shall include any service as a director, officer, employee or agent of the Company which imposes duties on, or involves services by, such director, officer, employee or agent with respect to an employee benefit plan, its participants, or beneficiaries.

11. Counterparts. This Agreement may be executed in one or more counterparts, each of which shall constitute an original.

12. Successors and Assigns. This Agreement shall be binding upon the Company and its successors and assigns, and shall inure to the benefit of Indemnitee and Indemnitee's estate, heirs, legal representatives and assigns.

13. Attorneys' Fees. In the event that any action is instituted by Indemnitee under this Agreement to enforce or interpret any of the terms hereof, Indemnitee shall be entitled to be paid all costs and expenses, including reasonable attorneys' fees, incurred by Indemnitee with respect to such action, unless as a part of such action, a court of competent jurisdiction enters a Final Judgment based on the Company's proof by clear and convincing evidence that each of the material assertions made by Indemnitee as a basis for such action were not made in good faith or were frivolous. In the event of an action instituted by or in the name of the Company under this Agreement or to enforce or interpret any of the terms of this Agreement, Indemnitee shall be entitled to be paid all costs and expenses, including reasonable attorneys' fees, incurred by Indemnitee in defense of such action (including with respect to Indemnitee's counterclaims and cross-claims made in such action), unless as a part of such action the court determines that each of Indemnitee's material defenses to such action were made in bad faith or were frivolous.

14. Notices. All notices, requests, demands and other communications under this Agreement shall be in writing and shall be deemed duly given (i) if delivered by hand and receipted for by the party addressee, on the date of such receipt, (ii) if delivered by facsimile, on the date of such delivery, provided that a written receipt of successful transmission is obtained, (iii) in the case of a nationally-recognized overnight courier, on the next business day after the date when sent, or (iv) if mailed by domestic certified or registered mail with postage prepaid, on the third business day after the date postmarked.

15. Consent to Jurisdiction. The Company and Indemnitee each hereby irrevocably consent to the jurisdiction of the courts of the State of California for all purposes in connection with any action or proceeding which arises out of or relates to this Agreement and agree that any action instituted under this Agreement shall be brought only in the state of the State of California.

16.   Choice of Law. This Agreement shall be governed by and its provisions construed in accordance with the laws of the State of California as applied to contracts between California residents entered into and to be performed entirely within California.

Appendix W
Individual Liability for Managers/ Directors and Officers

This memorandum outlines the various potential grounds for imposing potential personal liability on the board of directors, board of managers, or officers of a company. Accordingly, debtors should ensure that any such liabilities are adequately covered in a "windup" or "liquidation" budget during dissolution, or adequately covered via directors and officers liability insurance (including tail coverage).

Grounds for seeking to impose personal liability on directors, officers, and/or managers of a company include the following:

1.   **Alter Ego Claims**. Under the alter ego doctrine, a corporate entity may be disregarded (i.e., the corporate veil "pierced") and the officers and directors may be held personally liable for corporate debts, obligations, and other liabilities because of the manner in which they have dealt with the corporation by treating it as an alter ego. The regular observance of corporate formalities will help protect against the imposition of personal liability for alter ego claims which are usually due to a failure to respect the company's separate identity.

Managers of an LLC may likewise be liable for the debts, obligations, and other liabilities of the company due to a failure to respect the company's separate identity; however, personal liability will not be imposed for failure to follow corporate formalities in an LLC. Instead, the alter ego doctrine is usually applied where there is a: (1) failure to complete formation of the company; (2) failure to properly capitalize the company; (3) use of company assets for personal use; and/or (4) commingling of company funds with personal funds.

Even if you properly treated the company as a business entity, separate from yourself in your individual capacity, you should expect that you will be named personally in any collection action and will need to incur expenses out of your own pocket to defend yourself against the claim. Moreover, the risks from an alter ego claim will be higher if assets that could have been used to satisfy creditor claims end up in your hands or under the control of your family members.

2.   **Unpaid Wages and Compensation Owed to Employees**: The California Labor Code imposes various penalties and criminal sanctions for an employer's failure to pay the wages owed to employees. Wages for most purposes include not only regular wages, but earned vacation pay and benefits.

Section 215 of the Labor Code makes it a misdemeanor for any agent or officer of a company to violate those provisions of the California Labor Code which require that (i) wages to be paid accordingly to the weekly or bi-weekly payroll schedule and (ii) any check issued for wages to be for good funds. The Labor Code provides that the dishonorment of a check creates a presumption that the responsible person had knowledge of the insufficiency of funds. Section 216 makes it a misdemeanor for the company's agent manager or officer to willfully refuse to pay wages due after demand where the corporate has the ability to pay. Employees' wage claims may be enforced by the California Labor Commissioner.

While § 216 requires that the company have the ability to pay before liability attaches to individual officers, that same qualification is not present in § 215. While we have not seen the Labor Commissioner proceed under § 215 where the company did not have the ability to pay, it is possible that an aggressive Labor Commissioner could seek to do so.

The risk of personal liability for directors and officers is greatest in circumstances where they continue to let employees work after the point in time when such officers and directors know that the company does not have sufficient funds to pay the employees' accrued wages. While the provisions of the California Labor Code do not expressly address this situation, officers and directors may be liable for such wages on a fraud or intentional misrepresentation theory similar to that discussed below in connection with potential liability to trade creditors. Briefly stated, by continuing to employ the employees, the corporate management -- in the person of the officers and the board of directors -- is making an implicit representation that it intends to and has the ability to pay the employees their compensation. If corporate management knows that it does not have the ability to pay the employees' compensation, its implicit representation is knowingly false. The employees will be deemed to have relied on that false representation to their detriment. Thus, officers and directors could be found liable for fraud or intentional misrepresentation and the measure of damages would presumably be the unpaid wages.

3. **Federal Employee Withholding Taxes.** An employer is obligated to withhold from an employee's wages income and social security taxes and then pay over the withheld taxes on a quarterly basis. These withheld taxes are referred to as "trust fund taxes" because the employer is deemed to hold them in trust for the United States.

Section 6672 of the Internal Revenue Code imposes a penalty equal to the amount of the tax on the responsible persons -- those persons with a duty to collect and pay the trust fund taxes -- who willfully fail to collect such tax or truthfully account and pay over such tax. While "responsible person" is not defined in the Internal Revenue Code by reference to specific corporate officers, it generally includes the CFO, controller, president, CEO and may in some circumstances extend to directors.

4. **California Unemployment, Workers' Compensation and Disability Taxes/Contributions.** Section 1735 of the California Unemployment Insurance Code imposes personal liability on any officer, major stockholder or other person having charge of the affairs of a corporate employer who willfully fails to pay any contribution (employer portion) or withholding (employee portion) for unemployment, workers' compensation or disability taxes.

Note that the "responsible person" is personally liable for <u>both</u> the employer and employee portion of these obligations.

5. **California Sales and Use Taxes.** Section 6829 of the California Revenue and Taxation Code imposes personal liability on any officer, member, manager, partner or other person having control or supervision of, who is charged with responsibility for filing returns, or who is under a duty to act for the company with respect to California sales or use taxes to the extent such person willfully fails to pay or cause to be paid such taxes.

6. **Liability for "Bad" Checks.** Section 476(a) of the California Penal Code imposes criminal liability on an officer of a company who willfully issues a check with knowledge that at the time of issuance, the company does not have sufficient funds or credit with the bank on which the check is drawn to pay the check and other checks then outstanding. The officer can be sentenced to up to one year in jail, although restitution is the more common remedy.

7. **Improper Distributions and Loans.** Section 316 of the California Corporations Code imposes personal liability on directors for the following:

    a. **Improper Distribution to Shareholders.** The provisions of the Corporations Code prohibit a shareholder distribution which would render the corporation insolvent. Similarly, once corporate dissolution proceedings have commenced, there cannot be a distribution to shareholders unless the payment or adequate provision for payment of all known liabilities of the corporation.

    b. **Improper Loans or Guaranties.** Section 315 prohibits the making of loans to officers or directors or guaranteeing their obligations without prior disclosure and approval of a majority of shareholders.

8. **Liability for Plan Contributions Under ERISA Plans.** ERISA fiduciary liability can attach in two circumstances: The first is when the plan expressly designates a person as a fiduciary, generally as the plan administrator, plan trustee, or member of an administrative Committee. The second is when a manager performs a function that ERISA deems a fiduciary function. Such functions include (1) discretionary authority or control over the management of the plan or any authority or control over management or disposition of the plan assets, (2) the rendering of investment advice for a fee or other compensation, and (3) discretionary authority or control in the administration of the plan. If a court determines that a person is a fiduciary duty, personal liability attaches, and the fiduciary is personally liable to make good the losses to the plan.

Not every act by an officer, director, or manager affecting a benefit plan is a fiduciary act. The law distinguishes between purely "corporate" functions and "fiduciary" functions. Unfortunately, it is not always clear where company functions end and fiduciary functions begin. Liability may attach where monies withheld from employee's paychecks for contributions to the union's pension fund are deposited into the company's general account but not paid over to the pension fund. In such circumstances, the U.S. Department of Labor (DOL) and the pension trustee make the same argument they make when sponsors of single employer plans fail to timely segregate their employees' 401(k) plan deferrals: when the management fail to timely segregate the employees' contributions from the corporation's assets, they became fiduciaries under ERISA and are thus personally liable to make good the losses to the plan.

Once a required contribution comes due, it becomes a plan asset. Failure to segregate plan assets from general corporate funds may constitute a breach of fiduciary duty for which the officer, director, manager, or other employee is personally liable.

Generally speaking, employers must segregate from their general assets plan contributions that a participant pays to the employer or that have been withheld by the employer at the earliest date on which the contributions can reasonably be segregated. The latest possible date is the 15th business day of the month following the month in which the participant contributions are received by the employer or would have been payable to the participant in cash Moreover, any use of plan assets for corporate or business use once they become plan assets is a prohibited transaction under ERISA. Fiduciaries, as well as employers, officers, directors, and 10 percent shareholders, can be held personally liable for prohibited transactions.

9. **Liability for Termination of Single Employer Plan Under ERISA.** 29 U.S.C. § 1362 imposes liability on members of "control group" of a corporation which is a contributing sponsor of a single-employer retirement plan upon termination of the plan in certain circumstances. This liability is usually only a concern in the large corporate setting where there are large pension and retirement plans.

10. **CERCLA Responsible Party Liability.** CERCLA authorizes the EX PARTE APPLICATION to investigate and clean up hazardous waste sites and to recoup clean-up costs from "potentially responsible parties." The definition of a "potentially responsible party" is broad and may include corporate officers and directors.

11.   **Liability to Trade Creditors.** There is no statutory basis to impose personal liability for unpaid debt incurred by a company to trade creditors—unless they have obtained a guaranty—generally acknowledge that their only recourse is against the company and its assets. However, it is possible for a disgruntled trade creditor to seek to hold an agent or officer of the company liable on a fraud or intentional misrepresentation theory. In order to make a case for fraud or intentional misrepresentation, the creditor has to prove four elements:

   i.   a knowing or intentional misstatement;

   ii.   the misstatement is material;

   iii. the creditor reasonably relies on the misstatement; and

   iv.   the creditor is damaged as a result.

A trade creditor could argue that by purchasing its goods or services on credit terms, the officer made an implicit representation that the corporation intended to and had the ability to pay for the goods and services and that the trade creditor justifiably relied on the implicit representation. If the creditor can demonstrate that at the time the officer made the implicit representation that the officer knew that the corporation could not pay or did not intend to pay, the trade creditor will have established its case for fraud or intentional misrepresentation. Thus, the officers or director could be found liable on a fraud or intentional misrepresentation theory if at the time the corporation purchases goods or services on credit, the officer or director never intended for the corporation to pay or knew -- based on the funds on hand or their own cash projections -- that the corporation would not be able to pay for the goods or services.

As indicated above, these types of claims are relatively rare, but we have seen circumstances where the trade creditor has pursued them because it believed that management knowingly and deliberately allowed the creditor's exposure to increase without any prospect for repayment.

12.   **Guaranty of Corporate Obligations.** An officer and director may of course be personally liable for a corporate debt if the officer or director guaranteed the debt. An officer or director presumably is aware of whether he/she has guaranteed a debt. However, we have seen a number of leases and agreements where the guarantee was added as several lines at the bottom of

a long standard form document and the officer or director may have signed it without fully appreciating that it was intended to make him/her personally liable.

Officers are advised to review all equipment and real property leases they may have signed to make certain that no such guaranty was included. Officers should also always make sure that they are signing a document in their capacity as an officer rather than in their individual capacity.

13. **Expanded Scope of Fiduciary Duty.** As a corporation nears insolvency, the fiduciary duty owed by corporate management and the board of directors expands to include not just shareholders, but creditors and other parties interest. While the directors' decision should still be evaluated under the "business judgment rule," directors must take the priority of the interests of creditors into account in exercising their business judgment.

14. **401K Plan Administration.** An arrangement should be made to have any 401K Plan funds be distributed to participating employees. The Debtor may want to prepay the Plan Administrators for this task.

15. **Corporate Credit Card Liability**. Employees who use "corporate" credit cards may be held responsible for charges which they signed.

* *

We hope that the above information is useful in managing the potential individual risks associated with insolvency and dissolution. This memorandum is intended to be a general guide as to some of the legal matters that the officers and directors may face and is not intended to be comprehensive or otherwise constitute legal advice or opinion. If you have questions about a specific circumstance or legal matter, contact us immediately.

Appendix X

Tax Free Reorganizations

TYPE A REORGANIZATIONS – SECTION 368(a)(1)(A) STATUTORY MERGER

Shareholders

Target → **Acquiror**

- Statutory Merger – 2 or more corporations combined and only one survives (Rev. Rul. 2000-5)
- Requires strict compliance with statute
- Target can be foreign; Reg. 1.368-2(b)(1)(ii)
- No "substantially all" requirement
- No "solely for voting stock" requirement

Requirements:
- Necessary Continuity of Interest
- Business Purpose
- Continuity of Business Enterprise
- Plan of Reorganization
- Net Value

Tax Effect:
- Shareholders – Gain recognized to the extent of boot
- Target – No gain recognition
- Acquiror takes Target's basis in assets plus gain recognized by Shareholders
- Busted Merger – taxable asset sale followed by liquidation

TYPE A REORGANIZATIONS – SECTION 368(a)(1)(A) STATUTORY MERGER

Shareholders

Target → **Acquiror**

- Statutory Merger – 2 or more corporations combined and only one survives (Rev. Rul. 2000-5)
- Requires strict compliance with statute
- Target can be foreign; Reg. 1.368-2(b)(1)(ii)
- No "substantially all" requirement
- No "solely for voting stock" requirement

Requirements:
- Necessary Continuity of Interest
- Business Purpose
- Continuity of Business Enterprise
- Plan of Reorganization
- Net Value

Tax Effect:
- Shareholders – Gain recognized to the extent of boot
- Target – No gain recognition
- Acquiror takes Target's basis in assets plus gain recognized by Shareholders
- Busted Merger – taxable asset sale followed by liquidation

TYPE A REORGANIZATIONS – SECTION 368(a)(1)(A) STATUTORY MERGER

- Statutory Merger – 2 or more corporations combined and only one survives (Rev. Rul. 2000-5)
- Requires strict compliance with statute
- Target can be foreign; Reg. 1.368-2(b)(1)(ii)
- No "substantially all" requirement
- No "solely for voting stock" requirement

Requirements:
- Necessary Continuity of Interest
- Business Purpose
- Continuity of Business Enterprise
- Plan of Reorganization
- Net Value

Tax Effect:
- Shareholders – Gain recognized to the extent of boot
- Target – No gain recognition
- Acquiror takes Target's basis in assets plus gain recognized by Shareholders
- Busted Merger – taxable asset sale followed by liquidation

TYPE B REORGANIZATIONS – SECTION 368(a)(1)(B) STOCK FOR STOCK

- Acquisition of stock of Target, by Acquiror in exchange for Acquiror voting stock
- Acquiror needs control of Target immediately after the acquisition
- Control = 80% by vote and 80% of each class

- Acquiror's basis in Target stock is the same as the Shareholder's Solely for voting stock
- No Boot in a B
- Reorganization Expenses – distinguish between Target expenses and Target Shareholder expenses (Rev. Rul. 73-54)
- Creeping B – old and cold stock purchased for cash should not be integrated with stock exchange

TYPE C REORGANIZATIONS – SECTION 368(a)(1)(C) STOCK FOR ASSETS

Shareholders

Acquiror Stock

Acquiror Stock

Target ← Acquiror Stock → **Acquiror**

Target Assets

- Acquisition of substantially all of the assets of Target, by Acquiror in exchange for Acquiror voting stock

- "Substantially All" – at least 90% of FMV of Net Assets and at least 70% of FMV of Gross Assets

- Target must liquidate in the reorganization

- 20% Boot Exception – Acquiror can pay boot (non-stock) for Target assets, up to 20% of total consideration; liabilities assumed are not considered boot unless other boot exists

- Reorganization Expenses – Aquiror may assume expenses (Rev. Rul. 73-54)

- Assumption of stock options not boot

- Bridge loans by Acquiror are boot

- Redemptions and Dividends – who pays and source of funds

TRIANGULAR OR SUBSIDIARY MERGERS

Target Shareholders ← Acquiror Stock

Target   **Acquiror**

↓ 80%

Merger Sub Survives → **Merger Sub**

Tax Consequences
- Merger Sub takes Target's basis in assets increased by gain recognized by Target
- Acquiror takes "drop down" basis in stock of Merger Sub (same as asset basis)

Section 368(a)(2)(D) Forward Triangular Merger

- A statutory merger of Target into Merger Sub (at least 80% owned by Merger Sub)

- Substantially all of Target's assets acquired by Merger Sub

- Would have been a good Type A merger if Target had merged into Merger Sub

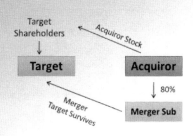

TRIANGULAR OR SUBSIDIARY MERGERS

Target
Shareholders

Acquiror Stock

Target

Acquiror

↓ 80%

Merger Sub

Merger
Target Survives

Tax Consequences
* Non-taxable to Target and carryover basis
* No gain to Acquiror and Merger Sub under Sections 1032 and 361
* No gain to Target shareholders except to the extent of boot
* Acquiror's basis in Target stock generally is the asset basis, but Acquiror can choose to take Target shareholders basis in stock (if it is also a B)
* If transaction is also a 351, Acquiror can use Target shareholders' basis plus gain

Section 368(a)(2)(E) Reverse Triangular Merger

* Merger of Merger Sub into Target where
  * (i) Target shareholders surrender control (80% of voting and nonvoting classes of stock) for Acquiror voting stock and
  * (ii) Target holds substantially all the assets of Target and Merger Sub
  * Shareholder loan issues

5

Appendix Y
Blind Option

Buy-out. Either Member ("Electing Member") may at any time make an election under this section 8 by Notice ("Election Notice") to the other Member ("Notice Member"). The Election Notice shall constitute an offer of the Electing Member to sell all of his or her interest in the Company to the Notice Member or to purchase all of the interests in the Company of the Notice Member, in either case at the Purchase Price determined in section 6.4 and payable as provided in section 6.5 of this Agreement. The first such Election Notice given shall be the only one considered. The Election Notice shall constitute an irrevocable offer for a period of 45 days. Within forty-five days after the giving of the Election Notice, the Notice Member shall give notice to the Electing Member as to whether the Notice Member will buy the interests in the Company of the Electing Member or will sell the interest in the Company of the Notice Member. In the event that the Notice Member does not respond to the Election Notice within such 45 day period, the Electing Member may elect to either buy the Notice Member's interest or sell his or her interest to the Notice Member under this section. Within sixty days after the giving of the Election Notice, such sale shall be closed. The Member making the purchase ("Purchasing Members") shall purchase all (but not less than all) of the interests in the Company of the Member selling such interests ("Selling Member").

END NOTES

1   *Dead on Arrival* is available online at https://rogerroyse.com/books/.

2   Malcolm Gladwell, *Outliers: The Story of Success* (Back Bay Books; 1st edition, 2011).

3   In the late 1990s, Google originally incorporated as a California corporation but then reincorporated as a Delaware corporation in 2002. Facebook and Uber both started off and continue to be registered as Delaware corporations (Facebook incorporated in 2004 and Uber in 2010).

4   The Code means Internal Revenue Code of 1986, as amended, at 26 U.S.C. ("IRC").

5   Earnings and profits or E&P is defined in Code Section 316.

6   Under current federal tax law, gain realized on the sale of certain qualified small business stock ("QSBS") held for at least five years may be exempted from income for federal tax purposes. QSBS, subject to a few exceptions, means stock in a domestic corporation if: (1) such corporation is a "qualified small business" ("QSB") at the time the stock is issued and (2) the taxpayer acquires the stock, in an original issuance of such stock, in exchange for money, other property, or as compensation for services to the issuing corporation.

7   S corporations must pay reasonable compensation to their officers, which will be subject to the Federal Insurance Contributions Act ("FICA"), the Federal Unemployment Tax Act ("FUTA"), and Medicare taxes. Distributions by the S corporation, however, are not subject to FICA, FUTA and Medicare taxes. Thus, the well-advised S corporation will be incentivized to pay less in compensation and more in distributions. LLCs do not have this advantage. The income of the LLC allocable to an active member will be self-employment income.

8   Watch out for this. Many off-the-shelf, boilerplate LLC operating agreements have an unlimited deficit restoration provision, which means that the LLC members must contribute to the LLC to the extent that they have a negative capital account. Many LLC members have discovered that they had liability on liquidation of the LLC because of imprudent drafting.

9   I say "mostly" because there are some differences. Most significantly, gain on a stock sale is usually capital and qualifies for a 20 percent federal tax rate if the requisite holding period is met. Gain on the sale of certain assets is ordinary, such as self-created intangibles, inventory, or cash basis receivables. If Ron is in California, he will also trigger an additional 1.5 percent state income tax (SIT) on the deemed asset sale that he would not incur on a stock sale. Finally, if Ron's corporation had earnings and profits from a year in which it was a C corporation, there may be an additional built in gains tax (BIG).

10 At the time of this writing, the corporate rate is a flat 21 percent. President Biden has proposed raising that rate.

11 The tax analysis is complex but, generally, if an LLC has debt in excess of tax basis or if a member has a negative capital account, there will likely be a recapture of losses or

income inclusion on incorporation. A taxpayer can avoid that result through the use of technical tax planning strategies.

12 For companies that are doing business in California, cumulative voting is a system where each shareholder has a non-waivable right to accumulate and cast their votes for one candidate or several. CAL. CORP. CODE § 708. Cumulative voting is intended to protect the rights of minority shareholders in board representation. It is not clear that cumulative voting would be avoided by incorporating in Delaware, but most companies act as if that is the case. *See* CAL. CORP. CODE § 2115; *Lidow v. Superior Court*, 206 Cal. App. 4th 351, 363 (2012) (agreeing with a Delaware court that the state of incorporation should govern corporate internal affairs).

13 Some states, like California, require class voting on important decisions. Class voting would require a majority of each class of shares to approve a transaction. *See, e.g.*, CAL. CORP. CODE § 117. In Delaware, class voting may be eliminated.

14 N.D. Cent. Code, Title 10, Corporations.

15 Wyoming has emerged as one of the most cryptocurrency friendly states by passing extensive legislation relating to the market. For example, Gov. Mark Gordon signed a comprehensive bill into existing law, titled SF0125, on February 26, 2019. Wyoming has consistently passed legislation regarding cryptocurrency and will likely continue this trend. Previous legislation includes, H.B. 70 64th Leg., Budget Sess. (Wyo. 2018); H.B. 101, 64th Leg., Budget Sess. (Wyo. 2018); H.B. 19, 64th Leg., Budget Sess. (Wyo. 2018); H.B. 1, 65th Leg., Gen. Sess. (Wyo. 2019); S.F. 125, 65th Leg., Gen. Sess. (Wyo. 2019); H.B. 62, 65th Leg., Gen. Sess. (Wyo. 2019); H.B. 70, 65th Leg., Gen. Sess. (Wyo. 2019); H.B. 185, 65th Leg., Gen. Sess. (Wyo. 2019); H.B. 57, 65th Leg., Gen. Sess. (Wyo. 2019).

16 A controlled foreign corporation ("CFC") is generally defined as a foreign corporation that is more than 50 percent owned by 10 percent or more US persons. IRC § 957.

17 A US trade or business means regular, substantial and continuous profit oriented activities in the *U.S. Comm'r v. Spermacet Whaling & Shipping Co.*, 281 F.2d 646 (6th Cir. 1960).

18 *See* the ABA Access to Justice Project.

19 Rule 701 of the Securities Act of 1933. Companies can offer their securities under a written compensatory plan without having to comply with federal securities registration requirements if total sales of stock under the plan do not exceed certain limits.

20 The gain on exercise of an ISO is an item of tax preference and will attract an alternative minimum tax when total preferences exceed applicable exemption amounts.

21 To be considered qualified stock, it must be transferred in connection with the exercise of an option or settlement of an RSU for the performance of services by an employee and during a year in which the corporation is an eligible corporation. A qualified employee is an individual who is not a 1 percent owner during the previous year or any of the preceding 10 calendar years, the CEO, the CFO or other acting in such a capacity at the time of the grant or prior or one of the four highest-compensated officers currently or during the previous 10 years, as determined by SEC shareholder disclosure rules. When qualified employees utilize the benefits of 83(i), they may elect out of the default rules that apply to stock options and RSU's and defer their taxable income for up to five years. This period, called the deferral period, may end prior to the expiration of a five-year period under a few circumstances. These include: the first date the qualified

stock becomes transferable (including if it becomes transferable to the employer); the date the employee becomes an excluded employee; the date any stock of the employer becomes publicly traded; or the date the employee revokes the 83(i) election.

22   Authorized shares means the maximum number of shares that can be issued under the corporation's articles or certificate of incorporation.

23   Fully diluted for this example means that all shares subject to issuance under options (convertibles, etc.) are treated as issued.

24   Thomas F. Hellmann & Noam Wasserman, *The First Deal: The Division of Founder Equity in New Ventures* (Nat'l Bureau of Econ. Research, Working Paper No. 16922, 2011).

25   Carta (www.carta.com); Pulley (https://pulley.com/); Captable.io aka LTSE Equity (https://captable.io/).

26   Analogizing to real estate deals, the amount of recourse might be as low as 20 or 25 percent in a more mature company. This is a facts and circumstances test and there are no hard and fast guidelines.

27   That wise man was Fargo, North Dakota Mayor Jon Lindgren.

28   Before there was LinkedIn, we used to keep track of who we know by collecting business cards and saving them in a circular physical file called a rolodex.

29   Quorum in this context, represents the minimum number of members of the board of directors required to be in attendance in order for the group to take official action. *"Quorum"*, Legal Information Institute, Cornell Law School.

30   Directors owe two core fiduciary duties:

(1)   The duty of care, which requires that directors be fully and adequately informed and act with care when making decisions and acting for the corporation.

(2)   The duty of loyalty, which requires that directors act and make decisions in the best interest of the corporation, not in their own personal interest. Directors owe these fiduciary duties to the corporation and its stockholders.

Practical Law Corporate & Securities, *Fiduciary Duties of the Board of Directors* (Thomson Reuters Practical Law).

31   The business judgment rule is a standard of judicial review of corporate director conduct; it is not a standard of conduct in itself. Model Bus. Corp. Act Annotated § 8-225 (4th ed. 2008). The rule sets forth a basic presumption that, "in making a business decision the directors of a corporation acted on an informed basis, in good faith and in the honest belief that the action was in the best interest of the company." *Brehm v. Eisner* (*In re Walt Disney Co. Derivative Litig.*), 906 A.2d 27, 52 (Del. 2006) (quoting *Aronson v. Lewis*, 473 A.2d 805, 812 (Del. 1984)). Thus, the business judgment rule is "a rule of law that insulates an officer or director of a corporation from liability for a business decision made in good faith if he is not interested in the subject of the business judgment, is informed with respect to the subject of the business judgment to the extent he reasonably believes to be appropriate under the circumstances and rationally believes that the business judgment is in the best interests of the corporation." *Am. Soc'y for Testing & Materials v. Corrpro Cos.*, 478 F.3d 557, 572 (3d Cir. 2007). "A hallmark of the business judgment rule is that, when the rule's requirements are met, a court will not substitute its own judgment for that of the corporation's board of directors." *Lamden*

v. La Jolla Shores Clubdominium Homeowners Ass'n., 21 Cal. 4th 249, 257 (1999) (citing *Katz v. Chevron Corp.*, 22 Cal. App. 4th 1352, 1366 (1994)).

32   The Fair Labor Standards Act (FLSA) requires that most employees in the United States be paid at least the federal minimum wage for all hours worked and overtime pay, at time and one-half the regular rate of pay, for all hours worked over 40 hours in a workweek. However, Section 13(a)(1) of the FLSA provides an exemption from both the minimum wage and overtime pay requirements for employees employed as bona fide executive, administrative, professional and outside sales employees. To qualify for the executive employee exemption, all of the following tests must be met:

-   The employee must be compensated on a salary basis (as defined in the regulations) at a rate not less than $455 per week.

-   The employee's primary duty must be managing the enterprise or managing a customarily recognized department or subdivision of the enterprise.

-   The employee must customarily and regularly direct the work of at least two or more other full-time employees or their equivalent.

-   The employee must have the authority to hire or fire other employees or the employee's suggestions and recommendations as to the hiring, firing, advancement, promotion or any other change of status of other employees must be given particular weight.

See 29 U.S.C. § 213 (detailing exemptions to the Fair Labor Standards Act); U.S. Department of Labor, Fact Sheet #17B: Exemption for Executive Employees Under the Fair Labor Standards Act (FLSA) (last updated on January 2018).

33   Though non-disclosure agreements are generally enforceable under California law they do not apply to salary disclosure. Under the California Labor Code, employers or their agents, are prohibited from asking job applicants about their salary history. This prohibition is strictly confined to applicants seeking employment and does not apply to individuals currently employed by a particular employer. CAL. LAB. CODE § 432.3. In addition, employers cannot "prohibit an employee from disclosing the employee's own wages, discussing the wages of others, inquiring about other employee's wages or aiding or encouraging any other employee to exercise his or her rights." CAL. LAB. CODE § 1197.5(k)(1).

34   *Dynamex Operations W. v. Superior Court*, 4 Cal. 5th 903 (2018).

35   *See* THE BIDEN PLAN FOR STRENGTHENING WORKER ORGANIZING, COLLECTIVE BARGAINING and UNIONS. "Ensure workers in the 'gig economy' and beyond receive the legal benefits and protections they deserve. Employer misclassification of 'gig economy' workers as independent contractors deprives these workers of legally mandated benefits and protections. Employers in construction, service industries and other industries also misclassify millions of their employees as independent contractors to reduce their labor costs at the expense of these workers. This epidemic of misclassification is made possible by ambiguous legal tests that give too much discretion to employers, too little protection to workers and too little direction to government agencies and courts. States like California have already paved the way by adopting a clearer, simpler and stronger three-prong 'ABC test' to distinguish employees from independent contractors. The ABC test will mean many more workers will get the legal protections and benefits they rightfully should receive. As president, Biden will work

with Congress to establish a federal standard modeled on the ABC test for all labor, employment and tax laws." *See also* the Worker Flexibility and Small Business Protection Act (S.4738), which creates an ABC test with no exemptions.

"An individual performing any labor for remuneration shall be considered an employee and not an independent contractor, unless—(A) the individual is free from control and direction; (B) the labor is performed outside the usual course of the employer's business; and (C) the individual is customarily engaged in an independently established business."

36 17 CFR § 230.701 (Exemption for offers and sales of securities pursuant to certain compensatory benefit plans and contracts relating to compensation).

37 Some practitioners will take the position that warrants, options, and convertible debt are not taxable to the contractor on issuance.

38 EBITDA stands for earnings before interest, taxes, depreciation and amortization and serves as a widely used metric to measure corporate profitability. Adam Hayes, *Earnings Before Interest, Taxes, Depreciation and Amortization – EBITDA*, Investopedia. com (June 25, 2019).

39 Lucy Handley, *Reid Hoffman: The billionaire philosopher*, CNBC, https://www.cnbc.com/linkedin-founder-reid-hoffman-on-investing-his-podcast-and-scaling-up/ (2018). For a full list of his investments see *Reid Hoffman*, Angel List, https://angel.co/reid-hoffman.

40 *Masters of Scale: Let Fires Burn* (July 18, 2017), https://mastersofscale.com/#/let-fires-burn/.

41 A class action is a procedural device that permits one or more plaintiffs to file and prosecute a lawsuit on behalf of a larger group or class. Put simply, the device allows courts to manage lawsuits that would otherwise be unmanageable if each class member (individuals who have suffered the same wrong at the hands of the defendant) were required to be joined in the lawsuit as a named plaintiff. Rule 23 of the Federal Rules of Civil Procedure provides the statutory authorization for class actions and lists 4 prerequisites:

(1) the class is so numerous that joinder of all members is impracticable;

(2) there are questions of law or fact common to the class;

(3) the claims or defenses of the representative parties are typical of the claims or defenses of the class; and

(4) the representative parties will fairly and adequately protect the interests of the class.

42 In an article titled "Homejoy Shuts Down After Battling Worker Classification Lawsuits," Carmel DeAmicis details the events leading up to Homejoy's shutdown that took place on July 31, 2015. Founded in 2012, Homejoy represented one of the earlier entrants into the developing gig economy. Homejoy successfully raised about $40 million from Y Combinator, PayPal founder Max Levchin, and a handful of angel investors due in part to the belief that the home-cleaning services industry was "ripe for an Uber-like overhaul." Less than two years later, the founders suddenly announced that they had run out of money and planned to shut down the company for good. According to CEO Adora Cheung, the deciding factor was the four lawsuits it

was fighting regarding whether its workers should be classified as employees or independent contractors. At the outset, the company classified the home-cleaning workers on its platform as independent contractors instead of employees. Numerous other gig economy companies employed (and still employ) the same worker classification practice. However, Homejoy simply did not have the war chest of Uber or other gig-economy giants to fight long, costly legal battles. Carmel DeAmicis, *Homejoy Shuts Down After Battling Worker Classification Lawsuits*, Vox (July 17, 2015), https://www.vox.com/2015/7/17/11614814/cleaning-services-startup-homejoy-shuts-down-after-battling-worker.

43   *Vasquez v. Jan-Pro Franchising International, Inc.*, 923 F.3d 575 (9th Cir. 2019) (*Dynamex* applies retroactively to all non-final cases that predate the decision).

44   *See* 8 Del. C. § 218 (voting trusts and other voting agreements).

45   Jungian Archetypes are universal patterns from the collective unconscious that manifest in behavior in the outside world.

46   Thanks to Gary Edwards and Marvin Glazer of Haynes & Boone, LLP for their helpful comments to this chapter.

47   Title 35 of the United States Code (35 U.S.C. §§ 1 et seq.) embodies the United States Patent Act. The United States Patent and Trademark Office (USPTO) defines a patent for an invention as "the grant of a property right to the inventor, issued by the United States Patent and Trademark Office." A patentable invention is defined as "any new and useful process, machine, manufacture or composition of matter or any new and useful improvement thereof." 35 U.S.C. § 101. Generally, the term of a new patent is 20 years from the date on which the application for the patent was filed in the United States. If the application claims the benefit of an earlier filed non-provisional application, then the term is 20 years from the date on which the earliest such application was filed. 35 U.S.C. § 154. The right conferred by the patent is, in the language of the statute and of the grant itself, the right to exclude others from making, using, offering for sale or selling the invention in the United States or importing the invention into the United States. 35 U.S.C. § 154. What is granted is not the right to make, use, offer for sale, sell or import but the right to exclude others from making, using, offering for sale, selling or importing the invention. Once a patent is issued, the patentee must enforce the patent without aid of the USPTO.

48   Copyright is a form of protection provided by U.S. law to the authors of original works of authorship fixed in any tangible medium of expression. Works of authorship include the following categories: (1) literary works; (2) musical works, including any accompanying words; (3) dramatic works, including any accompanying music; (4) pantomimes and choreographic works; (5) pictorial, graphic and sculptural works; (6) motion pictures and other audiovisual works; (7) sound recordings; and (8) architectural works. 17 U.S.C. § 102. No publication, registration or other action in the Copyright Office is required to secure copyright. Copyright is secured automatically when the work is created and a work is created when it is fixed in a copy or a phonorecord for the first time. For example, a song can be fixed in sheet music or on a CD or both. Under the 1976 Copyright Act, the copyright owner has the exclusive right to reproduce, adapt, distribute, publicly perform and publicly display the work. *See* USPTO, *Copyright Basics*, U.S. Patent and Trademark Office, https://www.uspto.gov/ip-policy/copyright-policy/copyright-basics. These exclusive rights are freely transferable and may be licensed,

sold, donated to charity or bequeathed to heirs. It is illegal for anyone to violate any of the exclusive rights of the copyright owner. If the copyright owner prevails in an infringement claim, the available remedies include preliminary and permanent injunctions (court orders to stop current or prevent future infringements), impounding and destroying the infringing articles and monetary remedies. 17 U.S.C. §§ 501-513 (Copyright infringement and remedies).

49   Service provider has been interpreted broadly to include basically any online service. Amazon and eBay, for example, are service providers.

50   Bret Cohen & Amanda Carozza, *Recourse for Trade Secret Misappropriation under the Federal Defend Trade Secrets Act*, LexisNexis Practice Advisor Journal (April 4, 2018).

51   A trademark or service mark includes any word, name, symbol, device or any combination, used or intended to be used to identify and distinguish the goods/services of one seller or provider from those of others and to indicate the source of goods/services. 15 U.S.C. § 1052 (Trademarks registrable on principal register; concurrent registration); *see also* 15 U.S.C. §§ 1051 - 1141n (section regarding trademarks in the United States code). It is not necessary to register a trademark on the federal trademark register. Federal registration, however, provides the trademark owner with substantial benefits and more expansive rights than are available for unregistered marks under the Lanham Act, which governs federal trademark law. Some of these primary advantages include (1) exclusive nationwide use of the mark and (2) availability of treble damages and recovery of attorneys' fees for any infringement claims. 15 U.S.C. § 1057 (certificates of registration); 15 U.S.C § 1117 (recovery for violation of rights).

52   For example, in California, an employee non-compete is unenforceable except in connection with the sale of the goodwill of a business. CAL. BUS. & PROF. CODE § 16600 ("Except as provided in this chapter, every contract by which anyone is restrained from engaging in a lawful profession, trade or business of any kind is to that extent void"). Also, under case law, even a non-solicit would be unenforceable. In November 2018, a California appellate court clarified the standard for employee non-solicitation agreements in *AMN Healthcare, Inc. v. Aya Healthcare Services, Inc.* In this case, the court analyzed whether the employer's non-solicitation provision was an improper restraint on individuals [employees'] ability to engage in their profession. In short, AMN required that their employees sign a Confidentiality and Non-Disclosure Agreement, which included a non-solicitation agreement, which prevented the employees from soliciting any employee of AMN to leave the service of AMN for at least a one-year period. The court concluded that this non-solicitation clause restrained individual defendants from engaging in their chosen profession in violation of California Business and Professions Code Section 16600. *AMN Healthcare, Inc. v. Aya Healthcare Services, Inc.*, 28 Cal. App. 5th 923 (2018). Furthermore, as some lawyers have learned the hard way, such clauses may be worse than worthless, since the courts in California may hold an employer liable in damages for unfair trade practices for trying to enforce these sorts of provisions. In *Application Group, Inc. v. Hunter Group, Inc.*, the court found that an employer who violated § 16600 by entering a non-compete agreement with a California employee also violated California's unfair trade practices law under California Business and Professions Code § 17200. *Application Group, Inc. v. Hunter Group, Inc.*, 61 Cal. App. 4th 882 (1998).

53   There was a time when the tax law incentivized IP development by allowing passive investors to claim tax credits or deductions for the costs of development through R&D

partnerships. The Code was changed in 1986 to largely limit those benefits through passive loss and alternative minimum tax rules but the strategy retained some viability in that certain taxpayers who actively participate could convert ordinary income to capital gains by deducting patent development costs at ordinary rates and paying tax on the gains from the sale of patents at capital gains rates. *See Scoggins v. Comm'r*, 46 F.2d 950 (9th Cir. 1995). The Tax Cuts and Jobs Act of 2017 finally plugged that hole by taxing gains from self-created intangibles at ordinary rates. Thus, while the structure still has tax benefits, its main use now is asset protection.

54 For example, there is the famous lawsuit between Facebook and the Winklevoss twins. The dispute dated back to 2003, when Mark Zuckerberg, at the time a sophomore at Harvard, agreed to help the Winklevosses program a social website called "Harvard Connection," later renamed ConnectU. Instead of following through on their verbal agreement, Zuckerberg delayed work on Harvard Connection and instead worked on his own project. In February 2004, Zuckerberg released "TheFacebook," which eventually became Facebook. The Winklevoss twins sued Zuckerberg and Facebook, claiming that Zuckerberg stole their social website idea. The case ended in a settlement, which included $20 million in cash and more than 1.2 million Facebook shares (the value of which has now reached some $180 million). Miguel Helft, *Court Upholds Facebook Settlement with Twins*, N.Y. TIMES (April 11, 2011), https://www.nytimes.com/2011/04/12/technology/12facebook.html. Snapchat encountered a similar legal issue. Reggie Brown, who attended Stanford with Evan Spiegel and Bobby Murphy (Snapchat co-founders), sued his former colleagues. He alleged that the two stole his original idea for a phone application that could send disappearing picture messages and subsequently excluded him from all participation and profit in the venture. The case was settled in September 2014 when Reggie Brown accepted a $157.5 million settlement agreement.

Ingrid Lunden, *Snapchat paid Reggie Brown $157.5M to settle his 'ousted founder' lawsuit*, TECHCRUNCH (February 2, 2017), https://techcrunch.com/2017/02/02/snapchat-reggie-brown/. Square, a financial services and mobile payment company based in San Francisco, California, dealt with a similar co-founder dispute that resulted in a pricey settlement for the company. Robert Morley sued Square and its co-founders Jack Dorsey and James McKelvey in early 2014, alleging patent infringement and breach of fiduciary duty. The college professor claimed that he actually invented the software that Square went on to use as its credit card reader and that Dorsey and McKelvey systematically cut him out of any ownership stake in the company. The company settled an ongoing lawsuit against Morley for $50 million in 2016. Leena Rao, *Square Settled Lawsuit with Refuted Co-Founder for $50 Million*, FORTUNE (May 5, 2016), https://fortune.com/2016/05/05/square-settled-lawsuit/.

55 David S. Almeling et al., *A Statistical Analysis of Trade Secret Litigation in State Courts*, 46 GONZ. L. REV. 57, 69 (2010).

56 The California Labor Code states as follows:

(a) Any provision in an employment agreement which provides that an employee shall assign or offer to assign, any of his or her rights in an invention to his or her employer shall not apply to an invention that the employee developed entirely on his or her own time without using the employer's equipment, supplies, facilities or trade secret information except for those inventions that either:

(1) Relate at the time of conception or reduction to practice of the invention to the

employer's business or actual or demonstrably anticipated research or development of the employer; or

(2) Result from any work performed by the employee for the employer.

(b) To the extent a provision in an employment agreement purports to require an employee to assign an invention otherwise excluded from being required to be assigned under subdivision (a), the provision is against the public policy of this state and is unenforceable. CAL. LAB. CODE § 2870.

57 The term trade secret means all forms and types of financial, business, scientific, technical, economic or engineering information, including patterns, plans, compilations, program devices, formulas, designs, prototypes, methods, techniques, processes, procedures, programs or codes, whether tangible or intangible and whether or how stored, compiled or memorialized physically, electronically, graphically, photographically or in writing if—

(A) the owner thereof has taken reasonable measures to keep such information secret; and

(B) the information derives independent economic value, actual or potential, from not being generally known to and not being readily ascertainable through proper means by, another person who can obtain economic value from the disclosure or use of the information. 18 U.S.C. § 1839.

58 In California, a trade secret means information, including a formula, pattern, compilation, program, device, method, technique or process, that: (1) Derives independent economic value, actual or potential, from not being generally known to the public or to other persons who can obtain economic value from its disclosure or use; and (2) Is the subject of efforts that are reasonable under the circumstances to maintain its secrecy. CAL. CIV. CODE § 3426.1(d).

59 *Waymo LLC v. Uber Techs., Inc.*, 870 F.3d 1350 (Fed. Cir. 2017).

60 18 U.S.C. §§ 1836, et. seq.

61 CAL. CIV. CODE §§ 3426 - 3426.11.

62 Paul M. Janicke & LiLan Ren, *Who Wins Patent Infringement Cases?* 34 AM. INTELL. PROP. LAW ASSOC. QUARTERLY J. 1 (2006).

63 Thanks to Gary Edwards and Marvin Glazer of Haynes & Boone, LLP for their helpful comments to this chapter.

64 A unicorn is a privately held startup company valued at over $1 billion.

65 California Business & Professions Code Section 17000.

66 Federal Trade Commission Act 15 U.S.C. §§ 41-58, as amended.

67 *LabMD, Inc. v. Federal Trade Commission*, 678 F. App'x 816 (11th Cir. 2016).

68 CACI No. 325. Breach of Implied Covenant of Good Faith and Fair Dealing - Essential Factual Elements, Judicial Council of California Civil Jury Instructions (2020 edition).

69 *Arkley v. Aon Risk Services Companies, Inc.* (US District Court, Central District of California, 2012).

70   Selena Larson, *Uber and Waymo settle trade secrets lawsuit*, CNN (February 9, 2018), https://money.cnn.com/2018/02/09/technology/uber-waymo-settlement/index.html.

71   Cyrus Farivar, *Waymo and Uber end trial with sudden $244 million settlement*, ARS Technica (February 9, 2018), https://arstechnica.com/tech-policy/2018/02/waymo-and-uber-end-trial-with-sudden-244-million-settlement/#:~:text=In%20a%20stunning%20turn%2C%20Waymo,payout%20of%20over%20%24244%20million.

72   Consumer Review Fairness Act, 15 U.S.C. §45b (2016).

73   Arielle Duhaime-Ross, *Driven: how Zipcar's founders built and lost a car-sharing empire*, The Verge (April 1, 2014), https://www.theverge.com/2014/4/1/5553910/driven-how-zipcars-founders-built-and-lost-a-car-sharing-empire.

74   Robert Frank, *Why Zipcar's Founder Didn't Get Rich in the Deal*, CNBC (Jan. 2, 2013), https://www.cnbc.com/id/100349819.

75   Noam Wasserman, *The Founder's Dilemmas: Anticipating and Avoiding the Pitfalls That Can Sink a Startup* (2013).

76   Larry David, *Curb Your Enthusiasm*.

77   *http://www.slicingpie.com/the-grunt-fund-calculator*

78   Mike Moyer, *Slicing Pie: Fund Your Company Without Funds* (2012).

79   The popular website Gust has a co-founder equity split calculator at https://cofounders.gust.com. The Founders Institute has an Equity Split Spreadsheet at https://fi.co/insight/how-to-split-equity-with-cofounders. The Founders Pie Calculator can be found at https://www.andrew.cmu.edu/user/fd0n/35%20Founders'%20Pie%20Calculator.htm and the Co-Founder Equity Calculator is at https://foundrs.com. *See also* the Hellerman and Wasserman working paper at https://www.hbs.edu/faculty/Publication%20Files/14-085_2bd67a49-bd41-4396-a69d-73a7f40829b8.pdf https://www.andrew.cmu.edu/user/fd0n/35%20Founders'%20Pie%20Calculator.htm.

80   "Class F" is an arbitrary distinction chosen by Adeo Ressi of The Founder's Institute. Similarly, Series FF stock was named after the Founders Fund by Sean Parker, the company's founder.

81   If founders buy Series FF preferred stock at less than its fair value (i.e., the price at which it is redeemed), the founders will have ordinary income equal to the difference between the amount paid for the stock and the amount received from the company in the redemption of the Series FF preferred.

82   Code Section 351 provides that no gain or loss will be recognized if property is transferred to a corporation by one or more persons solely in exchange for stock in such corporation and immediately after the exchange, such person or persons are in control (i.e., own 80 percent) of the corporation.

83   *United States v. Stafford*, 727 F.2d 1043 (11th Cir. 1984).

84   *E.I. DuPont de Nemours v. United States*, 471 F.2d 1211 (Ct. Cl. 1973).

85   Overhang includes stock options granted, plus those reserved for grant, as a percentage of the total shares outstanding.

86   The term "fully diluted capitalization" refers to the total number of shares that would

be outstanding if all options granted or reserved were exercised for stock and all convertible securities (such as convertible debt and warrants) were converted or exercised.

87 *See* IRC § 409A.

88 *See* Ellen Lee, *Options lawsuit gives up details/Shareholders suing Mercury Interactive over timing of grants*, SF Gate (February 21, 2007), https://www.sfgate.com/business/article/Options-lawsuit-gives-up-details-Shareholders-2647529.php.

89 Warrant coverage is sometimes calculated off a number other than the principal amount of the note or other debt instrument.

90 "Series A investors" in this scenario refers to the first equity investors, who will buy preferred stock for cash and trigger the conversion of the outstanding debt.

91 *See* the discussion on Internal Revenue Code Section 409A below.

92 Michael Rubinkam, *A proper portrayal of a Ponzi-polka king*, Associated Press (January 11, 2018), https://www.thespec.com/entertainment/movies/2018/01/11/a-proper-portrayal-of-a-ponzi-polka-king.html.

93 Jason Calacanis, Angel: How to Invest in Technology Startups--Timeless Advice from an Angel Investor Who Turned $100,000 into $100,000,000 (2017).

94 Muthu Singaram & Prathistha Jain, *What is the Difference between Proof of Concept and Prototype?* Entrepreneur India (January 13, 2018) https://www.entrepreneur.com/article/307454.

95 *See* The Lean Startup Methodology, http://theleanstartup.com/principles.

96 The Securities Act of 1933 and the Securities Exchange Act of 1934 contain standards of communication that limit risk factors to protect investors from ambiguous language. The Private Securities Litigation Reform Act of 1995 provides a safe harbor for certain forward-looking statements. 15 U.S.C § 78u–5.

97 *See* 15 U.S.C. § 78u–5(b).

98 *Ankle-Biter*, Urban Dictionary, https://www.urbandictionary.com/define.php?term=ankle-biter.

99 *Public Notification of U.S. v. Elizabeth Holmes, et al.*, Department of Justice (September 29, 2020), https://www.justice.gov/usao-ndca/us-v-elizabeth-holmes-et-al.

100 *See, e.g., Strategic Diversity, Inc. v. Alchemix Corp.*, 666 F.3d 1197 (9th Cir. 2012); *Rice v. McAlister*, 268 Ore. 125, 128, 519 P.2d 1263, 1265 (1975); *Heitman v. Brown Grp., Inc.*, 638 S.W.2d 316, 319; *Prince v. Bear River Mut. Ins. Co.*, 2002 UT 68 (Utah 2002).

101 Samuel W. Buell, *What is Securities Fraud?* 61 Duke L. J. 511, 541 (2011).

102 *United States v. Naftalin*, 441 U.S. 768, 774 (1979).

103 18 U.S.C. § 1348 (2006) (covers any person who knowingly executes or attempts to execute, a scheme or artifice (1) to defraud any person in connection with ... any security of an issuer (required to register or report under the '34 Act); or (2) to obtain, by means of false or fraudulent pretenses, representations or promises, any money or property in connection with the purchase or sale of ... any security of an issuer (required to register or report under the '34 Act)).

104 You can find your Idea to IPO chapter and meeting information at https://www.meet-up.com/Silicon-Valley-Startup-Idea-to-IPO/.

105 Pitch Globally, http://www.pitchglobally.com.

106 Royse AgTech Innovation Network, http://royseagtech.com.

107 Securities Act Rule 148

108 Venture Capital Roundtable, Silicon Valley, https://www.vcr-sv.com/?fbclid=I wAR0n7iDyZL9AyO1zKcFqwPWNNCGxvqEv6HEi3BzXvt7kK72uioLRYvL65As.

109 http://f50.io/events

110 Band of Angels, https://www.bandangels.com.

111 Sand Hill Angels, https://www.sandhillangels.com.

112 Keiretsu Forum, https://www.keiretsuforum.com.

113 Tiger 21, https://tiger21.com.

114 Jews For Entrepreneurship https://www.jfenetwork.com/

115 Securities Act Rule 148.

116 Bill Reichert and Angelika Blendstrup, Getting to Wow! Silicon Valley Pitch Secrets for Entrepreneurs (2020).

117 Bill Reichert, *Getting to WOW!*, Garage Technologies, (2014) https://www.garage. com/files/GettingToWow.pdf

118 Rule 506(b) of Regulation D is considered a safe harbor under Section 4(a)(2) of the Securities Act of 1933. Companies conducting an offering under Rule 506(b) can raise an unlimited amount of money and can sell securities to an unlimited number of accredited investors. An offering under Rule 506(b), however, is subject to the following requirements: no general solicitation or advertising to market the securities; securities may not be sold to more than 35 non-accredited investors and all non-accredited investors, either alone or with a purchaser representative, must meet the legal standard of having sufficient knowledge and experience in financial and business matters to be capable of evaluating the merits and risks of the prospective investment.

119 There is no federal statute sanctioning a rescission offer and it is not certain that an investor loses its right to assert a federal claim but there is case law on the matter. *See Meyers v. C & M Petroleum Producers, Inc.*, 476 F.2d 427 (5th Cir. 1973); *Topalian v. Ehrman*, 954 F.2d 1125 (5th Cir. 1992).

120 For example, under Ca. Corp. Code § 25507 (b) an investor has 30 days to accept the rescission offer or be barred from bringing an action for rescission.

121 NVCA Modern Legal Documents, https://nvca.org/model-legal-documents/ .

122 *See Halpin vs. Riverstone Inc.*, C.A. No. 9796-VCG (Del. Ch. Feb. 26, 2015) (minority stockholders were not prohibited from exercising their statutory appraisal rights despite the existence of a drag-along provision in a stockholders' agreement).

123 *Venture Associates Corp. v. Zenith Data Systems Corp.*, 96 F.3d 275 (7th Cir. 1996).

124 *SIGA Techs., Inc. v. PharmAthene, Inc.*, C.A. No. 2627 (Del. May 24, 2013).

125 Silicon Valley Bank, *Executing a Successful Startup Pivot*, https://www.svb.com/blogs/

silicon-valley-bank/breaking-down-startup-pivot-strategy; SAP, *SAP to Acquire Gigya, Market Leader in Customer Identity and Access Management* (September 24, 2017), https://news.sap.com/2017/09/sap-to-acquire-gigya-market-leader-in-customer-identity-and-access-management

126 Guilherme Barbosa, *Cool Hand Luke (1967) – The Captain's speech "what we've got here is failure to communicate"*, YOUTUBE (August 27, 2013), https://www.youtube.com/watch?v=452XjnaHr1A

127 For example, CFIUS may restrict foreign ownership pursuant to Section 721 of the Defense Production Act of 1950, as amended (Section 721) and as implemented by Executive Order 11858, as amended and the regulations at Chapter VIII of Title 31 of the Code of Federal Regulations.

128 Rory Crawford, *Restaurant Profitability and Failure Rates: What You Need to Know*, FSR MAGAZINE (April 2019), https://www.fsrmagazine.com/expert-takes/restaurant-profitability-and-failure-rates-what-you-need-know

129 *Yelp: Local Economic Impact Report*, YELP, https://www.yelpeconomicaverage.com/yelp-coronavirus-economic-impact-report.html (last updated June 25, 2020).

130 The Real Story of Twitter (April 14, 2011), https://www.forbes.com/sites/christianwolan/2011/04/14/the-real-story-of-twitter/?sh=58f2b93366af

131 Elvis Plesky, *Reid Hoffman, Linkedin Co-Founder, Tells His Story from Failure to Success* (February 10, 2020), https://www.plesk.com/blog/people-articles/reid-hoffman-linkedin-success/

132 Kaja Whitehouse, *Thiel's Hedge Fund Plummet*, N.Y. POST (July 8, 2009), https://nypost.com/2009/07/08/thiels-hedge-fund-plummet/

133 *See* CAL. CIV. PROC. CODE § 2856.

134 Barkley Clark & Barbara Clark, *The 24 Defenses of the Guarantor, Secured Lending Alert* (November – January 1987-88).

135 Sections 580a through 580e and 726 of the Code of Civil Procedure, prohibit a lender from obtaining a deficiency judgment from a borrower following a non-judicial foreclosure of real property.

136 *LSREF2 Clover Property 4, LLC v. Festival Retail Fund 1, LP*, 3 Cal. App. 5th 1067 (2016).

137 Roger Royse, *Donald Trump's Billion Dollar Loss: Good Tax Planning or Dubious Trick?* (November 2, 2016), https://rogerroyse.com/donald-trumps-billion-dollar-loss-good-tax-planning-or-dubious-trick/

138 The Great Recession was one of the worst economic declines in US history and lasted from December 2007 to June 2009.

139 *See* also Roger Royse, *Taxation of Real Estate* (January 30, 2013), https://www.slideshare.net/rroyse/taxation-of-real-estate

140 IRC § 108.

141 IRC § 108(a)(1)(A),108(d)(2).

142 IRC § 108(a)(1)(B).

143 *In re Miller*, T.C. Memo. 2006-125.

144　IRC § 108(a)(3).

145　IRC § 7501.

146　The Trust Fund Recovery Penalty (TFRP) is based on IRC § 6672(a) and provides as follows:

"Any person required to collect, truthfully account for and pay over any tax imposed by this title who willfully fails to collect such tax or truthfully account for and pay over such tax or willfully attempts in any manner to evade or defeat any such tax on the payment thereof, shall, in addition to other penalties provided by law, be liable to a penalty equal to the total amount of the tax evaded or not collected or not accounted for and paid over..."

147　*See* IRM Policy Statement 1.2.14.1.3 (June 9, 2003) and IRS Policy Statement 5-14 (June 9, 2003).

148　*See, e.g., In re Quattrone Accountants, Inc.,* (1988, Bktcy Ct PA) 88 BR 713, aff'd (1989, DC PA), aff'd (1990, CA3) 895 F.2d 921; *Dougherty v. U.S.,* (1989, Cl Ct) 18 Cl Ct 335, aff'd (1990, CA Fed Cir) 914 F.2d 271.

149　Robert B. Thompson, *Piercing the Corporate Veil: An Empirical Study,* 76 Cornell L. Rev. 1036 (1991).

150　Carol Baskin and Big Cat Rescue Awarded Possession of GW Zoo, Wynnewood Gazette (June 19, 2020), https://thewynnewoodgazette.com/articles/f/carol-baskin-and-big-cat-rescue-awarded-possession-of-gw-zoo

151　Exotic (aka Joseph Maldonado-Passage) is currently serving 22 years in federal prison for hiring a hitman to kill Baskin and for more than a dozen wildlife violations including the killing of five tigers. He asked President Trump for pardon but was ultimately not awarded one.

152　*See* Uniform Voidable Transactions Act. For example, California's version is codified at CAL. CIV. CODE § 3439 *et seq.*

153　11 U.S.C. § 548 (Fraudulent transfers and obligations).

154　11 U.S.C. § 547 (Preferences).

155　*See* CAL. PEN. CODE § 154.

156　*The Sopranos: The Happy Wanderer,* HBO (February 20, 2000).

157　The elements of fraud that will give rise to a tort action for deceit are: "(a) misrepresentation (false representation, concealment or nondisclosure); (b) knowledge of falsity (or 'scienter'); (c) intent to defraud, i.e., to induce reliance; (d) justifiable reliance; and (e) resulting damage." *Engalla v. Permanente Medical Group, Inc.* (1997) 15 Cal.4th 951, 974 (internal quotation marks omitted).

158　In California, deceit is defined in CIV. CODE §§ 1709 and 1710, while fraud is defined in CIV. CODE §§ 1572 (actual fraud) and 1573 (constructive fraud).

159　Negligent misrepresentation requires an assertion of fact, falsity of that assertion. and the tortfeasor's lack of reasonable grounds for believing the assertion to be true. It also requires the tortfeasor's intent to induce reliance, justifiable reliance by the person to whom the false assertion of fact was made, and damages to that person. An implied assertion of fact is 'not enough' to support liability. CAL. CIV. CODE § 1710; *SI 59 LLC v. Variel Warner Ventures, LLC,* (2018) 29 Cal.App.5th 146, 154 (internal citation omitted).

160   *See BRY Partners V, L.P. v. F & W Acquisition LLC,* 891 A.2d 1032 (Del. Ch. 2006) (sophisticated parties may disclaim fraud claims based on representations or promises not contained in the contract itself).

161   *North American Catholic Educ. Programming Found. v. Gheewalla,* 930 A.2d 92, 103 (Del. 2007).

162   *See Berg & Berg Enterprises, LLC v. Boyle,* 2009 Cal. App. LEXIS 1740 (October 29, 2009).

163   DEL. CORP. CODE § 145.

164   CAL. CORP. CODE § 316.

165   CAL. CORP. CODE § 315.

166   CAL. CORP. CODE § 500 provides:

(a)   Neither a corporation nor any of its subsidiaries shall make any distribution to the corporation's shareholders (Section 166) unless the board of directors has determined in good faith either of the following:

(1)   The amount of retained earnings of the corporation immediately prior to the distribution equals or exceeds the sum of (A) the amount of the proposed distribution plus (B) the preferential dividends arrears amount.

(2)   Immediately after the distribution, the value of the corporation's assets would equal or exceed the sum of its total liabilities plus the preferential rights amount.

167   CAL. LAB. CODE §§ 215, 216. Section 558 of the CA Labor Code: "[a]ny employer or person acting on behalf of an employer, who violates, or causes to be violated," provisions regulating wages or hours, may be held personally liable "as the employer." Section 1197.1(a) of the CA Labor Code: an employer "or other person acting either individually or as an officer, agent, or employee of another person" who pays or causes to pay an employee less that the state's applicable minimum wage shall be subject to a civil penalty.

168   California Assembly Bill (AB) 1003, if enacted, would criminally penalize a company's intentional theft of wages of more than $950 from any individual employee, or $2,350 total from 2 or more employees, in a 12-month period.

169   *See* Employee Retirement Income Security Act of 1974.

170   CAL. REV. & TAX. CODE § 6829.

171   CAL. PEN. CODE § 476(a).

172   According to the Oxford Dictionary, a doohickey is "noun INFORMAL • NORTH AMERICAN a small object or gadget, especially one whose name the speaker does not know or cannot recall." As an example, the dictionary provides, "a garage filled with electronic parts and other valuable doohickey."

173   The Bankruptcy Code appears in Title 11 of the United States Code, beginning at 11 U.S.C. § 101.

174   11 U.S.C. 547.

175 The ABC is defined in California in CAL. CIV. PROC. CODE § 493.010-493.060 (Effect of Bankruptcy Proceedings and General Assignments for The Benefit of Creditors).

176 UCC § 9-610(a).

177 Bo Burlingham, *Finish Big, How Great Entrepreneurs Exit Their Companies on Top* pp. 18-24 (Penquin Random House UK 2016).

178 IRC § 199A.

179 IRC §§ 338(h)(10), 336(e).

180 IRC § 368(a)(1)(A).

181 IRC § 368(a)(1)(B).

182 IRC § 368(a)(1)(C).

183 IRC §§ 368(a)(2)(D), (E).

184 This requirement is satisfied if at least 40 percent of the consideration received by the target's shareholders is in the form of the acquiror's stock. Treas. Reg. §1.368-1(e)(2)(v), Ex 1. The 40 percent threshold is established by the IRS. However, case law suggests that a lower percentage may be sufficient. *See, e.g., John A. Nelson Co. v. Helvering*, 296 U.S. 374 (1935) (38% of preferred stock).

185 The term "control" means the ownership of stock possessing at least 80 percent of the total combined voting power of all classes of stock entitled to vote and at least 80 percent of the total number of shares of all other classes of stock of the corporation.

186 In a Type C reorganization, the acquirer must acquire substantially all of the target's assets in exchange solely for voting stock. The assumption of the target's liabilities is not considered to result in taxable boot except that up to 20 percent of the consideration for the target's assets can be property other than voting stock but if any other consideration is used, the assumption of liabilities will be treated as boot.

187 Generally, the forward subsidiary merger must satisfy the same continuity requirement as a merger. In a reverse merger, target shareholders must receive voting stock of the acquirer's parent in exchange for control of the target.

188 Chris Voss and Tahl Roz, *Never Split the Difference: Negotiating As If Your Life Depended On It* (Harper Business, 2016).

189 I make an exception here for my law school roommate Justice Ralph Erickson, who sits on the 8th Circuit Court of Appeals, and who is one of the nicest guys you would ever want to meet.

190 IRC § 2702.

191 IRC § 2503.

192 CAL. BUS. & PROF. CODE §§ 16600, 16601.

193 Nathaniel Cahners Hindman, *Mark Zuckerberg: 'We Buy Companies to Get Excellent People'*, THE HUFFINGTON POST (October 19, 2010).

194 *In re Trados Incorporation Shareholder Litigation*, 2009 Del. Ch. LEXIS 128 (Del. Ch. 2009).

195 Martin Babinec, *More Good Jobs* (Lioncrest 2020)